Colorado

The Complete Municipalities

Volume 1

Amanda Blackwood

MANDOLIN PUBLISHING

Published by the Mandolin Publishing Group

Welcome to the Adventure

In embarking on this journey through the enchanting landscape of Colorado, we dive headfirst into the first of two volumes dedicated to the 273 municipalities that collectively form the tapestry of this diverse state. From the quirky charm of Akron to the vibrant pulse of Jamestown, each town tells a story—one that deserves to be explored, celebrated, and occasionally chuckled at. This isn't just a guide; it's an adventure filled with humor, history, and a touch of absurdity.

Have you ever wondered how a town got its name? Was it a poetic vision or perhaps an inside joke between settlers? As we traverse the alphabet from Akron to Jamestown, we'll uncover the often amusing origins of each name. Some may have grand historical significance, while others could very well have been the result of a late-night brainstorming session gone awry. Prepare for puns, plays on words, and a few downright head-scratchers along the way!

The history of these municipalities is as colorful as the Colorado landscape itself. From wild gold rush days to the sleepy farming communities of today, each town has a unique backstory that shapes its identity. You'll meet the pioneers, entrepreneurs, and everyday folks who played a part in crafting the communities we see today. With humor as our trusty guide, we'll explore the events that have defined these towns, making history not just informative, but entertaining.

Museums are often the custodians of local lore, and many of Colorado's towns boast unique collections that reflect their rich histories. Whether it's an extensive art collection, quirky artifacts from the Wild West, or a charming display of local memorabilia, we'll highlight the best spots to immerse yourself in the towns' stories. And yes, expect some delightful oddities that may leave you questioning how they made it into a museum in the first place!

Of course, no exploration of these municipalities would be complete without a nod to the best and worst things to see and do. Each town has its hidden gems—those unassuming eateries that serve the best green chili or breathtaking vistas that demand your camera's attention. But let's face it, there are also some questionable attractions that may make you think twice before stopping. Fear not; I'll be your trusty tour guide through this labyrinth of local offerings, ensuring you know where to feast and where to flee.

As we delve deeper, you'll find that every town has its quirks, idiosyncrasies, and local legends. Maybe you'll learn about a mysterious ghost story that has haunted the townsfolk for generations or an annual festival that started as a whimsical prank and turned into a beloved tradition. These anecdotes will breathe life into the pages, making each municipality feel less like a dot on a map and more like a character in a sprawling epic.

This journey isn't merely about locations; it's about the connections we form with these places and the people who inhabit them. The towns we'll encounter are vibrant communities, each with its own heartbeat and rhythm. By sharing their stories, we create a deeper understanding of the cultural fabric that binds Colorado together. Expect to laugh, shake your head in disbelief, and perhaps even find a place you'd love to visit someday.

You may also discover a newfound appreciation for the charming oddities that lie within these towns. Every community has its traditions and quirks, from peculiar statues to local competitions that defy all logic. These delightful eccentricities are what make Colorado's municipalities so enchanting and entertaining. You'll find that there's beauty in the bizarre, and you'll want to keep your eyes peeled for the unexpected at every turn.

So, grab your sense of humor and your adventurous spirit as we embark on this whimsical journey through Colorado, from Akron to Jamestown. This volume is your companion, filled with enough laughs, fun facts, and intriguing stories to keep you entertained as you navigate the landscape. Whether you're a local, a visitor, or just someone curious about the state, I invite you to join me in celebrating the spirit of these municipalities, where every name has a story and every street holds a history waiting to be uncovered.

With a mix of laughter and discovery, let's set out to explore the quirks and charms of Colorado's towns, one name at a time, making our way through the alphabet as we celebrate the rich tapestry that is the Centennial State. Buckle up; it's going to be a wildly entertaining ride!

Wild Beginnings: Denver's Gold and Grit

Welcome to Denver, Colorado, the Mile High City, where the air is thin, the views are breathtaking, and the history is as rich as the coffee you'll need to stay awake while reading about it. Grab your hiking boots and a craft beer—preferably both—because we're diving into the wild, wacky beginnings of a city that was born out of sheer audacity, a dash of luck, and a whole lot of gold fever!

Once upon a time in the mid-1800s, a group of ruggedly handsome adventurers (or at least, that's how they imagined themselves) stumbled upon the banks of the South Platte River. This was back when Colorado was still a "no man's land" of dusty trails and indignant squirrels. It was 1858, and folks were already whispering about the magical word: GOLD. Cue the dramatic music!

Our story begins with the "Pikes Peak Gold Rush," which can only be described as a gold rush of epic proportions—like the Black Friday of the 19th century but with fewer injuries and a lot more shovels. Thousands of miners, dreamers, and various characters who probably had more enthusiasm than common sense flocked to the area, believing they could strike it rich faster than you could say "Where's my gold?"

Now, a few enterprising folks—perhaps fueled by dreams of wealth or just an unshakeable belief in their own luck—decided to set up camp in what would eventually become Denver. They formed a town called "Denver City" in honor of James W. Denver, the territorial governor who, let's face it, was probably wondering what all the fuss was about. "Wait, what do you mean they named a town after me? I thought we were still figuring out how to deal with the pesky Native American tribes and the whole 'not having a proper government' thing!"

On December 3, 1859, the Territory of Jefferson (which sounds like a secret society but was actually a temporary governance effort) granted a charter to this fledgling settlement. You could say Denver was born out of chaos, like a toddler who learned to walk by toppling over every piece of furniture in the house. But instead of crying, the townsfolk just built a bar and threw a party.

Fast forward a bit, and the city was booming. Gold was being dug up like it was hiding from the sun, and the local merchants were selling everything from pickaxes to pies—because what's a gold rush without a slice of something sweet to keep the miners going? The streets filled with people, dust, and more questionable hairstyles than you could shake a stick at.

Of course, with the growth came some problems. Denver had all the charm of a town that was built in a hurry and decided that "infrastructure" was just a fancy word for "we'll figure it out later." Roads were little more than paths carved out by stampedes of hopeful miners, and the local law enforcement? Let's just say they were more focused on catching gold thieves than keeping the peace.

And then came the infamous "Sand Creek Massacre" in 1864, a tragic event that left a permanent scar on Colorado's history. It's a reminder that while Denver was growing, the struggle for territory and resources was fraught with conflict. Historians often say that the true wild west was about more than just cowboys and gold—it was about survival and tough choices that left a complicated legacy.

Despite its tumultuous beginnings, Denver soldiered on, and by the 1870s, it had transformed into a proper city. The railroads arrived, connecting it to the rest of the country, which meant more folks could flock to Denver to join the gold rush…or just enjoy the scenery and the burgeoning craft beer scene, depending on their interests.

So here we are, at the start of Denver's journey: a city that rose from dust and dreams, with a history that's as colorful as the sunsets over the Rockies. And if you're wondering how it all fits together, just know this: Denver didn't just emerge; it exploded onto the scene like a bottle of champagne—fizzy, messy, and absolutely worth celebrating!

As we plunge deeper into Denver's history, we must first acknowledge the city's unique charm—an irresistible blend of ambition, absurdity, and a certain, shall we say, "rustic chic" that only a frontier town could embody. Think of Denver in the 1860s as a high-stakes game of Monopoly, where the players are a mix of rugged miners, crafty merchants, and a few dreamers who probably thought they were the next John D. Rockefeller, except with worse haircuts.

Now, after the gold rush had settled down a bit (or at least after everyone had found out that gold wasn't actually lying around like lost change), the town started to develop some character. Picture this: saloons where the whiskey flowed like the South Platte River, and every corner had a new establishment with names like "The Gilded Pickaxe" or "The Dusty Nugget." Yes, they took their branding seriously.

In these saloons, you could find everyone from well-heeled prospectors to down-on-their-luck miners who'd spent their last dime on a game of poker and were now trying to figure out if they could bet their boots. And let's not forget the "ladies of the evening," who were probably wondering how they'd ended up in a place where the ratio of men to women was about 100 to 1. Imagine trying to find a decent dinner companion among a crowd of folks who were still figuring out how to wash their hands!

But the real drama unfolded outside the saloons. Picture a street brawl erupting over a spilled drink, only to have the sheriff intervene, not with handcuffs, but by shouting, "Hey, you all want to take this to the town square? We could use some entertainment!" And thus, impromptu boxing matches became a thing. Why have a town hall meeting when you can have a good ol' fistfight to settle disputes?

As the dust settled and Denver began to take shape, the city decided it needed some "real" infrastructure. They built roads, schools, and even a post office because what's a city without a way to send and receive mail—especially if you're hoping for letters from long-lost relatives begging you to come home and stop embarrassing the family?

But not everything was sunshine and roses. Enter the notorious "Denver Bootleggers." With alcohol being outlawed during Prohibition, enterprising locals turned to, shall we say, creative methods of obtaining and selling liquor. It was the Great American "How Do We Get Around This Law?" spirit at its finest! Picture secret tunnels, back-alley exchanges, and the occasional 'surprise' delivery that would make even the most experienced mobster nod in approval.

Meanwhile, the city was also grappling with another pressing issue: the need for a reliable water supply. So, naturally, they turned to the South Platte River, which had the combined charm of a murky puddle and the potential for "please don't drink that." But beggars can't be choosers, right? The river became the town's lifeblood—literally and figuratively—and they set to work creating irrigation systems that would make even the most seasoned engineer raise an eyebrow.

Let's not forget the spirit of community that blossomed amid the chaos. Denver was built on the principle of "we're all in this together"—and by "this," I mean surviving the whims of Mother Nature and each other. Whether it was the annual fairs, where you could enjoy everything from livestock shows to pie-eating contests, or the impromptu dance parties in the town square, Denverites found ways to come together, shake off the dust, and have a good time.

Fast forward to the late 1800s, and the arrival of the railroad completely transformed the city. Suddenly, Denver was no longer just a frontier town but a bustling hub of commerce and culture. People arrived from all over, bringing their stories, traditions, and, of course, their unique fashion choices. Imagine the scene: cowboys in boots mingling with elegant ladies in crinoline skirts, all while wondering who could sell the best apple pie.

Time passes here just like anywhere else on the planet. Welcome to the 1920s in Denver, where flappers flapped, jazz was the soundtrack to chaos, and the city was ready to embrace the modern age with the enthusiasm of a kid at a candy store—if that kid had just discovered a secret stash of chocolate bars! The air was thick with possibility, and the spirit of the age was infectious. Everyone was ready to shed their dusty frontier past and don the glitz and glam of the Jazz Age.

Now, let's be honest: Denver was already a bit of a character, but the arrival of the Roaring Twenties meant it was about to really let its hair down. Gone were the days of frontier grit; this was a time for stylish hats, flapper dresses, and a general air of "Let's party like it's 1929!" (Spoiler: they didn't know what was coming, but we'll get there).

First on the agenda was the birth of the iconic Denver Union Station. Originally built in 1881, it underwent a massive renovation in 1914, transforming it into a grand gateway for travelers. Imagine it bustling with people—suitcases in tow, jazz music playing, and the occasional traveler shouting, "Is this train even going to my destination, or did I just step into an episode of a wild mystery show?" With its ornate chandeliers and beautiful tile work, Union Station became the perfect backdrop for countless romantic escapades and tearful farewells.

Speaking of romance, let's not forget that with the 1920s came a liberating wave of social change. Women were throwing off the shackles of long skirts and corsets like they were about to take the stage in a vaudeville show. The right to vote? Check! Short hair and shorter hemlines? Double check! Denver ladies joined the fray, mixing it up in the speakeasies that popped up across town like mushrooms after a rainstorm. You can just imagine someone saying, "What's that sound? Oh, it's just the Prohibition agents knocking on the door! Quick, everyone act natural!"

Meanwhile, the Denver economy was riding high, with industries booming faster than you could say "capitalism." From mining to agriculture, the city was like a kid with a new bicycle—spinning out of control but enjoying every second. Businessmen strutted around town in suits that were probably tailored to perfection, while the locals debated over whether they should invest in stocks or just stick with good old-fashioned whiskey.

But, of course, the Roaring Twenties weren't all jazz and jiving. There was a bit of a dark side, too. The rise of organized crime meant that you had your share of unsavory characters lurking around, and not all of them were in town for the live music. Picture this: a prohibition-era speakeasy where the cocktails flow freely, but you had to keep an eye out for the "whiskey wars" between rival gangs. The phrase "you can't trust anyone" took on a whole new meaning, and keeping your cocktail glass half-full while dodging trouble was a talent in itself.

As the decade progressed, Denver was also making strides in education and infrastructure. Schools were popping up like daisies in spring, and the city was investing in parks and recreational areas—because what's the point of having all this urban growth if you can't enjoy a leisurely stroll or a good game of croquet on a sunny afternoon?

Now, let's take a moment to chat about the 1929 stock market crash, which brought a sudden halt to the roaring festivities. Picture the jazz music screeching to a halt, the confetti falling to the floor as folks realized their stock portfolios looked more like a sad grocery list than a promising investment. Denver wasn't immune to the economic downturn. Suddenly, that vibrant dance party turned into a slow shuffle as the city braced for the Great Depression.

But don't count Denver out just yet! The spirit of resilience was strong in the air. People banded together, finding ways to support one another and keep their heads above water, all while sharing stories over coffee that tasted a little more like despair than brew. There's nothing quite like the camaraderie born out of hardship—especially when it comes with a side of humor.

So, as we wrap up our romp through the Roaring Twenties, let's remember this: Denver was not just a city; it was a character in its own right, full of hopes, dreams, and the occasional nefarious plot twist. This era was a pivotal chapter in the city's story—a blend of wild parties, economic ambition, and the inevitable lessons learned when the music stops.

As we step into the 1930s, Denver was in the throes of a reality check that would make even the most hardened gold miner reconsider their life choices. The Great Depression had swept through the country like a wayward tumbleweed, leaving folks scrambling for jobs and the local economy looking like it had just stumbled out of a speakeasy at 2 a.m.—wobbly and slightly worse for wear.

Picture this: once bustling streets filled with the sounds of laughter and jazz now echoed with the solemnity of hard times. Denverites were adapting faster than you could say "economic downturn," trading in their fancy hats for well-worn caps and their evening gowns for sensible dresses. But if there's one thing Denver learned from its tumultuous past, it's that resilience is a city's best accessory.

As people gathered in coffee shops—where the "coffee" was often just a sad imitation of the real deal—conversations buzzed with innovative ideas. "What if we start a community garden?" one visionary proposed. "Or maybe we could host a talent show to raise some funds?" another chimed in, likely with visions of themselves as the next big star, singing their way out of hardship.

Local artists and musicians, perhaps sensing an opportunity, began filling the air with hope and creativity. Street performers took center stage—literally—playing everything from ragtime piano to spirited banjo tunes, reminding everyone that even when the economy is in the tank, a good tune can lift the spirits. Who knew that Denver had such talent? You could be sipping your less-than-stellar coffee and suddenly feel like you were at a Broadway show!

In a clever twist of fate, the New Deal programs introduced by President Franklin D. Roosevelt provided a much-needed boost to the struggling city. Denver welcomed initiatives aimed at job creation and public works projects, leading to the construction of new roads, parks, and buildings. Talk about a government-sponsored glow-up! "Look at us! We're getting new infrastructure while trying to figure out how to pay the rent!" It was like a community makeover, complete with fresh paint and a hint of optimism.

During this time, the iconic Red Rocks Amphitheatre was born—yes, the very venue where rock stars would later come to reign supreme. Originally constructed in the 1930s, the amphitheater was designed to showcase not only music but also the stunning beauty of Colorado's landscape. It was a perfect spot for people to gather, share stories, and forget about their worries—if only for a moment. Who wouldn't want to watch a concert in nature's very own arena, where the mountains seem to nod along to the beat?

And then there were the festivals! The local communities started hosting events that celebrated everything from arts and crafts to local produce. Picture vibrant markets springing up where folks could trade their homemade goods, swap gossip, and maybe even barter for some fresh veggies—talk about a precursor to today's farmers' markets!

As the decade wore on, folks began to find ways to cope with their new normal. Denver's inhabitants displayed a sense of humor that could rival any stand-up comedian. "You know it's a tough time when your biggest worry is whether your car will start or if your neighbor's cat is plotting to steal your lunch!" Laughter became a coping mechanism, one that turned shared adversity into a community bond stronger than steel.

By the time the 1940s rolled around, the winds of change were beginning to blow once again, as the nation geared up for World War II. Denver, ever the adaptable spirit, started contributing to the war effort. Factories opened up, producing everything from munitions to airplanes. Suddenly, the city was back in action, proving that it had more than just grit—it had the kind of determination that could weather any storm.

Welcome to the fabulous 1950s and 1960s, when Denver was not just recovering from the Great Depression but also stepping into a new era that could only be described as "Let's get groovy!" The post-war years were like a new pair of roller skates—exciting, a little wobbly, and sure to bring a few spills along the way.

As soldiers returned home, Denver found itself welcoming a wave of new residents, many of whom had the classic post-war dream: a cozy home with a white picket fence, two kids, and a dog named Sparky. All of a sudden, the suburbs sprang up like mushrooms after a rainstorm, turning the surrounding areas into a veritable patchwork of cul-de-sacs and driveways. If you ever wanted to play "spot the lawn gnome," this was the golden age!

And let's talk about the automotive boom. With more families hitting the road than ever before, highways expanded like they were trying to win a game of "who can go bigger?" The construction of I-25 and I-70 turned Denver into a transportation hub, making it easier for folks to zip in and out of the city. But with great highways came great responsibility—specifically, the responsibility to ensure that everyone could parallel park without causing a multi-car pileup. Spoiler: they couldn't.

This was also the era when Denver really started to embrace its inner culture vulture. The city became a canvas for the arts, with murals popping up and galleries opening their doors wider than a child on Christmas morning. People were getting creative and expressing themselves in every corner, whether it was through dance, painting, or that infamous "modern art" phase that left everyone wondering, "Is that really a sculpture, or did someone just throw some scrap metal together and call it a day?"

Then came the 1960s, a decade of social upheaval, and Denver was right in the thick of it. Young people flocked to the city like it was the latest fashion trend, embracing a counterculture movement that demanded change. Peace signs, bell-bottoms, and the unmistakable sound of folk music filled the air. If you thought the 50s were calm, the 60s were like someone threw a glitter bomb in the middle of a quiet library!

In 1965, the founding of the Denver Center for the Performing Arts meant that the city was officially ready to shine on the national stage. No longer content to be a frontier town, Denver was now putting on a show—literally! People flocked to see everything from Broadway productions to modern dance performances. And just like that, the city found its voice, and it was singing!

Speaking of voices, let's talk about the impact of sports in Denver during this era. The Broncos, born in 1960, quickly became a staple of the community, bringing fans together in a way that was more unifying than a Sunday potluck. The excitement of game day spread like wildfire, turning every Sunday into a mini-holiday where folks donned their orange and blue, prepared to cheer, and mentally fortified themselves against the inevitable heartache of a close loss. "We'll get 'em next time!" they'd shout, clutching their nachos like precious trophies.

And just when you thought the fun couldn't get any more electric, the 1976 Winter Olympics rolled into town. Denver was chosen as the host city, and the buzz was palpable. The world was about to get a glimpse of Colorado's stunning mountains and the hospitality of its people—like inviting friends over for a party, only this time, the world was coming to your backyard!

However, in a twist of fate that could only be described as "classic Denver," the city eventually decided to bow out of hosting due to the rising costs. The residents were left scratching their heads, wondering if they'd accidentally entered an alternate universe where the Olympics were hosted without an actual host city. The upside? All that publicity without the headache of cleaning up afterward! Talk about a savvy move!

As we dive into the late 20th century, Denver was like a teenager going through an awkward growth spurt—growing taller, but not quite sure how to handle it. With its burgeoning population and a growing reputation as a hub for culture and commerce, the city was ready to strut its stuff, albeit with a few missteps along the way.

The 1970s kicked off with Denver embracing its inner environmentalist. The city began to realize that all those lovely people moving in meant it had to figure out how to manage everything—from housing to transportation to, you know, the occasional need for clean air. This was the decade of activism, and locals took to the streets, protesting for better urban planning, public transportation, and those essential green spaces that everyone now swore they would absolutely use for picnics—eventually.

Enter the infamous "Denver Mint" saga. In 1906, the U.S. Mint built a branch in Denver, but by the 1970s, it became a symbol of just how much the city was worth—both literally and figuratively. As demand for silver coins surged, the mint saw itself drowning in work, proving that Denver was, in fact, serious about its economic growth. But with great minting power came great responsibility—particularly when it came to ensuring that local smugglers weren't trying to sneak bags of silver out like it was a high school graduation party!

Meanwhile, the economy had its ups and downs, and the oil crisis of the late 1970s shook things up. Gas prices soared, leading many to rethink their transportation habits. Suddenly, the once-proud Denverites who had paraded around in their shiny new cars began considering the virtues of carpooling, biking, and—gasp—public transport! Picture a city where everyone was suddenly very interested in bus schedules and where the term "commuter" didn't just mean "someone who drives everywhere and hopes for the best."

As the 1980s rolled in, Denver was ready to embrace its new identity. A cultural renaissance took root as the city welcomed a wave of artists, musicians, and entrepreneurs, eager to sprinkle some color into the urban landscape. Think of it as a giant arts and crafts project where the only rule was to go wild with creativity. Murals adorned buildings, music festivals popped up like daisies, and the local food scene exploded. Suddenly, everyone was a critic—and a self-proclaimed "foodie." "Is that a new taco truck? I must sample its wares!"

Of course, not all was rosy in the Mile High City. With growth came the challenge of managing gentrification, which left many residents feeling squeezed out. The struggle between maintaining Denver's unique character while welcoming new development became the talk of the town. It was like watching a family argue over how to decorate their living room—there were bound to be disagreements!

As we danced into the 1990s, Denver began to polish its image even further. The Denver International Airport (DIA) opened in 1995, instantly becoming the largest airport in North America and giving Denver bragging rights like a champion at a county fair. "Look at us, we've got an airport that's bigger than some small countries!" Travelers flocked in, excited to discover all that Denver had to offer.

And let's not forget the sporting renaissance! The Denver Nuggets, Colorado Rockies, and Denver Broncos all solidified their places in the hearts of fans. Game days transformed into city-wide celebrations. "Win or lose, we're all here for the nachos!" became the mantra of the day. The city was buzzing with pride, and the local bars and restaurants thrived as they served up everything from buffalo wings to locally brewed beers—because what's a game without a solid beverage?

However, amidst the excitement, there were lessons to learn. The city faced its fair share of challenges, from economic recessions to social issues, but the Denver spirit—defined by resilience and humor—never faded. Denverites proved they could weather any storm, whether it was a blizzard that left everyone stuck in their homes with nothing but a good book and a questionable supply of snacks or a political debate that turned into a lively neighborhood discussion at the local coffee shop.

Welcome to the dazzling 21st century, where Denver emerges from its chrysalis, fully equipped with organic kale smoothies, craft beers, and the kind of technology that makes you wonder how we ever lived without smartphones. It's a wild ride of innovation, nature-loving, and the occasional existential crisis at a hip coffee shop—because what's the point of a city if you can't contemplate life while sipping a pour-over?

As the new millennium dawned, Denver was ready to embrace its transformation into a modern metropolis. Tech companies began flocking to the Mile High City like bees to honey, drawn by the promise of a creative workforce, a stunning landscape, and a lifestyle that encouraged both productivity and play. "Why work in Silicon Valley when you can code with a view of the Rockies?" became the rallying cry for new-age entrepreneurs. The startup scene exploded, and suddenly every coffee shop was filled with individuals in hoodies, busily typing away on laptops, fueled by caffeine and dreams.

But let's not forget the outdoorsy spirit that defines Denver. With the Rocky Mountains just a hop, skip, and a jump away, residents embraced their inner adventurer. Hiking trails became the ultimate escape from the hustle and bustle, and Instagram exploded with photos of stunning vistas. "This is me summiting Mount Bierstadt! #Blessed," they'd post, while the rest of us were just trying to figure out how to find our car keys.

Of course, with great mountains come great responsibility. The influx of new residents brought challenges, particularly when it came to housing. Denver's real estate market began to resemble a competitive game of musical chairs, where everyone wanted a seat, but there weren't enough chairs to go around. "Wait, that cute little bungalow is how much?!" became the common refrain. Rents skyrocketed, and the search for affordable housing turned into a full-time job—complete with interviews, applications, and the occasional dramatic sigh.

In response, the city began to prioritize sustainability, seeking ways to ensure that its growth didn't come at the expense of its beautiful surroundings. Eco-friendly initiatives sprang up like wildflowers, from urban farms to bike-sharing programs. Denverites were determined to be good stewards of the environment, even if it meant cycling uphill in spandex shorts—because who doesn't love a little uphill struggle with their morning coffee?

And speaking of coffee, the culinary scene in Denver took off like a rocket! The city's food landscape became a delightful mix of traditional and avant-garde. From farm-to-table restaurants that prided themselves on using local ingredients to quirky food trucks serving everything from gourmet tacos to artisan grilled cheese, it felt like every meal was a culinary adventure. "You mean I can get a bacon-wrapped avocado taco? Sign me up!" became the mantra of hungry locals.

In addition to its culinary delights, Denver also embraced its arts and culture scene with open arms. Museums, theaters, and music venues sprang up, creating a rich tapestry of entertainment options. The Denver Art Museum began hosting blockbuster exhibitions, while venues like the Fillmore Auditorium brought in bands that spanned every genre imaginable. It was a cultural buffet—just be sure to wear your stretchy pants!

And let's not overlook the sports scene, which remained a staple of Denver life. The Broncos continued to rally fans around their orange and blue, while the Rockies and Nuggets solidified their presence in the hearts of locals. Game day became a full-on celebration, complete with tailgating that often looked more like a block party than a pre-game ritual. "What do you mean I can't bring my homemade guacamole to the stadium?!" became a cry of outrage heard throughout the parking lots.

As we approached the late 2010s, Denver was not without its trials. The city grappled with issues of equity and social justice, as communities pushed for changes to ensure that growth and prosperity were shared by all. Activism and advocacy became buzzwords as residents rallied to make their voices heard, reminding everyone that a vibrant city is one that uplifts all its inhabitants—not just those who can afford a fancy latte.

By the time we hit the 2020s, Denver had firmly established itself as a place of opportunity, creativity, and community spirit. The pandemic may have thrown a wrench into the works, but Denverites adapted once again, discovering new ways to connect, support local businesses, and enjoy the great outdoors—safely, of course. "Let's hike! Who needs a crowded bar when you can have fresh air and nature?" became the rallying cry as trails filled with determined adventurers.

So, as we wrap up this chapter on Denver's 21st-century journey, let's celebrate its unique blend of innovation, culture, and outdoor spirit. The city has weathered challenges and embraced change with humor and resilience, proving that while it may be growing rapidly, it never loses its distinctive personality.

As we launch ourselves into the future, we find Denver standing at the edge of a precipice, looking out over a horizon filled with possibilities and challenges. Picture it: the city has donned its best aviator sunglasses, ready to soar into uncharted territory like a high-flying eagle that's just discovered it can take selfies. The future is bright, but it's also filled with a mix of excitement, uncertainty, and the occasional "Wait, what are we doing?"

First up, let's talk about sustainability—because, really, what's a modern city without an eco-friendly plan? Denver is all about embracing its green credentials, from ambitious goals to reduce carbon emissions to innovative initiatives like urban gardening and renewable energy projects. "We're going solar! Who needs a fossil fuel dependency when you can have sunshine and a very hip vibe?" became the motto of the eco-warriors taking over the city.

Public transportation also got a facelift, as residents recognized that relying on cars was about as trendy as wearing bell-bottoms in a yoga class. Enter the expansion of the RTD light rail system, making it easier for folks to get around without turning into a traffic jam. "Why sit in rush hour when you can kick back and enjoy a podcast on the train?" became a valid question as the light rail transformed commutes into a time for self-care and relaxation—complete with a side of people-watching, of course.

But it's not all about getting from Point A to Point B—let's talk about Point C: community. Denver has been diving headfirst into the concept of inclusivity, with efforts to ensure that everyone—regardless of background—has a seat at the table. Grassroots organizations have sprung up, advocating for social justice, affordable housing, and equitable access to resources. "No one gets left behind on this ride!" became the battle cry for those rallying for change.

And speaking of community, let's shine a spotlight on the tech boom that continues to sweep through Denver like a refreshing mountain breeze. Startups and established companies alike are flocking to the city, creating a buzz that rivals the excitement of a Broncos victory. Remote work has shifted the landscape, with people realizing they can work from anywhere—with a view of the Rockies, of course. "Why sit in an office when you can run Zoom meetings from a mountain cabin?" became the new mantra for many Denverites.

However, as with any growth spurt, challenges remain. The influx of new residents has led to concerns about gentrification and the preservation of Denver's rich cultural heritage. Long-time residents often find themselves reminiscing about the "good old days" when neighborhoods had a distinct flavor and everyone knew their neighbor's dog by name. "Did I mention that my grandma lived here before the hipster invasion?" became a nostalgic refrain heard over brunch as people reminisced about simpler times.

And let's not forget about the role of arts and culture in shaping the future of Denver. The arts community is alive and kicking, continuously pushing boundaries and challenging norms. New galleries, theaters, and performance spaces are popping up like mushrooms, each one more eclectic than the last. "Is that performance art or just my friend's new dance routine?" became a running joke among those trying to keep up with the fast-paced creative scene.

As the 2030s approach, Denver has established itself as a city that not only embraces change but thrives on it. From tech innovations to cultural movements, the Mile High City is on a trajectory that promises continued growth and transformation. Local leaders are focusing on smart city initiatives that incorporate technology to improve quality of life, making it easier for residents to engage with their community and access services. "Alexa, what's the best taco truck in Denver?" might just become the new way to navigate the culinary landscape.

From here on out, I'll be discussing the fascinating history of Colorado cities in alphabetical order, just so it's easy for you to find in the book the next time you roll through a town with a population of 162 people and want to know more without stopping.

Akron

Not to be confused with Akron, Ohio, which is a real place but doesn't have the charm of our little gem in the Centennial State. If you're looking for a big city vibe, you might want to keep driving. But if you're ready for some small-town adventure, pull up a chair and let's dive into the delights of this not-so-bustling haven.

First things first, getting to Akron is a journey in itself. You'll need a good map, a reliable GPS, or perhaps an old-school compass if you're feeling particularly adventurous. As you drive through the vast Colorado plains, you might start to question your life choices—like why you thought a weekend getaway to a town with a population smaller than your college dorm was a good idea. But fear not! As you approach, you'll be greeted by the kind of welcome that makes you feel like a celebrity. In Akron, you're not just another face in the crowd; you're the star of the show!

Once you arrive, it's time to explore. Your first stop should definitely be the Akron Historical Society Museum. Now, don't let the word "historical" scare you off. This museum is less about dusty relics and more about quirky exhibits that'll make you chuckle. Picture yourself walking through a room filled with vintage farming equipment, each piece with its own hilarious backstory. "This here is a plow that was used in the 1800s. Legend has it that the farmer lost a bet and had to use it to plow the neighbor's yard on a dare." You'll leave with a newfound appreciation for the rural lifestyle and a burning desire to start your own farming YouTube channel.

Next, you must visit the Washington County Courthouse. But before you walk in, practice your best dramatic courtroom entrance. Adjust those imaginary glasses, take a deep breath, and stride through the doors like you're about to deliver a groundbreaking closing argument. Of course, you'll quickly realize that it's just a courthouse and not an episode of Law & Order, but hey, a little imagination never hurt anyone. Plus, the architecture is stunning—just try not to accidentally step into a legal meeting and declare, "I object!" because you've just realized there's no coffee being served.

After all that exploring, you're bound to be hungry. Head over to The Blue Sky Cafe, where the food is so comforting it should come with a blanket. This is the kind of place where locals gather to share stories, gossip about the weather, and indulge in meals that taste like a hug. The menu is filled with classic comfort food that would make even the toughest food critic shed a tear. Just make sure to save room for dessert—legend has it their pie could single-handedly cure homesickness. You might find yourself saying, "One slice isn't enough; I'll take a whole pie to go!" But good luck explaining that to the TSA on your flight back home.

Now, if you think Akron is all about food and history, think again. The great outdoors awaits you! The Platte River runs nearby, offering a perfect backdrop for hiking, fishing, or simply sitting quietly while contemplating the mysteries of life—like why you still can't find a matching sock. Hiking the trails is a great way to experience nature, but beware of the local wildlife. If you see a deer staring at you, don't take it personally. It's not judging your life choices; it's just as confused as you are about why you decided to wear sandals on a hike.

If you happen to be in Akron during the annual rodeo, consider yourself lucky. The Akron Rodeo is a spectacle unlike any other, where cowboys and cowgirls come together to show off their skills in a way that will leave you both entertained and slightly terrified. You'll witness barrel racing, bull riding, and probably a few mishaps that will make you question your own athletic abilities. Just remember to keep your "Yeehaw!" ready; it might come in handy if you accidentally get caught up in a lively conversation about which cowboy has the best mustache.

As your visit winds down, you may find it hard to say goodbye to Akron. You'll be armed with hilarious stories and a deeper appreciation for small-town life. The locals are incredibly friendly, and as you drive away, don't forget to wave goodbye. They'll likely wave back, wondering who that out-of-towner was that just spent a weekend living their best small-town life.

So, whether you came for the quirky museum, the delectable pie, or the unforgettable rodeo, Akron, Colorado, has a charm that'll linger long after you leave. It's a reminder that sometimes, the best adventures are found in the most unexpected places. Go ahead, spread the word about this hidden gem! You might just inspire a travel trend that has people flocking to Akron for all the right reasons. Now, pack your bags and get ready for your next small-town adventure—you never know what laughter and stories await you in Akron!

Alamosa

Alamosa, Colorado, where the elevation is higher than your wildest dreams and the charm is as abundant as the nearby sand dunes! Nestled in the San Luis Valley, Alamosa is a place that'll make you wonder why you haven't packed your bags and moved here already. Seriously, once you visit, you'll be telling your friends, "I'm thinking of becoming a professional Alamosa enthusiast."

Let's start with how to get there. If you're traveling from the city, prepare yourself for a journey that feels longer than waiting for your friend who says they're "five minutes away." The scenery is beautiful, though, with mountains that look like they're flexing just for you. You'll wind through some picturesque landscapes, and before you know it, you'll catch a glimpse of the town and think, "Wow, it looks like I just stepped into a postcard!" Spoiler alert: it looks even better in person.

Once you arrive, your first stop should definitely be the San Luis Valley Museum. Don't let the word "museum" scare you off; this is not your average dusty place filled with artifacts that nobody cares about. No, no! This museum is like a treasure trove of local history and culture, featuring exhibits that will make you laugh, cry, and possibly question why you ever took a history class. You'll learn about everything from the region's agricultural history to the bizarre tale of a local inventor who tried to create a self-propelling bicycle that, let's just say, didn't quite take off. You can't help but admire the optimism!

Next on your itinerary should be the Alamosa Farmers Market. Imagine a place where the local farmers gather to show off their produce, homemade goods, and an alarming number of ways to enjoy zucchini. This is where you can sample everything from fresh salsa to baked goods that taste like they were made with a secret ingredient: love. Just be prepared for a friendly competition among the vendors, each one trying to outdo the other with quirky product names and larger-than-life personalities. You might hear someone yelling, "Try my pickles! They're so good they should be illegal!"

Now that you're fueled up with local goodies, it's time to get outside and explore the nearby Great Sand Dunes National Park. Yes, you heard that right—sand dunes in Colorado! It's like Mother Nature decided to toss a beach into the mountains just to confuse everyone. The dunes are massive, rising over 700 feet tall, and they provide the perfect setting for some truly unique adventures. You can hike, sled down the dunes, or just roll around in the sand like a kid who's just discovered the beach for the first time. Just remember, while sand might be great for making castles, it's less enjoyable when it finds its way into your shoes, car, and snacks.

After a long day of hiking and frolicking in the sand, you'll want to refuel, and there's no better place than one of Alamosa's local diners. The food here is so hearty you might need a forklift to get up from the table. You'll find classic diner fare that'll make your taste buds dance. Just when you think you've had your fill, the pie comes out. Local lore has it that the pies are so good they could persuade even the most ardent dieter to throw caution to the wind. "A slice won't hurt, right?!" you'll convince yourself, as you dive into a piece of homemade cherry pie that tastes like pure happiness.

If you're feeling particularly adventurous, why not check out the Rio Grande Scenic Railroad? This is not just any train ride; this is a scenic journey through some of the most breathtaking landscapes you can imagine. The train rolls through mountains, valleys, and all the scenic spots that make you go, "Wow, I really need to take more pictures." You'll find yourself grinning like a kid on a roller coaster as you chug along, and if you're lucky, you might even catch a glimpse of wildlife. Just be careful not to wave at a deer too enthusiastically; it might think you're trying to challenge it to a race.

As your time in Alamosa comes to a close, you might find it hard to say goodbye. You'll be filled with stories that you'll regale your friends with, like the time you attempted to sled down the sand dunes and ended up rolling down like a tumbleweed, or when you discovered that one of the local farmers doubles as an expert joke teller. "Why did the tomato turn red?" they'll ask you. "Because it saw the salad dressing!"

In the end, Alamosa is not just a destination; it's an experience. From the rich history to the vibrant community and stunning natural beauty, you'll leave with memories that'll last a lifetime. So, whether you came for the sand dunes, the food, or the quirky local charm, know that Alamosa has a special place in the heart of anyone who visits. And who knows? You might just find yourself planning your next trip before you even leave! Now, go forth and spread the word about this hidden gem—you might just inspire a new wave of Alamosa enthusiasts!

Allenspark

Nestled in the foothills of the Rocky Mountains, this charming little town is the kind of place where the air is fresher, the mountains are taller, and the residents might just be slightly friendlier than your average bear—well, the bear might be friendly too, but let's not push our luck. If you're looking for a peaceful getaway from the hustle and bustle, you've found it. Just prepare for the inevitable "where in the world is Allenspark?" question that'll come from anyone you tell about your adventure.

Getting to Allenspark is half the fun. You'll wind through roads that twist and turn like they're trying to perform a magic trick, leading you through stunning landscapes that will have you pulling over for a thousand photos. And don't worry if you get lost; just follow the sound of laughter and the smell of fresh pie, and you'll eventually stumble upon this hidden gem.

As you arrive, the first thing you'll notice is the overwhelming beauty of the area. With towering trees, majestic mountains, and enough natural scenery to make a postcard jealous, you'll feel like you've stepped into a Hallmark movie. And don't forget your camera, because this place is Instagram gold. Just try to avoid posing in front of every tree; you don't want your followers to think you're auditioning for the role of "Tree Hugger Extraordinaire."

Now, once you've soaked in the sights, it's time to dive into Allenspark's history. Founded in the late 1800s, this town has seen more than its fair share of colorful characters and stories. Legend has it that early settlers were so enchanted by the beauty of the landscape that they vowed to build a community where everyone could appreciate the great outdoors. Or maybe they just wanted a place to escape the hustle and bustle of city life—who's to say? Either way, Allenspark became a haven for those seeking peace, quiet, and possibly a good place to grow a beard.

For a taste of local culture, head to the Allenspark Community Center. This is where the magic happens—well, as much magic as a small-town community center can muster. From potluck dinners to pancake breakfasts, you'll find events that'll make you feel like a local in no time. Just don't be surprised if someone tries to get you to join the "Allenspark Book Club," which is really just an excuse to drink wine and discuss whether the dog in the book should've gotten a happy ending.

Feeling outdoorsy? You're in luck! Allenspark is surrounded by some of the most stunning natural landscapes in Colorado. A visit to Rocky Mountain National Park is a must. As you hike through the trails, you'll encounter breathtaking vistas and possibly a few squirrels who have clearly never heard of personal space. Keep your eyes peeled for wildlife, but remember, if you see a moose, take a picture—just don't try to pet it. They have a reputation for being a bit standoffish, and you definitely don't want to be the human who thought it would be a good idea to become BFFs with a wild animal.

Once you've had your fill of hiking, it's time to explore the local art scene. Allenspark is home to several talented artists, and you can find galleries showcasing everything from breathtaking landscapes to quirky sculptures made from recycled materials. You might even stumble upon an art fair where the locals proudly display their creations. Just don't be surprised if someone tries to sell you a painting of a cow wearing sunglasses; in Allenspark, that's just a Tuesday.

After a day of adventures, it's time to refuel. Allenspark might be small, but it has a few dining options that'll satisfy your hunger. Check out the local diners where you can indulge in hearty meals that feel like they were made by your grandma. Expect comfort food served with a side of warmth—just like Grandma used to make, minus the overly long stories about "back in my day." And if you're lucky, the pie will be fresh out of the oven. Remember, in Allenspark, "one slice" is merely a suggestion; you might find yourself ordering three and pretending to share with friends.

If you happen to be in town during the summer, you might want to check out the local festivals. The Allenspark Music Festival is a real treat, featuring local bands and enough good vibes to last you until the next festival season. Just imagine dancing under the stars, sipping local brews, and getting swept up in the joyous atmosphere. You might even find yourself doing the chicken dance with a stranger, and let's be honest, it'll be a bonding experience you'll never forget.

As your time in Allenspark comes to a close, you'll be filled with stories to share about your adventures. You'll tell your friends about the breathtaking hikes, the quirky art, and that time you mistook a moose for a friendly dog. And let's not forget the food—who could forget those legendary pies? You might even start to contemplate packing up your life and moving to this delightful little town, where the pace is slower, the air is cleaner, and every day feels like a new adventure waiting to happen.

So, whether you came for the scenery, the history, or just to escape the chaos of daily life, Allenspark, Colorado, has a special way of capturing your heart. It's a reminder that sometimes, the best experiences are found in the most unexpected places. Now go forth and tell the world about Allenspark—you might just inspire someone else to pack their bags and experience the magic for themselves!

Antonito

Nestled in the San Luis Valley, Antonito is like that quirky friend who always knows where the best pizza is hidden and tells the funniest stories. If you're looking for a place that's off the beaten path, where the locals are friendlier than your favorite childhood teddy bear, and where adventure awaits at every turn, then buckle up, because you're in for a ride!

First things first, let's talk about how to get there. The journey to Antonito is an experience in itself. You'll wind through breathtaking landscapes that will have you singing along to your favorite road trip songs, or perhaps composing an impromptu ballad about how you've finally escaped the city. As you drive, keep an eye out for the scenery; you might spot a few llamas lounging in the fields. Yes, llamas. Antonito is famous for them, and if you don't see one, consider your trip incomplete.

Upon arrival, you'll find Antonito is not just any small town—it's the kind of place where time feels like it's taking a leisurely stroll. The streets are lined with colorful buildings, and you might even feel like you've stepped onto a movie set. Don't be surprised if you start humming the theme song from a classic Western as you stroll through the town. It's that kind of place.

Your first stop should be the Antonito Train Depot. This isn't just any train station; it's the gateway to the Cumbres & Toltec Scenic Railroad, one of the most scenic train rides in the country. As you board the train, you'll feel like you're about to embark on a grand adventure, possibly involving pirates, treasure, and a talking parrot. Okay, maybe not the pirates, but the views are definitely worth it. The train chugs along through the mountains, giving you a front-row seat to some of the most stunning landscapes you've ever seen. Just make sure to bring your camera, because if you don't document it, did it even happen?

After your scenic train ride, it's time to dive into the local history. Antonito has a rich past that's as colorful as the town itself. Founded in the late 1800s, it started as a railroad town and has seen its fair share of characters and stories. Legend has it that the town was once a bustling hub for travelers and adventurers, with tales of cowboys and gold seekers echoing through the streets. Just think about all the stories these old buildings could tell if they had mouths—well, and maybe a few less splinters.

Feeling hungry? Antonito has some dining spots that'll make your taste buds do a happy dance. Head over to one of the local diners, where the food is served with a side of warmth and maybe a little gossip. You'll find hearty meals that could only be described as "grandma-approved." The green chili here is legendary—so good that people have been known to start spontaneous food fights over it. Just kidding, but be careful not to eat too much; you don't want to end up in a food coma while trying to explore the rest of the town.

Now, if you're looking for a little adventure, why not take a detour to the nearby Conejos River? This hidden gem is perfect for fishing, kayaking, or just splashing around like a kid who has just discovered the joy of water. The river is beautiful, and you might find yourself lost in the moment, wondering why you don't live here permanently. Just be sure to keep your phone dry; no one wants a soggy smartphone during a spontaneous photo op.

After a day of exploring, you'll want to wind down at one of Antonito's local shops. You might find yourself in a store filled with handmade crafts, locally sourced goods, and quirky souvenirs that you never knew you needed. Think of it as a treasure hunt where every item has its own story. Who wouldn't want to bring home a llama-shaped keychain as a reminder of your Antonito adventures? It's the perfect conversation starter for all those awkward "What's that?" moments.

If you're lucky enough to be in town during one of the local festivals, you're in for a treat. The Antonito Potato Festival is a highlight, where you can enjoy everything from potato sack races to potato-themed culinary delights. You'll laugh, you'll eat, and you might just find yourself wondering how many different ways a potato can be prepared. Spoiler alert: it's more than you think. Just don't challenge the locals to a potato-eating contest unless you're prepared to face the consequences—like having to roll yourself home afterward.

As your time in Antonito draws to a close, you might find it hard to say goodbye. You'll leave with a heart full of laughter, a camera full of memories, and a stomach that may or may not be permanently lined with green chili. You'll be filled with stories to share about the scenic train rides, the llamas, and that time you accidentally ordered three servings of fries because the waiter was just so darn charming.

In the end, Antonito is more than just a small town; it's a place where you can escape the chaos of everyday life and find joy in the simple things. It's a reminder that sometimes the best adventures are found in the most unexpected places. So go ahead, tell your friends about Antonito, the quirky crossroads of adventure. You might just inspire them to pack their bags and join you on your next escapade!

Arboles

The population is small, but the adventures are larger than life! Nestled near the banks of the tranquil Navajo Lake, this little town is the perfect spot for anyone looking to escape the hustle and bustle of city life. If you've ever dreamed of a place where the biggest decision you'll make all day is whether to go fishing or hiking, you've found your paradise.

Getting to Arboles is part of the fun. As you drive through the scenic landscape, you might feel like you're in a postcard—lush greenery, mountains in the background, and maybe even a few cows grazing nonchalantly like they own the place. Keep your eyes peeled for local wildlife! You may spot everything from deer to the occasional curious squirrel that seems to have a personal vendetta against your car's windshield. Don't take it personally; they just want to know what you're doing in their neck of the woods.

Once you arrive in Arboles, the first thing you'll notice is that it's small. I mean really small. So small that you might miss it if you blink, but don't let that fool you! This tiny town is packed with charm, and you'll feel right at home the moment you step out of your car. The locals are friendly and might even give you a warm smile or wave, which is standard practice in small-town America—especially if you're holding a slice of pie.

Speaking of pie, your first stop should definitely be at the local diner. It's a quintessential small-town spot that serves everything from burgers to breakfast all day. As you walk in, the smell of frying bacon and fresh coffee will hit you like a warm hug. Grab a seat, and prepare for a menu filled with comfort food that could make even the pickiest eater weep tears of joy. Don't skip dessert! The pie here is legendary, and if you're lucky, you might catch the owner telling stories about how she once beat a bear in a pie-eating contest. Or at least that's how the story goes; who are we to question it?

After you've fueled up, it's time to explore the great outdoors. Arboles is right next to Navajo Lake State Park, a beautiful place perfect for fishing, kayaking, and simply basking in the sun like a lizard on a rock. If you're feeling adventurous, rent a kayak and paddle out onto the lake. Just be prepared for some friendly competition with the local ducks, who will surely try to race you for bragging rights. Remember, ducks don't play fair—they might use some serious quackery to distract you.

If fishing is more your style, grab a pole and head to the water. The lake is known for its abundance of fish, and there's nothing quite like the thrill of reeling in a big one. Just remember, if you catch a fish that's bigger than your boat, it's totally acceptable to take a victory lap around the lake while shouting, "I'm the king/queen of the fish!" But be careful; you might just scare the fish away for good.

After a day of outdoor adventures, it's time to check out some local history. Arboles may be small, but it has a rich past that's worth exploring. The town has deep roots in the old railroad days, and you can still see remnants of the past scattered throughout. There's something magical about walking down streets that have witnessed countless stories and characters. Just don't be surprised if you feel like you're in a Western movie—cowboys may or may not ride by on horseback.

If you're into art, swing by one of the local galleries. You'll find everything from beautiful landscapes to quirky sculptures that make you scratch your head and think, "What on earth?" The local artists are passionate about their work, and you might even strike up a conversation that leads to a discussion about the meaning of life—don't worry; you won't need to know the answer, just nod and smile.

As evening approaches, head back to the diner for dinner and some live music. On certain nights, local musicians gather to showcase their talents, and you'll find yourself tapping your feet to the rhythm while enjoying some mouthwatering comfort food. You might even be inspired to jump up and show off your best dance moves, which will undoubtedly make you the life of the party. Just be ready for the locals to cheer you on or—better yet—join in with their own dance steps, making it an impromptu small-town hoedown!

As your visit to Arboles comes to an end, you'll be filled with laughter, memories, and maybe a few extra pounds from all that pie. You'll leave knowing that this tiny town has a big heart and a community that's eager to welcome you back anytime. Whether it was the friendly faces, the stunning scenery, or the unforgettable food that captured your heart, one thing is for sure: Arboles has a special place in your travel tales.

So, go ahead and share your newfound love for Arboles with everyone you know. Tell them about the charming diner, the serene lake, and the quirky local art scene. Maybe even write a postcard or two—just make sure to send one to yourself as a reminder of the simple joys found in small towns. After all, life's greatest adventures often happen when you least expect them, and Arboles is just waiting for your next visit!

Arriba

Arriba, Colorado, a tiny town that proves size doesn't matter when it comes to charm. Situated along the plains and surrounded by the kind of open space that makes you feel like you're in a movie about the Wild West, Arriba is a hidden gem waiting to be discovered. If you've ever dreamt of a place where the only traffic jam is caused by a cow slowly crossing the road, then grab your cowboy hat and let's dive into this quirky slice of Americana.

Getting to Arriba is a journey worth taking. The drive through the Colorado plains is serene and will remind you of all those picturesque postcard images. As you roll down the highway, you might even catch yourself singing along to your favorite road trip tunes, with the windows down and the wind in your hair. Just watch out for tumbleweeds; they have a knack for appearing out of nowhere and can ruin the vibe if you're not careful.

When you finally roll into Arriba, you'll notice the town's population isn't much larger than your family reunion. In fact, Arriba is so small that if you blink, you might miss it. But don't let its size fool you! This town is bursting with personality, and the locals are as friendly as a golden retriever at a petting zoo. As you stroll through the town, don't be surprised if you're greeted with a wave or a cheerful "Howdy!"—it's just their way of saying, "Welcome to our little slice of paradise!"

Your first stop should be the Arriba Community Center. This is the heart of the town, where the magic happens. From potluck dinners to bingo nights, the community center is where the locals gather to share stories, laughter, and possibly a few embarrassing moments. Grab a slice of homemade pie and settle in for a night of good old-fashioned fun. Just be prepared for some friendly competition during bingo; these folks take their games seriously!

After soaking up the local camaraderie, it's time to explore Arriba's rich history. Founded in the late 1800s, the town started as a railroad hub and has seen its fair share of characters and stories. You might find yourself captivated by tales of early settlers who braved the wild frontier to build a community. As you wander through the town, you can almost hear the echoes of horse-drawn wagons and see the ghostly figures of cowboys tiptoeing down the streets, hats pulled low over their eyes. Okay, maybe that last part is just your imagination, but who doesn't love a good ghost story?

Once you're well-versed in Arriba's history, it's time to step outside and enjoy the great outdoors. The surrounding plains offer a fantastic playground for hiking, biking, and even birdwatching. Strap on your hiking boots and head out to explore the nearby trails. You'll be greeted by beautiful vistas and the kind of quiet that makes you realize how much you miss nature when you're stuck in the city. Keep your eyes peeled for wildlife; you might spot a curious prairie dog peeking out of its burrow or a majestic hawk soaring overhead. Just remember, no matter how cute they are, they're not great at sharing snacks.

If you're feeling adventurous, take a short drive to the nearby Jumbo Reservoir. This hidden gem is perfect for fishing, boating, or just relaxing by the water with a good book. If you're lucky, you might even catch the sunset reflecting off the water, creating a scene so picturesque you'll be tempted to start painting. Just be careful not to drop your sandwich in the water while you're trying to capture the moment—nothing ruins a peaceful day like a soggy lunch!

When hunger strikes, it's time to head back to Arriba for some good ol' American diner fare. The local diner is where you'll find food so hearty it could fuel a small army. From burgers to fries and milkshakes that are bigger than your head, the menu will have you feeling like you're in a classic 1950s movie. Don't skip the chance to order the daily special; it's always a delicious surprise. Just don't be alarmed if your server tries to engage you in a passionate debate about the best way to cook a steak; it's a rite of passage in Arriba.

As the day winds down, consider stopping by one of Arriba's local shops. While the options may be limited, you'll find unique treasures that could make perfect gifts—or that quirky item you never knew you needed. You might stumble upon hand-crafted goods, local art, or even that one-of-a-kind souvenir that makes you say, "I have to have this!" Just be prepared to explain to your friends back home why you decided to buy a decorative cowbell.

If you're lucky enough to be in Arriba during one of the town's annual events, you're in for a treat. The community comes alive with celebrations that showcase local culture, food, and, of course, some friendly competition. Whether it's a rodeo, a county fair, or a pie-eating contest, you'll find events that'll have you laughing and enjoying the small-town spirit. Just remember to stretch before participating; you don't want to be that person who tries to eat five slices of pie only to end up in a food coma.

As your visit comes to a close, you'll find it hard to say goodbye to Arriba. You'll leave with your heart full of laughter and your mind buzzing with memories. From the friendly locals and the delicious food to the stunning landscapes and rich history, Arriba has a way of capturing your heart. You might even start plotting your return trip before you've even left the parking lot!

So, go ahead and tell your friends about Arriba, the little town with a lot of character. Share your tales of pie contests and prairie dog sightings, and let them know that sometimes the best adventures are found in the most unexpected places. Who knows? You might just inspire them to join you on your next escapade to this charming corner of Colorado!

Arvada

Arvada, Colorado, a vibrant suburban enclave that is so much more than just a place to rest your head after a long day of work. Nestled just northwest of Denver, Arvada has carved out a niche for itself as a hub of history, outdoor adventure, and quirky charm. If you're looking for a spot where the streets are lined with beautiful parks, the local coffee shops have more personality than your last blind date, and the craft beer flows like a mountain stream, then buckle up, because Arvada is ready to show you a good time.

Let's start with how to get there. The drive to Arvada will take you through the picturesque Colorado landscape, where you'll see everything from towering mountains to sprawling plains. As you approach the city, keep an eye out for the iconic windmill at the entrance to Arvada. You might think it's a beacon guiding you to a hidden treasure, and in a way, it is—because the treasure is all the fun you're about to have.

Once you arrive, the first thing you'll notice is the delightful mix of old and new. Arvada has a rich history dating back to the Gold Rush days, and the town embraces its past while also thriving in the present. The historic Olde Town Arvada district is a must-see, with its charming storefronts, delicious eateries, and an atmosphere that feels like stepping into a movie set. As you stroll down the streets, you might find yourself humming an old-timey tune, just to match the ambiance. Be careful, though; you might attract the attention of a street performer who will insist you join their impromptu band.

Speaking of Olde Town, this area is not just a feast for the eyes—it's also a feast for your stomach. Grab a bite at one of the many local restaurants, each boasting unique flavors that could make your taste buds sing in harmony. From artisanal pizzas to mouthwatering tacos, you'll be tempted to try everything on the menu. Just remember, this isn't a contest to see how many meals you can consume in one sitting; it's about enjoying the experience. Although, if you do accidentally order four entrees, at least you'll have plenty of leftovers to impress your friends with later.

As you explore further, don't miss the Arvada Center for the Arts and Humanities. This cultural gem hosts everything from art exhibits to theater performances. You'll feel like a cultured individual just by walking through the doors. Whether you want to catch a local theater production or admire the latest art installations, this place has it all. And if you're feeling brave, consider signing up for a class. Just imagine telling your friends back home that you're now a "watercolor enthusiast." Who needs to be a professional when you can create something that's interpretatively called "abstract disaster"?

Now, if you're in the mood for some fresh air, head to one of Arvada's many parks. The city is home to over 100 parks, each with its own unique charm. You can wander through the beautiful trails of the Majestic View Nature Center, where you might encounter everything from wildflowers to the occasional squirrel that seems to be plotting its next acorn heist. Don't forget to take in the stunning views of the Rocky Mountains while you're there—it's a sight that will make you want to whip out your phone and snap a million pictures. Just make sure you don't drop it while trying to capture that perfect sunset shot!

If you're looking for a little adventure, Arvada is conveniently located near some fantastic hiking and biking trails. You can hop on your bike and explore the Ralston Creek Trail, which winds through beautiful landscapes and offers plenty of spots to stop and enjoy a picnic. Just be warned: if you see a family of ducks crossing the path, they don't adhere to the rules of the road. You might have to stop and wait while they strut their stuff like they own the place. Honestly, they probably do.

After all that outdoor fun, you'll want to relax, and what better way to unwind than by sampling the local craft beer scene? Arvada boasts several breweries that are worth checking out. Each one offers its own unique brews, from hoppy IPAs to rich stouts. You might even discover your new favorite beer, which will undoubtedly lead to passionate discussions about hops and malt when you get back home. And if you're feeling adventurous, ask for a flight of their best beers—you'll be a connoisseur in no time. Just be sure to pace yourself; nobody wants to be "that person" who thinks they can keep up with the locals after a few too many samples.

As the sun sets and the stars begin to twinkle, consider catching a show at the Arvada Center or checking out a local music venue. The nightlife here is vibrant, with live music and events happening throughout the week. Whether it's a local band playing the latest hits or a cover band rocking out to your favorite classics, you're bound to have a great time. Just remember to warm up your dance moves; you wouldn't want to embarrass yourself on the dance floor.

If you happen to be in town during the summer, don't miss the annual Arvada Harvest Festival. This event is a fantastic celebration of community, featuring a parade, carnival rides, and a whole lot of fun. You can enjoy delicious food, shop from local vendors, and maybe even find yourself in a pie-eating contest. Yes, you read that right—a pie-eating contest! If you ever wanted to channel your inner competitive eater, this is your chance. Just be sure to stretch beforehand; nobody wants to pull a muscle while diving into a pie.

As your time in Arvada comes to an end, you'll find it hard to leave. You'll be filled with stories of charming streets, delicious meals, and unexpected adventures. From the friendly locals to the rich history and vibrant culture, Arvada has a way of sneaking into your heart. You might even start planning your next trip before you've left the city limits, just to experience it all over again.

So go ahead, share your newfound love for Arvada with your friends and family. Tell them about the incredible food, the stunning parks, and the vibrant culture. You might just inspire someone to pack their bags and join you on your next adventure. After all, life is too short to stay in one place for too long, especially when places like Arvada are waiting to be explored!

Aspen

Aspen, Colorado, a place where the air is crisp, the slopes are legendary, and the coffee shops are filled with more designer winter gear than a Vogue runway show. If you've ever wanted to experience a town that feels like a Hollywood set, complete with breathtaking mountain views and enough boutiques to make your wallet weep, then pack your bags because Aspen is calling.

First off, getting to Aspen is an adventure in itself. As you wind your way through the Rocky Mountains, the scenery will have you questioning if you've accidentally stumbled into a postcard. Trees, mountains, and maybe even a deer or two will greet you, giving you that wholesome feeling that nature is welcoming you with open arms. Just be careful driving; if you see a moose, you may want to pull over and take a selfie—though let's be honest, they don't usually cooperate for photos.

Arriving in Aspen, you'll instantly notice the juxtaposition of rustic mountain charm and upscale luxury. The town is filled with gorgeous historical buildings that look like they belong in a fairytale, interspersed with high-end shops where you can buy a pair of ski goggles that cost more than your last vacation. You might feel a little out of place as you wander into a boutique and are greeted by a sales associate wearing what looks like a designer snowsuit, but don't worry! Just act like you know what "après-ski" means, and you'll fit right in.

Your first stop should be the famous Aspen Mountain, or Ajax as the locals call it. Whether you're an expert skier or someone who just likes to pretend they know how to ski while sipping hot cocoa at the lodge, Aspen Mountain has something for everyone. The views from the slopes are nothing short of jaw-dropping, and you'll find yourself pausing to take a million photos—because who doesn't want to show off their "I'm an adventurous outdoorsy person" persona on social media? Just make sure you don't drop your phone while trying to capture that perfect selfie; trust me, the only thing worse than a broken phone is a broken dream of being an influencer.

If skiing isn't your jam, don't fret! Aspen also offers plenty of alternative activities. You could go snowshoeing or take a scenic gondola ride that will make you feel like you're gliding through the air like a majestic eagle—or at least a slightly less graceful bird. The ride offers stunning views of the surrounding mountains, and if you're lucky, you might spot a few adventurous souls skiing down slopes that look like they're straight out of a ski magazine. You'll likely have a fleeting moment of envy before you remember that you just enjoy the hot tub and marshmallows by the fire more than being a professional athlete.

After a day of fun in the snow, it's time to indulge in some local cuisine. Aspen is known for its culinary scene, which boasts restaurants that can make even Gordon Ramsay shed a tear of joy. You'll find everything from fancy fine dining to cozy spots serving up comfort food that feels like a hug in a bowl. Treat yourself to a meal at one of the renowned establishments, where the prices might be steep, but the flavors will make your taste buds dance like they just won the lottery. Just make sure to bring your best "I totally belong here" outfit because no one wants to show up in ski gear looking like a lost penguin.

And speaking of penguins, if you happen to be in Aspen during the off-season, the town transforms into a different kind of wonderland. The summer months bring a whole new set of activities—hiking, biking, and festivals that will have you celebrating everything from music to art. The Aspen Music Festival is a highlight, where you can sit back and enjoy some incredible performances while pretending you're a cultured individual who knows the difference between Bach and Beethoven. Just don't ask me; I still get them confused!

Now, let's talk shopping. Aspen's shopping scene is a whole experience in itself. You'll find boutiques that sell everything from luxury winter wear to one-of-a-kind art pieces. If you're feeling particularly brave, you might even step into a store that sells clothing so trendy you'll wonder if you've accidentally walked into an alien spaceship. Just remember, if you buy that $400 jacket, you'll have to explain to your friends why it's more expensive than their entire wardrobe combined. A good story about how it will make you ski better might help.

As the sun sets over the mountains, the nightlife in Aspen begins to sizzle. The town is known for its vibrant nightlife, with bars and clubs that cater to everyone from the après-ski crowd to those who want to dance the night away. Just be prepared for some serious people-watching; you might spot a celebrity or two mingling among the crowd. If you play it cool, you might even share a dance with someone who looks suspiciously like they just walked off a movie set. Just remember not to gawk—acting like you belong is the key to fitting in here.

If you're lucky enough to be in Aspen during one of its famous festivals, like the Aspen Ideas Festival or the Food & Wine Classic, you're in for a treat. These events attract some of the brightest minds and culinary talents, making for a weekend filled with inspiring talks, delicious tastings, and the chance to feel a little smarter just by being in the vicinity of geniuses. Who knows? You might walk away with a newfound passion for gourmet cooking or a deep understanding of the universe. Or, at the very least, some really cool Instagram photos.

As your adventure in Aspen comes to a close, you'll find yourself filled with memories of breathtaking views, exquisite food, and perhaps a little too much hot cocoa. You might even have a few new friends who also appreciate the art of people-watching and pretending to know what they're doing on the slopes. The charm of Aspen lies in its ability to welcome everyone—whether you're a seasoned skier, a foodie, or just someone who appreciates a good mountain view.

So go ahead, share your love for Aspen with everyone you know. Tell them about the incredible food, the breathtaking slopes, and the vibrant culture that makes this town so special. You might even inspire someone to book their next vacation and experience the magic of Aspen for themselves. After all, in a place as beautiful as this, the only thing missing is you and your sense of adventure!

Ault

Ault, Colorado, a charming little town that proves good things come in small packages. Nestled just a stone's throw from the bustling city of Greeley, Ault may not be the first place that springs to mind when you think of travel destinations, but trust me—this hidden gem has enough quirky charm and local flavor to make even the most seasoned traveler raise an eyebrow in delight. So, buckle up as we dive into the delightful world of Ault, where the motto seems to be "Why be famous when you can be fabulous?"

First off, let's talk about how to get there. The journey to Ault is filled with picturesque views of the Colorado countryside. Rolling fields, golden sunsets, and the occasional curious cow will greet you along the way. If you're lucky, you might even encounter a flock of geese waddling across the road, giving you that brief moment of "Am I in a Disney movie?" Just remember to keep your eyes on the road; you don't want to end up on the local news for stopping to take selfies with a herd of livestock.

As you roll into Ault, you'll be greeted by the kind of small-town charm that feels like a warm hug. The town has a population that's so cozy, you might wonder if you've stumbled into a family reunion instead of a community. Ault's history dates back to the late 1800s, when it was founded as a railroad town. Back then, it served as a hub for farmers and ranchers, and it's been growing its unique character ever since. You'll quickly realize that the spirit of the Old West still lingers in the air, along with a healthy dose of friendly smiles.

Your first stop should definitely be the Ault Historical Society. This local treasure trove of history will give you a glimpse into the town's past, complete with exhibits that'll make you feel like you're in a time capsule. You can learn about the early settlers who braved the wild frontier and even see artifacts that date back to the town's founding. Just be careful not to get too carried away asking questions; you might accidentally end up volunteering to help catalog their collection. You know you've hit rock bottom when your friends have to rescue you from an afternoon of sorting dusty old items.

After getting your history fix, it's time to explore the great outdoors. Ault boasts beautiful parks that are perfect for picnics, leisurely strolls, or just soaking up the sunshine while contemplating the mysteries of life, like why your sandwich always tastes better when someone else makes it. Head over to the Ault Community Park, where you can take a leisurely walk, throw a frisbee, or let your inner child loose on the playground. And if you're feeling ambitious, consider renting a bike and cruising around town. Just make sure you have a helmet—safety first, folks! Plus, it makes you look extra cool.

As you meander through the park, you might notice the friendly locals going about their day. If you're lucky, you'll strike up a conversation with one of them. Ault residents are known for their hospitality, and you might find yourself invited to join a community barbecue or asked if you want to join the local book club. Just be prepared to read some questionable literature; you might end up discussing the finer points of a romance novel that sounds like it was written in the 1800s.

Now, let's talk about food because, let's be honest, it's one of the best parts of traveling. Ault may be small, but its culinary scene is surprisingly delightful. Stop by one of the local diners for a classic American breakfast that will have you feeling like a superstar. You can't go wrong with pancakes the size of your head, and the coffee flows like a mountain river. If you're feeling adventurous, ask for the daily special—you might just discover a dish that will make you question why you don't live in Ault permanently.

And speaking of adventures, if you happen to visit in the summer, make sure to check out the Ault Harvest Festival. This annual event brings the community together for a celebration of local agriculture, crafts, and all things fun. You can enjoy live music, delicious food, and games that will make you feel like a kid again. Just be warned—participating in a pie-eating contest might sound fun until you realize you're more of a spectator than a champion.

If you're still looking for more local flavor, take a short drive to the nearby Pawnee National Grassland. This stunning area offers incredible hiking opportunities and chances to see wildlife in their natural habitat. Picture yourself trekking through the tall grasses, binoculars in hand, waiting for the perfect moment to spot a prairie dog or a majestic hawk soaring overhead. Just remember to pack plenty of snacks because nothing ruins a nature hike faster than a rumbling stomach.

As the sun begins to set, it's time to wind down and enjoy Ault's laid-back vibe. You might stumble upon a local watering hole where the drinks are cold, the company is warm, and the conversations flow as easily as the beer. Strike up a conversation with a local about their favorite fishing spots or the best fishing tales; you'll likely hear stories that are more entertaining than anything you'll find on Netflix. Just be prepared to laugh, especially if someone gets carried away and starts showing off their fishing trophies.

As your adventure in Ault comes to a close, you'll find it hard to leave this little slice of heaven. The warmth of the community, the charm of the town, and the sheer delight of experiencing something new will have you feeling nostalgic before you've even hit the road. You might start plotting your return before you've even left the parking lot, thinking about all the meals you'll miss and the locals you'll want to catch up with.

So, go ahead and share your newfound love for Ault with your friends and family. Tell them about the friendly faces, the delicious food, and the stunning landscapes. You might just inspire someone to hop in their car and experience the joy of this small town for themselves. After all, life is too short to overlook places like Ault, Colorado—a town that reminds us all that sometimes, the best adventures are found off the beaten path.

Aurora

Aurora, Colorado, a city that could easily be mistaken for the "Other Denver" if you squint hard enough and ignore the fact that it's actually the third largest city in Colorado. Yes, Aurora is like that middle child who finally decided to step out of the shadows and say, "Hey, I'm here too!" This vibrant community is filled with enough charm, history, and quirky attractions to keep even the most discerning traveler entertained—or at least moderately amused. But let's not sugarcoat it: Aurora has its share of challenges, including a reputation for gang violence that makes wandering alone at night feel like a game of Russian roulette. So grab your sunscreen, a snack, and maybe a buddy, and let's dive into the wild world of Aurora.

First, let's talk about how to get to Aurora. The journey is straightforward, but be prepared for a little bit of existential dread as you navigate the Denver traffic. It's like playing a real-life version of Frogger, but instead of dodging cars, you're trying not to be late for brunch. You might even contemplate the meaning of life as you sit at a red light for what feels like an eternity. But fear not! Once you arrive, the first thing you'll notice is Aurora's unique blend of suburban tranquility and urban excitement, making it the perfect place for anyone who wants to feel like they're part of the action without actually having to deal with the chaos of Denver.

Now, let's get into some history because nothing screams "fun" like a brief lesson on the past. Aurora's roots date back to the late 1800s when it was originally founded as a small railroad town called Fletcher. Yes, that's right, it was named after a guy who probably had a penchant for mustaches and long-winded speeches about railroads. Fast forward a few decades, and the city grew like a weed in a garden full of daisies, eventually changing its name to Aurora, which means "dawn" in Latin. It's as if the city decided it was time to wake up and smell the coffee—thankfully, there's plenty of that to go around.

As you wander through the city, you might want to start your day at the Aurora History Museum. It's a quaint little place where you can learn about the city's past while admiring exhibits that will make you think, "Wow, I never knew this was a thing!" You might even stumble upon artifacts that will leave you questioning the fashion choices of past generations—seriously, what were they thinking with those hats? Just be careful not to get too lost in the exhibits; you don't want to be the person who gets trapped in a museum overnight, only to be found by the morning staff, clutching a mannequin and mumbling about the 1800s.

After your history fix, it's time to embrace the outdoors because Colorado is famous for its stunning landscapes, and Aurora is no exception. Head over to the stunning Cherry Creek State Park, where you can hike, bike, or just lounge around pretending to be a nature-loving Instagram influencer. As you traverse the trails, be on the lookout for the local wildlife. You might spot deer, rabbits, or the elusive jogger who insists they "love running in nature" but looks like they'd rather be binge-watching a series on the couch.

Feeling adventurous? Rent a paddleboat and take to the water! There's nothing quite like the thrill of paddling in circles while pretending to be a majestic swan. Bonus points if you can convince a friend to join you for an impromptu race. Just be prepared for the reality check that comes with realizing you haven't exercised since that New Year's resolution three years ago. If you're lucky, you might even impress some ducks with your newly discovered "paddle prowess"—or they'll just look at you like you're the weird human who thinks they're a bird.

Once you've worked up an appetite, it's time to explore Aurora's culinary scene. The city is home to a diverse array of restaurants, offering everything from classic American comfort food to international flavors that will make your taste buds do the cha-cha. Head over to the Aurora Town Center, where you can sample some local delights. You'll find places that serve tacos so good you might end up questioning every taco you've ever eaten elsewhere. And if you happen to spot a food truck, be sure to chase it down—food trucks in Aurora are like unicorns; you never know when you'll see one again.

For those of you who consider shopping a sport, you're in luck! Aurora offers plenty of shopping options, from large malls to quaint boutiques that could easily double as a set for a rom-com. At the Aurora City Place, you can stroll through stores that range from trendy clothing to quirky home goods that you didn't know you needed until you saw them. Just be prepared to explain to your friends why you suddenly "need" that decorative garden gnome that looks suspiciously like a famous movie character.

Now, let's not forget about the art scene! Aurora has an impressive collection of public art installations that could rival some major cities. As you walk around, keep your eyes peeled for murals that are as colorful as they are confusing. There's something about modern art that seems to be shouting, "Look at me! I'm deep!" while you stand there trying to decipher whether it's a commentary on society or just a bunch of paint splatters. Either way, it's sure to spark a conversation—especially if you throw in a "What do you think the artist was trying to convey?" to sound sophisticated.

As the day winds down, consider catching a show at the Aurora Fox Arts Center. This venue hosts a variety of performances, from theatrical productions to live music. It's like stepping into a world where people are suddenly talented and have perfected the art of speaking in dramatic tones. You'll find yourself laughing, crying, and wondering why you didn't pursue a career in the arts. If nothing else, you'll walk away with a newfound appreciation for the magic of live performances—plus a few inside jokes you'll likely never understand fully.

But let's not gloss over the reality of Aurora's nighttime scene. As charming as the city is during the day, things can take a turn after sunset. While many neighborhoods are perfectly safe, some areas have a reputation for gang activity, making it a little less "Happiest Place on Earth" and more "Proceed with Caution." So, if you find yourself in Aurora after dark, it's best to stick to well-lit areas and keep your phone charged—just in case you need to call for a ride or, you know, summon the ghost of your bravest friend to come pick you up.

And if you happen to be in town during one of Aurora's many festivals, you're in for a treat! The city hosts events throughout the year that celebrate everything from culture to food. The Aurora Arts

Festival is a highlight, showcasing local artists and performers while giving you the perfect excuse to eat your weight in cotton candy. Just be sure to pace yourself; there's nothing worse than feeling like you've just run a marathon after indulging in too many snacks at a festival.

As your adventure in Aurora comes to a close, you might find yourself feeling a little sad to leave this charming city. The quirky charm, friendly locals, and delightful experiences have a way of making you feel right at home—just remember to keep your wits about you. Who knew that the "Other Denver" would turn out to be such a delightful destination?

So, go ahead and share your newfound love for Aurora with your friends and family. Tell them about the quirky attractions, the delicious food, and the friendly faces you encountered along the way. You might even inspire someone to pack their bags and experience the magic of Aurora for themselves—just make sure they bring a buddy for the nighttime adventures! After all, life is too short to overlook places that might just surprise you, but it's also too short to be wandering the streets alone at night.

Avon

Avon, Colorado, a town that feels like a postcard come to life, nestled snugly in the breathtaking Rocky Mountains. You might think Avon is just a cute little stop on the way to more popular ski destinations like Vail, but oh boy, you're in for a surprise. Avon is like that underdog character in a feel-good movie who ends up winning the big game, all while wearing an adorable smile and a cozy sweater. So grab your beanie, lace up those hiking boots, and let's dive into what makes Avon a must-visit spot.

First, getting to Avon is an experience in itself. As you drive along the winding roads flanked by towering pine trees, you'll likely feel a rush of excitement mixed with the mild panic of wondering if you'll encounter a bear or a moose on your journey. Seriously, if you find yourself stuck behind a slow-moving vehicle, just take a deep breath and remember that it's probably just a family of tourists who've never seen a mountain before and are trying to figure out how to take the perfect selfie with their rental car.

Once you roll into Avon, you might notice that it has the kind of charm that makes you want to unpack your bags and stay forever—or at least until you realize you need to pay for a lift ticket at the ski resort. The town has a rich history that dates back to the 1800s when it was primarily a mining town. Yes, Avon was once a place where dreams of striking it rich were common, much like those dreams you had of becoming a pop star in your high school talent show. Spoiler alert: they both often end in disappointment.

Today, Avon is more about luxury and leisure than gold rush dreams. The town is home to the famous Beaver Creek Resort, which is like the champagne of ski resorts—bubbly, upscale, and a bit intimidating if you're more of a "pizza in the lodge" kind of person. If you're visiting in winter, you'll find yourself amidst powdery slopes and stunning views that could make even the most jaded Instagram influencer weep tears of joy. Whether you're an expert skier or someone who spends more time on the ground than on their skis, Avon has something for everyone.

But skiing isn't the only thing to do here. In the warmer months, Avon transforms into a haven for hikers, bikers, and anyone who enjoys pretending they're an outdoorsy person for a weekend. The Eagle Valley Trail is a delightful path that runs through Avon, allowing you to soak in the natural beauty while simultaneously trying to convince yourself that your workout is "totally worth it." Keep an eye out for local wildlife, but remember that no matter how cute the deer look, you're not actually supposed to feed them—unless you want to be known as "that person" in the local gossip circles.

Feeling adventurous? You can also try white-water rafting in the nearby rivers, where you'll be thrust into a foam-filled frenzy of adrenaline that will have you questioning all of your life choices. Just remember to wear sunscreen, as nothing says "I had a great time" like a sunburn that resembles a lobster.

Now, let's talk about food, because if there's anything that can lure you away from a beautiful view, it's a delicious meal. Avon boasts a diverse culinary scene that offers everything from gourmet dining to laid-back eateries serving up the best comfort food you can imagine. Try some local Colorado cuisine at one of the many restaurants that pride themselves on farm-to-table goodness, or you can grab a quick bite at a food truck. Just make sure you follow the golden rule of food trucks: if there's a long line, it's probably worth the wait.

If you find yourself wandering around town, be sure to stop by the Avon Public Library. Yes, a library might not seem like a thrilling destination, but hear me out. This place often hosts community events, art shows, and even storytime for adults. That's right—storytime for adults. Imagine sitting back with a cup of coffee, listening to someone read you a story like you're in kindergarten again, but this time you can actually enjoy it without worrying about the kids stealing your crayons.

And speaking of events, Avon knows how to throw a party. The town hosts various festivals throughout the year, including the Avon Arts Festival and the annual Avon Winter Market. You'll find everything from local crafts to live music that might make you want to break out your best dance moves—even if your best moves resemble those of a particularly enthusiastic giraffe.

As the sun begins to set and the sky turns a brilliant shade of orange, take a moment to enjoy the beauty of Avon. The mountains silhouetted against the sunset create a picture-perfect backdrop that will make you feel like you've stepped into a travel magazine. Just make sure you have your camera ready—though be warned, trying to capture the perfect shot might take you longer than you expect. You'll need about twenty photos before you find one where your hair isn't blowing in your face.

But let's not forget the fun little fact that Avon is not just a beautiful place; it's also the site of one of life's biggest adventures: eloping. Yes, you read that right. My husband and I chose Avon as the backdrop for our secret wedding, escaping the chaos of planning a big event and opting for a romantic ceremony in this enchanting town. With the mountains as our witnesses and the promise of a great adventure ahead, we made it official in the most picturesque way possible. So, if you find yourself in Avon and see a couple sneak away into the sunset, just know they might be on their way to the happiest moment of their lives—hopefully with a good restaurant in mind for dinner afterward.

Avondale

Ah, Avondale, Colorado. A place that manages to fly under the radar like a ninja in a room full of clowns. Nestled between Pueblo and the Arkansas River, this tiny town is the kind of spot that makes you question how you didn't know it existed until now. As you pull into Avondale, you might think you've stepped into a time capsule where the speed limit is optional and life moves at the pace of a leisurely Sunday drive.

Historically speaking, Avondale is as unpretentious as it gets. Founded in the late 1800s, it started as a small agricultural community. Picture it: farmers planting crops while the rest of the country was trying to figure out what to do with all those newfangled inventions. If you ever wondered what life was like before the internet, just take a stroll through Avondale, where "streaming" means you're standing by the river with a fishing pole, waiting for a catch.

The town has embraced its agricultural roots, and you can almost smell the cornfields in the air. If you find yourself craving fresh produce, Avondale is just a hop, skip, and a jump from some of the best farms around. And by hop, skip, and jump, I mean drive your car at a leisurely pace while contemplating how much you appreciate vegetables that don't come from the grocery store. Trust me, you'll feel like a culinary pioneer when you bring home a sack of fresh tomatoes, even if you have no idea how to cook them.

Once you've satisfied your farm-fresh cravings, it's time to explore what Avondale has to offer. The first stop on this whimsical journey should be the Avondale Park. It's not exactly Disneyland, but it does boast some green space where you can sit and contemplate the mysteries of life, like why socks always disappear in the laundry. There are picnic tables where you can lay out a spread worthy of a food critic, or just a couple of sandwiches and a bag of chips if you want to keep it real. Just don't forget your sunscreen; you don't want to leave Avondale looking like a lobster.

If you're feeling particularly adventurous, hop on over to the Arkansas River. This isn't just any river; it's the kind of place where people go to fish, kayak, or pretend they know how to paddleboard. If you're up for it, renting a kayak could lead to the kind of adventure that involves a lot of splashing, laughter, and maybe a mild existential crisis as you try to navigate the currents. Just be sure to keep your phone in a waterproof case—nobody wants to explain how their phone ended up in the river during an epic battle with nature.

And if you happen to be in Avondale during the summer, don't miss the local farmers' market. It's like a mini festival where you can stock up on fresh produce, homemade jams, and artisanal crafts—all while engaging in the sport of people-watching. You'll encounter friendly locals who might tell you their life story, whether you asked for it or not. Just nod, smile, and take mental notes of the best gossip in town. You might even walk away with some incredible new recipes or a bizarre but beautiful hand-knit sweater that you never knew you needed.

Speaking of local charm, let's not overlook the Avondale community. The residents here are about as welcoming as your grandma's hug—warm, slightly overwhelming, and full of love. There's a sense of camaraderie that makes you feel like you're part of a big family, even if you're just passing through. If you're lucky, you might even stumble upon a community event. It could be a potluck where you can sample everyone's famous dishes or a festival that celebrates, well, who knows what. The important thing is to join in and pretend you know what's going on while secretly hoping for some homemade pie.

Now, let's get real for a second. Avondale may not have the flashy attractions of big cities, but what it lacks in glitz, it makes up for in heart. The small-town atmosphere allows you to kick back and relax while enjoying the simple pleasures in life. Picture yourself sitting on a porch with a cold drink, chatting with a neighbor about the weather—classic Americana at its finest.

For those with a penchant for history, be sure to stop by the local library. Libraries are the unsung heroes of small towns, and Avondale's is no exception. Here, you can dive into local history, get lost in books you'll probably never read, and occasionally discover some gem of information that will impress your friends back home. Who knew you could learn so much while pretending to be productive?

As the sun begins to set and paints the sky in hues of orange and pink, take a moment to enjoy the tranquility that envelops Avondale. There's a certain magic that happens at dusk, where everything seems to slow down, and you might just catch a glimpse of the stars beginning to twinkle. If you find yourself pondering life's big questions, such as why your favorite snacks are always on the top shelf, you're in good company.

So, if you ever find yourself wandering through Avondale, know that beneath its unassuming exterior lies a world of charm, adventure, and perhaps a few tales of adventure. Just remember to take it easy, soak in the local flavor, and maybe grab a slice of pie from a friendly neighbor along the way.

Basalt

Nestled between Aspen and Glenwood Springs, Basalt, Colorado, is like that hidden track on your favorite album that you didn't know you needed until it started playing. This quaint little town, named after the volcanic rock that's as interesting as your friend who just returned from a two-month trip to Europe, has a history that's as colorful as its surrounding landscape. Founded during the gold rush in the late 1800s, Basalt was originally a mill town where folks tried to strike it rich while simultaneously trying to avoid becoming a character in a Western film that didn't end well.

Today, Basalt boasts the kind of charm that makes you want to pack your bags and settle down in a cozy cabin—preferably one with a fireplace and a view of the Roaring Fork River. The river itself is a key player in Basalt's narrative, offering outdoor enthusiasts a playground for kayaking, fishing, and pretending to be an expert fly fisherman, even if you've never held a rod in your life. There's something undeniably appealing about standing in waders, looking vaguely confused while others seem to effortlessly cast their lines. Just remember: it's all about attitude. If you look the part, people will assume you know what you're doing.

If you happen to be in town during the summer, make your way to the Basalt Farmers Market. It's like a carnival of produce where locals gather to show off their best tomatoes, artisanal cheeses, and, of course, baked goods that could make even a dietician weep with joy. The market is a perfect spot for people-watching as you take in the eclectic mix of locals, tourists, and that one guy who always shows up in a cowboy hat, no matter the season. Grab some snacks and chat with vendors who might share tips on everything from gardening to the best secret fishing spots—because nothing says small-town camaraderie like bartering over zucchini.

After you've filled your bag with fresh goodies, it's time to explore Basalt's stunning scenery. The nearby Roaring Fork River Trail offers a picturesque pathway for hiking or biking, depending on whether you're feeling ambitious or just want to stroll while contemplating the mysteries of life, like why your favorite shirt always shrinks in the wash. As you meander along the trail, keep an eye out for local wildlife—if you're lucky, you might spot a deer looking as confused as you feel about your life choices. Just be careful not to get too distracted by the scenery; tripping over a rock while admiring the mountains is an all-too-common rookie mistake.

Now, if you're seeking a bit of culture, Basalt is home to several art galleries that showcase local talent. Stroll through these spaces, and you'll find pieces that range from breathtaking landscapes to abstract works that will have you questioning your understanding of reality. It's the kind of art that makes you nod knowingly while secretly wondering if you could replicate it with a few paint splatters and a robust Instagram filter. Whether you leave with a newfound appreciation for the arts or just a headache from overthinking every piece, it's bound to be an enlightening experience.

For those who enjoy a little thrill, Basalt offers various outdoor activities year-round. In winter, you can hit the slopes at nearby Aspen or Snowmass, where you'll find trails that will challenge even the most seasoned skier. Or you could opt for snowshoeing—because nothing says "I'm adventurous" quite like strapping large tennis rackets to your feet and trudging through the snow. Just remember to take breaks; no one wants to be the person who gets stuck in the snow while trying to take a selfie.

When it comes to dining, Basalt doesn't disappoint. The local eateries serve up a smorgasbord of options that could make your head spin faster than a merry-go-round. From upscale dining experiences to cozy cafés that serve the best coffee this side of the Rockies, there's something for everyone. And if you're in the mood for something sweet, make a beeline for one of the bakeries. You'll find pastries that are so delightful they should come with a warning label: "May cause uncontrollable happiness."

As the day winds down, don't miss the opportunity to take a stroll through Basalt's charming downtown area. The historic buildings add a touch of character, making you feel like you've stepped into a scene from a movie. You might even find yourself daydreaming about opening your own quirky little shop selling handcrafted goods or artisanal jams—because who wouldn't want to live that small-town dream? Just be prepared for the reality of long hours and constant customer service.

If you're feeling adventurous, check out the local breweries. Basalt has embraced the craft beer movement with open arms, offering several establishments where you can sample local brews while enjoying the laid-back atmosphere. You can chat with locals who will happily share stories about the town, the river, and their latest fishing adventures. Just be sure to pace yourself; nothing kills a good vibe like realizing you can't remember how you got home.

And let's not overlook the fact that Basalt is home to some stunning natural hot springs. If you've ever wanted to soak in water heated by the earth while surrounded by mountains, this is your chance. Just picture yourself relaxing in a steaming pool, sipping a cold drink while contemplating the meaning of life. Or, if you're like most people, you'll just be trying not to think about how much sunscreen you forgot to apply.

As the sun sets behind the mountains, casting a golden glow over Basalt, you might find yourself reflecting on the beauty of this little town. With its rich history, stunning scenery, and delightful locals, Basalt has a way of capturing your heart. It's a place where you can slow down, savor the moment, and maybe even lose track of time while contemplating how you ever lived without fresh produce from the farmers market.

In a twist of fate, Basalt holds a special place in my heart. It's the town where my husband and I eloped in secret, surrounded by the breathtaking beauty that this hidden gem offers. With the mountains standing guard and the river whispering sweet nothings, it was the perfect backdrop for a day that would forever change our lives. So, as you explore Basalt, just know that beneath its unassuming exterior lies a world of charm and adventure waiting to be discovered.

Battlement Mesa

Battlement Mesa, Colorado, is like that quirky uncle at a family reunion: not everyone knows him, but those who do have a great time swapping stories and sharing laughs. Tucked away in Garfield County, this unassuming community has a history that's as rich as a chocolate cake left out in the sun. It all began in the 1970s when a group of visionaries decided that a planned community perched on a mesa would be just the thing to draw in folks looking for a slice of the good life. And why not? Who wouldn't want to live on a mesa, where the views are breathtaking and the chances of bumping into a tumbleweed are significantly higher?

Before we dive into the delights of Battlement Mesa, let's take a quick look at the history. Originally, this area was populated by the Ute tribe long before anyone thought of building golf courses and housing developments. They likely had a much more peaceful existence, living off the land and probably not worrying about how to assemble IKEA furniture. In the 19th century, as settlers moved in, the land transformed into a vibrant community, with Battlement Mesa being officially recognized in the 1970s. That's right: it took a while for people to decide that living on a mesa was a fantastic idea. Who knew that elevation could be such a game changer?

Today, Battlement Mesa boasts a plethora of activities that can keep you entertained while you ponder the mystery of how it has managed to stay under the radar for so long. The first stop on this whimsical adventure should be the Battlement Mesa Golf Club. Whether you're a golf pro or someone who thinks a birdie is just a cute little songbird, this course is sure to delight. Picture yourself swinging away at the pristine greens while simultaneously trying to figure out which club is which. Spoiler alert: if you're ever unsure, just pick the one that's the heaviest and hope for the best. Just be careful not to slice the ball into someone's backyard, unless you're keen on making new friends in an awkward way.

After a round of golf, why not head to the local community center? It's the heart of Battlement Mesa, where you can participate in everything from yoga classes to bingo nights. You'll discover that bingo isn't just a game for your grandma; it's a competitive sport that can bring out the fiercest of rivalries. Just be prepared for some serious side-eye from seasoned players if you call out "bingo" too early. Nothing says "I'm new here" quite like a room full of disappointed seniors.

Feeling adventurous? Take a hike on one of the many trails that wind through the area. The Battlement Reservoir Trail offers stunning views and a chance to reconnect with nature—if by reconnect you mean getting lost for an hour before finally finding your way back. You'll likely encounter other hikers along the way, and you'll all share a knowing glance that says, "Yes, we're all here trying to remember where we parked." Just be sure to pack water and snacks, or risk becoming that person who scavenges for trail mix in their backpack while praying to the snack gods for sustenance.

If you're in the mood for some water fun, head over to the Battlement Mesa Swimming Pool. It's not quite a water park, but it'll do the trick when you want to cool off. The laughter of kids splashing around will remind you of your own childhood, when the biggest concern was how many snacks you could cram into your pockets before heading to the pool. Just try to resist the temptation to cannonball into the water; adulting has a way of making such moves seem far less impressive than they once were.

When hunger strikes, don't fret. Battlement Mesa has dining options that will make your taste buds do a little happy dance. Local eateries serve up everything from hearty burgers to mouthwatering pizzas that are perfect after a long day of exploration. Try to avoid staring too hard at the menu; that's just a rookie move that'll only result in an awkward silence while you try to decide between a cheeseburger or the special of the day. Go with your gut—literally and figuratively.

And let's not forget the glorious local events that pop up throughout the year. Farmers markets, craft fairs, and seasonal festivals transform the community center into a hub of activity where you can mingle with locals and feel like part of the family. You might even leave with some homemade jam or a hand-knit sweater that makes you question your fashion sense. Just remember: small-town gossip travels faster than a speeding bullet, so don't say anything you wouldn't want your grandma to hear.

For those interested in history, take a moment to appreciate the beautiful views of the surrounding mountains, which have seen more action than a soap opera. Battlement Mesa's geological formations have stories to tell—if only they could talk. You might find yourself pondering the epic battles of the past while standing on the edge of a mesa, feeling like a character in a Western film. Just watch your step; nobody wants to become the next dramatic moment in a nature documentary.

As evening falls and the sun dips behind the mountains, the sky lights up with a brilliant array of colors. The sunsets in Battlement Mesa are nothing short of legendary, creating a backdrop that will have you reaching for your camera in a frenzy. Snap some pictures, but don't forget to take a moment to just breathe it all in. There's something magical about witnessing a sunset that transforms a mundane day into a memorable one.

Now, here's a little secret: Battlement Mesa holds a special place in my heart because it's where my husband and I decided to tie the knot in an intimate ceremony. Surrounded by the stunning landscape and the comforting sound of nature, it was the perfect escape from the chaos of wedding planning. So while you explore this hidden gem, just know that you're walking in the footsteps of love stories and adventures that are waiting to unfold.

Battlement Mesa may not be the first name on everyone's lips when they think of Colorado, but that's part of its charm. It's a place where you can truly unwind, enjoy the great outdoors, and appreciate the simple pleasures in life. So take a seat on a park bench, watch the world go by, and maybe contemplate your next move—like how to perfect that golf swing or whether it's time to try your hand at bingo. In the end, Battlement Mesa is all about living life at your own pace, surrounded by stunning scenery and the kind of charm that makes you feel right at home.

Bayfield

This little town is like the cousin you never knew you had: charming, a bit quirky, and just a touch off the beaten path. Nestled between the San Juan Mountains and the Pine River, Bayfield is where the pine trees whisper secrets and the locals have stories that could fill a novel—if only someone would write them down and publish them for the world to enjoy.

Founded in the late 1800s, Bayfield started as a railroad town. Picture it: rugged pioneers with dirt under their nails, hustling to create a community while simultaneously trying to dodge the occasional bear. The railroad brought in settlers and supplies, allowing the town to flourish faster than a weed in a garden that hasn't seen a gardener in years. As time marched on, Bayfield transformed from a scrappy little settlement into the cozy gem it is today. And it's still scrappy; that's part of the charm.

Now, let's dive into the local attractions. First up is the Bayfield Heritage Museum. This isn't your run-of-the-mill museum filled with dusty artifacts. Oh no, this place is packed with local history and characters so colorful they could give crayons a run for their money. You'll learn about everything from the town's railroad days to tales of eccentric residents who probably had a wild conspiracy theory or two. Just remember to keep your voice down; you wouldn't want to disturb the ghosts of the past—especially if they're the chatty type.

Once you've soaked up some history, it's time to embrace the great outdoors. Bayfield is surrounded by natural beauty that would make even a postcard blush. Head over to the San Juan National Forest for hiking, biking, or just wandering aimlessly while trying to remember where you parked your car. Don't be surprised if you encounter a deer or two who seem to be judging your hiking attire; they've seen it all, from shorts in snow to the classic "I'll just wear my flip-flops" mistake. If you're feeling particularly adventurous, you can tackle one of the many trails, where you'll have the chance to yell "Eureka!" upon finding a breathtaking view or "Why did I think this was a good idea?" when faced with a steep incline.

If you're in the mood for some water fun, the Pine River is calling your name. Grab a kayak, canoe, or even an inflatable flamingo if you're feeling particularly whimsical, and float your cares away. Just be careful not to end up like the infamous "flamingo guy" who got stuck in a tree after trying to navigate a rapid. If you do encounter any fishermen, they might be less than impressed with your bright pink flotation device, but that's half the fun.

When hunger strikes after a long day of outdoor adventure, Bayfield has got you covered. Local eateries serve everything from classic American fare to Mexican food that will make your taste buds do the salsa. Make sure to check out a taco joint where the salsa is hotter than your last breakup. You'll find that nothing says "I love this town" quite like devouring a plate of nachos while engaging in heated discussions about who makes the best green chili. You'll quickly discover that everyone has an opinion, and it's usually very passionate.

As the sun sets over the mountains, transforming the sky into a riot of colors, it's the perfect time to explore Bayfield's nightlife—or lack thereof. This isn't a town that thrives on wild parties or late-night shenanigans. Instead, you might find a local bar where you can enjoy a cold drink while listening to live music or a group of folks playing cards in a cozy setting. If you're lucky, you might catch a local legend sharing tales of days gone by, complete with exaggerated hand gestures and dramatic reenactments that will leave you in stitches.

Speaking of legends, let's talk about the Bayfield BBQ Festival, a beloved local event that draws in crowds like moths to a flame. Here, the aroma of smoked meat fills the air as locals showcase their culinary skills in a fierce but friendly competition. You'll see barbecue enthusiasts sporting aprons that proclaim their allegiance to their secret sauce recipe, while judges sample ribs and pulled pork with the seriousness of a Supreme Court hearing. You might want to come hungry, as the food here is worth every calorie. Just be sure to bring some antacids if you plan to go all out; no one wants to have to explain why they're chugging Tums at a family-friendly festival.

And if you're a fan of crafts, the local artisans will make your heart sing. Bayfield is home to numerous craft fairs where you can find everything from hand-knit sweaters that look like they were designed by someone's overly ambitious grandma to pottery that might or might not contain a small, hidden curse. The locals are incredibly talented, and if you're lucky, you might even snag a piece of art that becomes the conversation starter at your next dinner party. Just be prepared to tell everyone the backstory of how you found it in a charming little town where the pine trees whisper secrets.

As you wrap up your adventure in Bayfield, don't forget to take a moment to appreciate the stunning scenery that surrounds you. The mountains stand tall, the river flows gently, and the locals have an uncanny ability to make you feel like you belong—if only for a weekend. You might leave with a full belly, a heart full of laughter, and a newfound appreciation for small-town life.

To add a little personal touch, let me reveal that Bayfield holds a special place in my heart because it's where my husband and I decided to tie the knot. With the beauty of nature as our backdrop, we exchanged vows surrounded by the whispers of the pine trees and the supportive laughter of our closest friends. It was a moment that perfectly encapsulated the charm of this little oasis, reminding us that sometimes, the best adventures happen in the most unexpected places.

Bayfield may not be the most famous destination in Colorado, but it's a hidden gem that offers a little bit of everything. Whether you're exploring the great outdoors, indulging in delicious food, or simply soaking up the local culture, you'll find that this town has a way of wrapping you in its warm embrace, leaving you with stories and memories that will last a lifetime. So, grab your sense of adventure, pack your bags, and head to Bayfield—you never know what delightful surprises await you in this enchanting corner of Colorado.

Bennet

Bennett, Colorado, is like the charming little bookstore you stumble upon in a city filled with flashy chain stores. You walk in expecting nothing much, and suddenly you're lost in a world of delightful oddities. Nestled in Adams County, this small town has a history that's as fascinating as your great-uncle's fishing tales—full of unexpected twists and a few questionable details.

Originally founded as a railroad town in the late 19th century, Bennett was named after the Bennett family, who were instrumental in its development. Imagine a bunch of determined pioneers working tirelessly while trying not to trip over each other's dreams of gold and glory. The town's location made it an ideal stop for travelers, and the arrival of the railroad turned it into a bustling little hub—if bustling can be defined as three shops, a post office, and a local diner that served the best pie you'd ever taste.

Fast forward to today, and Bennett still retains that small-town charm. It's the kind of place where everyone knows your name, and if they don't, they'll make sure to find out quickly—so you might want to be on your best behavior unless you want to become the town's latest gossip. One of the first places to check out is the Bennett Park. Picture a lovely green space where you can picnic, play frisbee, or contemplate the mysteries of life, like why socks always disappear in the dryer. If you're lucky, you might even catch a local dog trying to catch a frisbee while simultaneously tripping over its own feet. It's the kind of wholesome entertainment that brings a smile to your face.

Once you've soaked up the sunshine and the occasional dog-related shenanigan, it's time to explore the local dining scene. Bennett isn't exactly a culinary hotspot, but it does offer some delightful options. One local diner serves up breakfasts that could fuel an army. Their pancakes are so large they could double as pizza bases. You'll find yourself wondering if you should take a picture for Instagram or just dive right in. Pro tip: order the "Big Plate Special" if you want to leave feeling like a champion—or in a food coma.

For the more adventurous eater, try the small town's take on Mexican food. You'll discover that even the tiniest of towns can have a surprisingly good taco joint, complete with vibrant decor that screams "we love salsa!" Just be prepared for the salsa to be hotter than a sunbather in July. The locals have strong opinions about the best place to get a burrito, so tread carefully in conversations. You wouldn't want to accidentally spark a town-wide debate that lasts longer than a family reunion.

If you're in the mood for some local culture, Bennett occasionally hosts community events that will make you feel like part of the family. From farmers markets to holiday celebrations, the town knows how to bring people together. At the farmers market, you'll find fresh produce, homemade goodies, and an array of hand-crafted items that you never knew you needed. There's nothing quite like buying a jar of "mystery jam" from someone who swears it'll change your life.

For the more artistically inclined, Bennett also has a vibrant community of local artisans. Check out the craft fairs that pop up throughout the year, where you can find everything from handmade jewelry to artwork that will leave you wondering, "What exactly is that supposed to be?" Nothing says small-town charm quite like a sculpture made of recycled materials, possibly including what looks suspiciously like an old bicycle.

As the sun sets, don't miss the chance to explore Bennett's nighttime scene—or rather, the lack thereof. This isn't a town known for wild parties or raucous nightlife, but there's something comforting about gathering with friends at a local bar where everyone knows each other's life story. Enjoy a cold drink while sharing tales of your latest adventures, all while keeping an eye on the local dart league. You'd be amazed at how seriously people take their dart games; it's practically a competitive sport.

And if you happen to be in town during the summer, you might stumble upon the Bennett Days festival. This annual event is a celebration of everything that makes Bennett unique, complete with games, music, and plenty of food. You'll see families competing in the infamous three-legged race, where people inevitably trip over themselves and become instant internet sensations—or at least, the talk of the town for a week. Just be prepared for the obligatory pie-eating contest, which always ends in laughter and questionable decision-making.

Bennett is also a stone's throw away from some stunning outdoor adventures. Take a short drive to nearby parks where you can hike, bike, or just stare in awe at the beautiful scenery. If you're lucky, you might even catch a glimpse of some local wildlife—assuming they don't see you first and decide to hide behind a tree. Just remember to bring your camera; the Instagram opportunities are endless, even if you're standing next to a particularly unphotogenic cactus.

For a bit of history, don't forget to explore the town's historical landmarks. There are a few buildings that date back to the early days, each with a story waiting to be uncovered. You might feel like a character in a historical drama as you walk through the town, contemplating the lives of those who came before you and their questionable fashion choices.

And let's not forget the lovely people of Bennett. The locals are friendly and welcoming, ready to share their stories and their favorite places to eat. They might also share their secret fishing spots or the best way to navigate life in a small town. Just be prepared for some exaggerated tales about the biggest fish caught—or that time someone bravely fought off a bear with nothing but a fishing pole and sheer determination.

As you wrap up your journey in Bennett, you'll likely leave with a heart full of fond memories and a newfound appreciation for the beauty of small-town life. This isn't just a place to visit; it's a tapestry of experiences that reflect the quirks and charm of the people who call it home. And if you're lucky, you'll walk away with a "mystery jam" that may or may not change your life, a few new friends, and a stack of stories that will have you chuckling for years to come.

In the end, Bennett, Colorado, is a hidden gem that offers a little bit of everything. It's a place where you can unwind, connect with nature, and perhaps even find a slice of pie that's as large as your dreams. So, take a deep breath, embrace the quirks, and enjoy every delightful moment this small town has to offer.

Berthoud

Nestled snugly between the majestic Rockies and the delightful plains, this charming little town is like the unexpected plot twist in a rom-com—you didn't see it coming, but once you're in, you're hooked. With a history that dates back to the late 1800s, Berthoud has transformed from a railroad stop to a delightful community filled with stories, character, and perhaps a few too many garden gnomes.

The town was named after the founder, Edward Berthoud, who must have had an extraordinary talent for naming things. He set up shop here in 1877, convinced that this little spot was destined for greatness, or at least a decent coffee shop. The arrival of the railroad turned it into a bustling hub—if bustling means three shops, a post office, and a town square that could double as a friendly game of dodgeball. Fast forward a century or so, and Berthoud has evolved into a haven for outdoor enthusiasts, art lovers, and people who just really, really enjoy a good slice of pie.

Let's start with the outdoor escapades. The nearby Lory State Park is an adventurer's dream. Hiking, biking, and just generally pretending you know how to navigate nature are all on the agenda. You might find yourself standing at the edge of a trail, staring at a sign that reads "Advanced Hikers Only," while internally screaming, "What does that even mean?" Fear not! The trails are often just as welcoming as the locals, who seem to believe that everyone deserves a shot at getting lost. Just remember to pack snacks; nothing fuels a hiker like a pocket full of granola bars and the occasional protein bar that tastes like cardboard.

Once you've returned from your trek—hopefully not having wandered too far off the beaten path—it's time to explore downtown Berthoud. Picture a quaint main street where vintage shops and local eateries line the road, each with a personality as vibrant as its storefront. The Berthoud Historical Society is a must-visit, showcasing the town's past with exhibits that make you feel like a time traveler. You'll learn about the pioneers who shaped the area, and maybe even stumble upon a few curious artifacts, like a dusty old typewriter or an unidentifiable farming tool that looks like it could double as a medieval weapon.

After your historical journey, it's time to indulge in some local cuisine. Berthoud is home to several eateries that serve everything from classic burgers to gourmet sandwiches that are so artfully presented, they might as well be on the cover of a food magazine. One beloved spot has a reputation for its breakfast burritos that are so large they could double as a flotation device. It's the kind of place where you can order something called the "Kitchen Sink" burrito and leave feeling like you just conquered a mountain—or at least a sizable breakfast challenge.

For those with a sweet tooth, Berthoud offers dessert options that are downright heavenly. The local bakery has pastries that will make you weep with joy. Be sure to try their famous cinnamon rolls, which are so decadent that you'll wonder if you've accidentally stumbled into Willy Wonka's chocolate factory. Just a word of advice: don't look at the calorie count. Ignorance is bliss, especially when it comes to baked goods.

Feeling creative? Check out the Berthoud Art Gallery, a quaint little place that showcases local artists and their work. You'll find everything from paintings that speak to your soul to sculptures that leave you wondering what the artist was thinking. It's the perfect spot to spend an afternoon pondering the deeper meaning of life—or at least deciding whether that abstract piece would clash with your living room decor.

If you happen to be in town during the summer, make sure to swing by the Berthoud Heritage Day celebration. This annual event is a fantastic way to experience local culture and perhaps witness a pie-eating contest that turns competitive in a way you didn't know was possible. You'll see families gathered, cheering for their favorite contestants, while a local band provides a soundtrack of classic tunes. And if you're lucky, you might even witness the crowning of the "Pie Queen" or "King," complete with a crown made of pastry. Now that's a title worth striving for.

As night falls, the local watering holes come to life. Berthoud isn't exactly known for a wild nightlife, but there are a few cozy spots where you can enjoy a drink while engaging in conversations with the friendly locals. They'll likely regale you with tales of the town's quirky characters and past shenanigans. You might even hear about that one time someone attempted to set a record for the largest snowman, only to realize that it requires more than just ambition and a whole lot of snow.

And let's not overlook the natural beauty surrounding Berthoud. The town is just a short drive from stunning mountain vistas and scenic views that could make even a seasoned traveler pause in awe. Whether you're hiking, biking, or simply taking a leisurely drive, the landscapes are a reminder that Colorado is indeed the Centennial State, not just because of its history but because it continually takes your breath away.

For those who appreciate a good mystery, there's even an intriguing urban legend about a ghost that roams the old train depot. Rumor has it that if you visit at midnight, you might catch a glimpse of the spirit trying to catch the train that never arrives. Now that's a story that could make your next campfire gathering a hit!

As you wrap up your exploration of Berthoud, take a moment to reflect on the charm that this little town exudes. It may not be the biggest player on the map, but its heart is as big as the Rockies themselves. From its rich history to its quirky events and outdoor adventures, Berthoud offers a little slice of everything that makes Colorado special.

You might leave with a newfound appreciation for small-town life, a belly full of burrito, and a heart warmed by the stories shared by the locals. Berthoud, with its unique blend of history, adventure, and a dash of humor, is a hidden treasure waiting to be discovered. So grab your sense of curiosity, put on your walking shoes, and enjoy all that this delightful town has to offer.

Bethune

Bethune, Colorado, is a little town that could. Nestled in the eastern plains, it's like that one friend who shows up to the party with the most unusual snack, and you realize you can't stop eating it. Founded in the early 20th century, this town has a history that's as colorful as its sunsets, but with fewer Instagram filters.

The story of Bethune began in 1910, when the railroad decided it was time to grace this area with its presence. Named after a local railroad engineer, the town quickly blossomed into a hub for farming and commerce. If you've ever wondered where your wheat and corn come from, this is the place to thank—though the locals might prefer you just to buy them a drink instead. The original settlers faced all the usual challenges, like weather that couldn't make up its mind and a distinct lack of social media to distract them.

As you roll into town, you'll notice the population is less than that of a small college class. Bethune has a certain charm that makes it feel like a cozy coffee shop—only instead of lattes, you get small-town gossip served with a side of homemade pie. The locals are friendly, but don't be surprised if they ask you a million questions about why you're here. It's all in good fun, really. They're just making sure you're not a wandering ghost or an undercover reality TV star.

For those looking to explore, the first stop should be the Bethune Community Center. It's not just a community center; it's the beating heart of the town. Here, you'll find residents organizing potlucks, town meetings, and the occasional dance that can only be described as "enthusiastic." Picture a gathering where everyone is invited to show off their best moves, even if their best moves resemble an uncoordinated chicken trying to take flight.

Now, if you're feeling adventurous, head to the local parks. They're not quite the sprawling landscapes of national parks, but they do offer a peaceful respite from the bustling world outside. You can take a stroll, bring a picnic, or simply ponder the meaning of life while watching a squirrel attempt to claim dominance over a particularly impressive acorn. Just remember, nature can be unpredictable. One moment, you're enjoying the serenity, and the next, a rogue wind might send your sandwich flying into the next county.

When hunger strikes, it's time to discover Bethune's culinary scene, which is a delightful mix of small-town charm and unexpected flavors. Local diners serve up dishes that would make your grandma proud, with a side of fries that could easily qualify as a food group. You might stumble upon a burger joint where the special of the day is a towering behemoth that leaves you questioning all your life choices, particularly the choice to order extra fries. And just when you think you can't possibly eat another bite, dessert shows up, usually in the form of a pie that has its own fan club. If you can manage to finish it, you'll earn a place in local lore—a story that will be told for generations to come.

Now, let's talk about events. Bethune knows how to throw a party, even if it sometimes feels like a gathering of folks who just really enjoy potlucks. The town celebrates various festivals throughout the year, and each one is a chance for the community to come together, share laughter, and engage in competitions that range from baking contests to good old-fashioned horseshoe throwing. Don't underestimate the intensity of the horseshoe competition. You may find yourself witnessing friendships tested and rivalries ignited over who can toss a horseshoe the farthest.

One highlight is the annual fair, which is essentially a small-scale county fair but with all the charm of a community barbecue. You'll find carnival rides that look like they were built in someone's backyard but still manage to thrill. You can grab a corn dog the size of your arm and indulge in games that will have you questioning your coordination, like tossing ping pong balls into cups while trying to dodge the laughter of spectators.

As the sun sets, the nightlife in Bethune becomes a quaint affair. Don't expect a raging club scene; instead, think of a cozy bar where the regulars know each other's life stories and are eager to share. You might find yourself at a local watering hole, swapping tales with friendly strangers who are just as curious about you as you are about them. The conversation can veer into the hilariously bizarre, covering topics like UFO sightings, the best fishing spots, and why the town's mascot—a particularly fierce-looking prairie dog—was chosen.

For those who enjoy history, a visit to the local museum is a must. It's filled with artifacts that tell the tale of Bethune's past, including photographs that might induce fits of laughter or bewilderment. You'll find treasures like old farming tools that look suspiciously like medieval torture devices and black-and-white photos of residents who proudly displayed hairstyles that would make a modern stylist weep. The museum is a treasure trove of history, a place where the past comes to life, often accompanied by chuckles at the fashion choices of yesteryear.

And if you're feeling particularly adventurous, venture outside of town to explore the surrounding plains. The scenery is stunning in its simplicity, offering sweeping views that remind you just how beautiful the American heartland can be. Don't forget your camera; you'll want to capture the moments when the sunset paints the sky in shades of orange and pink, making even the most mundane of landscapes look like a postcard.

As your time in Bethune comes to a close, you'll find yourself reflecting on this quirky little town that somehow manages to combine history, charm, and just the right amount of weirdness. It may not be the glitziest destination in Colorado, but it's filled with warmth, laughter, and a community that feels like family. Here, you'll discover a little slice of life that proves small towns can pack a big punch in terms of stories, friendships, and unforgettable moments.

Blanca

Nestled at the foot of the majestic Sangre de Cristo Mountains, this tiny town is like the underdog of Colorado—quiet, humble, and often overlooked. Founded in the early 1900s, Blanca has a history that is as rich as a double chocolate cake but without the calories, assuming you don't count the local chili cook-off. Named after the Spanish word for "white," this charming town got its moniker from the nearby snow-capped peaks that could double as a backdrop for a holiday card.

Blanca is the kind of place where life moves at a leisurely pace, as if everyone collectively decided that the rush hour should be replaced with a good cup of coffee and a chat about the weather. The population hovers around the size of a small family reunion, which means you're likely to know everyone by the time you finish your first cup of coffee. And if you're lucky, you might even be invited to the next community potluck, where the local gossip is served alongside homemade casseroles that might make you rethink your entire culinary repertoire.

Start your exploration at the Blanca Fort, which isn't so much a "fort" as it is a charming reminder of the town's past. Built in the late 1800s, it served as a military outpost and a trading hub. The fort stands as a testament to the town's resilient spirit, much like that one person at every family gathering who insists on playing the accordion despite no one really wanting to hear it. You can wander around and imagine the hustle and bustle of the old days, while secretly hoping you don't accidentally stumble into a reenactment involving very serious historical figures and even more serious mustaches.

If you're feeling adventurous, don your hiking boots and take a trip to the nearby Blanca Peak. This stunning mountain offers trails that will have you questioning your life choices and fitness level simultaneously. One moment, you're feeling like a nature-loving warrior, and the next, you're gasping for breath, contemplating whether this is what they meant by "fresh air." The views, however, are worth it—provided you're not too busy wondering why you thought climbing a mountain was a good idea in the first place.

Once you've conquered (or at least hiked partway up) the mountain, it's time to explore the local dining scene. Don't expect five-star restaurants here; instead, think small-town diners that serve food with love and perhaps a sprinkle of that small-town magic. The local café is known for its hearty breakfasts that will make you reconsider the very notion of portion control. You might find yourself eyeing a plate of huevos rancheros that could double as a small car, while the locals casually sip their coffee, oblivious to your dietary crisis.

As you savor your meal, make sure to ask about the local specialty: green chili. This dish is more than just food; it's practically a rite of passage. If you can handle the heat, you'll earn the respect of the locals, who will likely bestow upon you a title like "Chili Conqueror" or "Spice Warrior." Just be prepared for the aftermath; your taste buds might stage a protest, and you'll have a new understanding of what it means to "live life on the edge."

After you've stuffed yourself silly, explore the art scene—or lack thereof. Blanca might not be a hub of artistic genius, but you can find local crafts and handmade items that reflect the town's quirky character. You might stumble upon a shop selling handcrafted jewelry made from local stones, or perhaps some decor items that could easily become conversation starters at your next dinner party. "Yes, that is a life-sized statue of a prairie dog made from recycled materials. No, I don't know why it's wearing a sombrero."

Speaking of quirky, don't miss the chance to check out the Blanca/Chama Historic Railroad. While it may not be a full-fledged tourist attraction, it offers a glimpse into the past that would make any history buff swoon. It's a classic case of a small-town treasure; a place where you can learn about the railroad's significance in shaping the community. Just be prepared for the locals to give you a detailed history that might include a few tall tales, like the one about the time a train managed to get lost for a week due to a particularly overzealous snowstorm.

As the sun begins to set, find yourself a cozy spot to watch the sky transform into a masterpiece of oranges and purples. It's the kind of sunset that makes you want to hug a cactus (though I wouldn't recommend it) and reflect on life, love, and why you didn't bring your camera. There's something incredibly peaceful about the open skies and the quiet of the town that makes you feel like you've stepped back in time—minus the lack of Wi-Fi, of course.

If you happen to be in town during the summer, keep an eye out for the local festivals. These events are a delightful mix of food, fun, and perhaps an overly competitive pie-eating contest. You'll find locals gathering to celebrate with music, games, and the kind of camaraderie that can only come from living in a small town. And if you're lucky, you might even catch a glimpse of the "Great Bean Bag Toss Championship," an event that brings out the most serious of competitors and the most ludicrous of strategies.

As your adventure in Blanca draws to a close, you'll find that this small town has a lot to offer, from its picturesque scenery to its warm community spirit. It's a place where everyone knows your name—or at least your face—and where the stories flow as freely as the coffee. You might even leave with a newfound appreciation for the simple joys in life, like a perfectly cooked breakfast and a heartwarming chat with a local who insists on telling you about their pet llama.

Blanca may not be the bustling metropolis you initially dreamed of, but it's a town filled with character, charm, and a few eccentricities that make it truly special. So, pack your sense of humor and your appetite for adventure, and get ready to embrace the delightful quirkiness that is Blanca, Colorado.

Boulder

A place where the scenery is stunning, the air is crisp, and the political climate is more colorful than a tie-dye T-shirt at a peace rally. Nestled against the foothills of the Rockies, this town is a blend of outdoor enthusiasts, intellectuals, and folks who might just be one yoga class away from enlightenment. Founded in 1859, Boulder began as a mining town and quickly evolved into a hub for those seeking the "good life" and a gluten-free lifestyle that even quinoa would envy.

As you roll into Boulder, the first thing that hits you is the view. Seriously, it's hard to focus on the road with the Flatirons looming majestically in the background like nature's version of a motivational poster. But don't let the beauty distract you; there's plenty of local culture and quirky charm waiting to be discovered, and maybe some heated debates about the best way to compost.

Start your adventure at Pearl Street Mall, a pedestrian-only street that's basically the heartbeat of Boulder. It's lined with shops, street performers, and an abundance of artisanal cheese shops that will make you question whether you've ever really tasted cheese before. Here, you can witness everything from musicians playing soulful tunes to an intense competition between performers trying to out-weird each other. One moment you'll be enjoying a guy juggling flaming torches, and the next, there's someone dressed as a giant avocado doing interpretive dance. Welcome to Boulder.

For foodies, Boulder is a veritable smorgasbord. There's no shortage of organic cafes, farm-to-table restaurants, and vegan-friendly eateries that cater to just about every dietary whim. You can savor dishes made from local ingredients, which might make you feel like a true environmental hero. Just be prepared for the servers to ask if you want your kale salad tossed or massaged. Yes, massaged. Apparently, there's a difference, and you'll need to decide just how much pampering your greens need.

Now, if you're in the mood for some intellectual stimulation, head over to the University of Colorado Boulder. It's not just a school; it's a breeding ground for some of the most passionate (and sometimes overly opinionated) students you'll ever meet. Campus life is vibrant, with students engaging in discussions that range from the importance of sustainable living to why pineapple on pizza should be considered a crime against humanity. Feel free to join in, but be ready to defend your stance because nothing gets a Boulderite fired up like a culinary debate.

If you're feeling adventurous, lace up your hiking boots and tackle one of the many trails in the area. The Chautauqua Trail is a local favorite, offering breathtaking views that make your heart sing and your legs scream. Just be careful; you might find yourself in a group of hikers who take their "soul-searching" seriously, pausing every ten minutes to do some deep-breathing exercises or meditate on a rock. If you're not careful, you'll end up surrounded by a circle of people chanting, "Om" while you try to figure out how to discreetly sneak a granola bar.

As you wander through Boulder, you'll quickly realize that the political climate here is as dynamic as the landscape. It's a town where conversations about environmental policy can turn into debates that rival any political discourse you've seen on cable news. Local elections can feel like the Super Bowl, complete with campaign buttons and yard signs that take up more real estate than some of the houses. Don't be surprised if you encounter passionate activists passionately advocating for everything from climate action to local pet adoption—often at the same time. It's the kind of place where "save the bees" stickers adorn eco-friendly water bottles alongside slogans about social justice.

Now, let's not forget about the cultural attractions. The Boulder Museum of Contemporary Art is a must-visit for anyone looking to expand their horizons or simply pretend to understand modern art. You'll find pieces that make you think, "I could do that," followed by a sudden realization that you probably wouldn't even know where to begin. The museum often features installations that are both thought-provoking and perplexing, ensuring that your visit will be a topic of conversation for at least three brunches to come.

When the sun begins to set, the nightlife in Boulder comes alive, but not in the way you might expect. Instead of wild parties, you'll find a more laid-back scene filled with breweries, wine bars, and cozy cafes. Boulder has a reputation for being craft beer central, so don't miss the chance to sample local brews that might just make you a believer in the power of hops. You can enjoy a pint while chatting with locals who have opinions on everything from the best hiking trails to the merits of their favorite band. Just be careful not to mention that one band that always seems to spark a heated debate—nobody wants to see a friendship ruined over musical tastes.

If you're in the mood for something more active, try bowling at the local alleys, where the atmosphere is less "rock star" and more "let's have a fun time without taking ourselves too seriously." Here, you can unleash your inner competitor, but be prepared for the occasional game of "bowl and debate," where discussions about the best pizza toppings inevitably arise.

As your time in Boulder comes to an end, you'll find yourself reflecting on this unique town that manages to combine natural beauty with a vibrant cultural and political scene. It's a place where hiking boots meet yoga mats, and where every conversation feels like it could spark a movement. You might leave with a greater appreciation for organic farming, an armful of artisan cheese, and perhaps a newfound ability to discuss the finer points of climate policy—while eating your kale salad, of course.

So, there you have it. Boulder, Colorado, is a town where the mountains are breathtaking, the opinions are abundant, and the coffee is strong enough to fuel even the most spirited debates. Whether you're hiking, dining, or simply engaging in lively discourse, this quirky town offers a little something for everyone—even if you don't leave with a clear answer on whether pineapple belongs on pizza.

Breckenridge

Breckenridge, Colorado, is a town that wears its charm like a cozy sweater. With a history rooted in gold mining, it's a place where adventure and nostalgia collide in a delightful fashion. Founded in 1859, Breckenridge started as a bustling mining camp during the Colorado Gold Rush, attracting dreamers and schemers alike. If you've ever wanted to visit a place that could have been the backdrop for a classic Western film but also doubles as a ski paradise, this is it.

As you roll into Breckenridge, the first thing you'll notice is the breathtaking mountain scenery. Picture this: majestic peaks towering over quaint Victorian buildings that look like they've stepped right out of a postcard. It's the kind of view that makes you want to grab a cup of hot cocoa, sit by the fire, and reflect on your life choices—like why you didn't move here sooner. Just be warned: the altitude might leave you gasping for breath and questioning why you thought climbing the stairs was a good idea.

The heart of Breckenridge is its historic Main Street, a vibrant stretch filled with shops, restaurants, and an endless supply of charm. Here, you can wander from store to store, admiring everything from locally crafted jewelry to ski gear that costs more than your last car. Don't forget to stop by one of the many chocolate shops, where you'll discover confections so rich they could make a gold miner weep with joy. You might even feel like you've struck gold yourself—until you see the price tag and realize you'll be living off ramen for the next week.

Breckenridge isn't just a pretty face; it's also home to some serious outdoor fun. In the winter, the town transforms into a ski resort paradise, boasting over 2,900 acres of skiable terrain. Whether you're a seasoned pro or a novice who's still trying to figure out how to put on ski boots, there's something for everyone. Just be prepared for the inevitable embarrassment of falling on your backside—preferably in a way that doesn't end with you colliding into a snowman or, worse, an unsuspecting child.

If skiing isn't your jam, fear not! Breckenridge offers plenty of alternatives. Snowshoeing is a fantastic option for those who prefer to move at a leisurely pace, allowing you to admire the beautiful scenery while pretending you're in a nature documentary. Just make sure you don't get too caught up in your thoughts and wander off the trail; nobody wants to be the subject of the local news because they got lost trying to commune with nature.

When the snow melts, Breckenridge transforms into a hiking and biking paradise. There are trails that range from "Hey, I can handle this" to "Am I in a fitness magazine?" You can enjoy stunning views without the risk of frostbite, though you might encounter the occasional friendly deer that seems to judge your choice of hiking gear. "Is that what you're wearing?" they seem to say with their big, doe eyes. But fear not, they're friendly; just don't expect them to help you with directions.

Now, let's talk food. Breckenridge has a culinary scene that is as diverse as its inhabitants. You can feast on everything from gourmet burgers to organic, gluten-free quinoa bowls, because nothing says "vacation" quite like counting carbs. The local breweries are worth a visit, too. After a long day on the slopes, nothing beats a cold craft beer that has more flavor than the average small talk you'll find at your family reunions. Plus, the breweries often host events that range from trivia nights to live music, making them the perfect spot to unwind.

If you're feeling extra adventurous, check out the Breckenridge Distillery, where you can indulge in tastings of small-batch spirits. You'll learn about the distillation process and sample drinks that might just have you questioning your loyalty to that bottle of vodka you've had since college. The distillery even offers tours, so you can feel like a true connoisseur while secretly trying to remember which cocktail you liked best.

As the day winds down, head to one of the many local establishments that offer live music. You'll find everything from country bands to acoustic duos, often performing in cozy venues where you can sip on your drink and pretend you're not judging the guy in the front row who thinks he's the next big thing. It's a magical experience that will make you feel like you're part of a community, even if you can't quite keep up with the latest local bands.

No visit to Breckenridge would be complete without taking a trip to the Breckenridge Arts District. This creative enclave is home to galleries, studios, and workshops where you can channel your inner Picasso—though it's wise to remember that not every attempt at art is destined for greatness. Participate in a class, but don't be surprised if you leave with a piece that's better suited for the fridge than the living room wall.

For a taste of history, visit the Edwin Carter Museum. Edwin was a legendary local figure who, in the 1800s, amassed one of the largest collections of taxidermy in Colorado. It's a quirky little museum that will have you questioning not only the history of the town but also the origins of that oddly realistic bear in the corner. You might even find yourself having deep philosophical discussions with your friends about the ethics of taxidermy while trying to decide who gets to take the next selfie with the bear.

As night falls, don't forget to explore the local nightlife. Breckenridge has a way of luring you into its bars and dance floors, where you can let loose after a day of outdoor adventures. The vibe is casual and welcoming—just like that one friend who insists on wearing socks with sandals. You might find yourself enjoying a game of pool or dancing to a live band, but remember to pace yourself. The last thing you want is to wake up the next morning wondering how you ended up in a hot tub with three strangers and a half-eaten slice of pizza.

In the end, Breckenridge is a town that captures the essence of Colorado—breathtaking beauty, quirky charm, and a community that thrives on adventure. It's a place where you can embrace the outdoors, indulge in culinary delights, and experience a blend of history and modernity. So pack your bags and your best sense of humor, and get ready to embrace everything this mountain town has to offer, because in Breckenridge, every day truly is a snow day—just with a little more flair and a lot more laughter.

Brighton

Brighton, Colorado, is like that friend who shows up to the party unexpectedly but turns out to be the most entertaining person in the room. Established in the late 1800s, this charming little town started off as a farming community, complete with fields of crops and plenty of horses. Today, it's a bustling suburb just north of Denver, where you can find a delightful mix of agricultural roots and modern suburban quirks. Think of it as a blend of rustic charm and suburban sprawl, like a cowboy wearing a "We love our HOA" T-shirt.

When you first arrive in Brighton, the scenery is a mix of wide-open prairies and picturesque mountain views that make you wonder how anyone could ever complain about their commute. Just don't get too comfortable in that car of yours; Brighton is a town where the local traffic can resemble a snail race, especially during rush hour when everyone suddenly decides that leaving for work at the same time is a good idea. You might find yourself pondering life's big questions, like why you didn't bring snacks for this journey.

Brighton is home to the historic downtown area, which features buildings that look like they've been plucked right out of a Western film set. Strolling down Main Street feels like a delightful trip back in time—if time had a lot more coffee shops and quirky boutiques. You can pop into the local antique shops, where you might find everything from vintage furniture to strange trinkets that raise more questions than they answer. Is that a ceramic frog with a top hat? Yes, yes it is, and it's just waiting for you to take it home and start a new collection that will confuse your friends.

Speaking of friends, Brighton has plenty of community events that will make you feel like you've joined a large, slightly dysfunctional family. The Brighton Farmer's Market is a local favorite, showcasing everything from fresh produce to handmade crafts. Here, you can snag some locally grown corn while trying to avoid that one vendor who insists on giving you unsolicited advice about gardening. "You know, if you just talk to your tomatoes, they'll grow better," they'll say, and you'll nod politely while wondering if you've accidentally wandered into a gardening cult.

If you're in the mood for some outdoor fun, head to the Brighton Recreation Center. It's the kind of place that has something for everyone, from swimming pools to fitness classes. Just be cautious about joining a yoga class unless you want to feel deeply inadequate when the instructor effortlessly moves into a pose that makes you question whether you should even be attempting yoga in the first place. One minute you're feeling zen, and the next you're contemplating a career change to interpretive dance—something less likely to involve flexibility.

Brighton is also known for its parks, which are perfect for picnicking, playing frisbee, or contemplating your life choices while lying in the grass. Don't miss the opportunity to visit Barr Lake State Park, where you can enjoy nature in all its glory—provided you can avoid the local geese, who seem to think they own the place. These feathered fiends will hiss at you as if you've just insulted their lineage, which is ironic considering they are literally just waddling around in search of breadcrumbs.

As for dining, Brighton offers a smorgasbord of options that reflect its diverse population. You can find everything from classic American diners to Mexican restaurants that serve up tacos so good you might consider changing your name to "Taco Enthusiast." Just be careful when ordering; the last thing you want is to accidentally end up in a spicy food contest. Nothing quite like a mouthful of fire to make you question your culinary decisions while the entire restaurant cheers you on, recording the whole event for social media.

Brighton has also embraced its artsy side, with local galleries showcasing the works of talented artists from the area. The Brighton Arts District is a gem where you can find everything from paintings that make you ponder life's deeper meanings to sculptures that might just be the result of an ambitious art student's late-night binge. It's the kind of place where you can marvel at creativity while simultaneously pretending you understand modern art.

Now, let's not forget about the local history, which is as colorful as the town itself. Brighton has a rich agricultural background, and one of its most notable historical landmarks is the Brighton Depot, which dates back to the early 1900s. This old train station was once a bustling hub for farmers and townsfolk, transporting goods and gossip alike. Today, it's a charming reminder of the town's roots, complete with a gift shop that's filled with quirky souvenirs. Want a miniature train set that you'll never assemble? You got it!

For those who enjoy a bit of excitement, Brighton is home to the annual Brighton Daze Festival, a local celebration that brings the community together for a weekend of fun. Think carnival rides, live music, and enough fried food to make your heart skip a beat—literally. You can witness the bizarre tradition of the "Bizarre Bazaar," where local vendors sell handmade crafts that range from cute to completely inexplicable. Ever wanted a necklace made from bottle caps? This is the place for you.

As night falls, Brighton's nightlife kicks in, and the town transforms into a place where friends gather for a good time. The local bars and breweries offer a relaxed atmosphere where you can unwind with a craft beer or a cocktail that's as colorful as your friend's last breakup story. The camaraderie in these places is palpable, with laughter and stories shared over clinking glasses. Just be prepared for a lively debate about whether the "old school" way of doing things is better than whatever trend the younger crowd is trying to start.

In the end, Brighton, Colorado, is a town that embodies the spirit of community and charm. It's a place where the past meets the present, where laughter is abundant, and where every day feels like an adventure waiting to happen. So pack your sense of humor and your appetite for quirky experiences, because Brighton will entertain you in ways you never expected, leaving you with stories to tell and maybe even a ceramic frog wearing a top hat to take home.

Broomfield

Broomfield, Colorado, a suburb that feels like the friend you never knew you needed until you stumbled into a surprisingly fun house party. Established in 1961 as a city, it quickly became a delightful patchwork of residential neighborhoods, parks, and more corporate offices than you can shake a stick at. It's like the kid who was picked last for dodgeball suddenly became the overachiever of the group, and now everyone wants to hang out with them.

As you roll into Broomfield, you might notice that it's not quite like your typical Colorado town. Sure, it has the requisite beautiful views of the Rockies, but it also boasts a unique blend of suburban charm and modern conveniences that can make you forget you're only a short drive away from the great outdoors. Broomfield is where the mountains meet the mall—yes, you can have it all, including a latte and a side of stunning scenery.

Let's start with the local attractions. One of the main highlights is the Flatiron Crossing Mall, a shopping center so vast it could probably be seen from space. Here, you can find everything from high-end retailers to discount stores, all conveniently located under one roof. It's the kind of place that makes you feel like a kid in a candy store, except the candy is overpriced clothing and gadgets you didn't know you needed. And let's be real, you might find yourself in a staring contest with a mannequin that looks better in that outfit than you ever could.

When you need a break from shopping, head to the Broomfield County Commons Open Space. This park is a real gem, offering wide-open spaces and trails that beg to be explored. Here, you can engage in classic outdoor activities like walking, jogging, or wondering if you really need to bring your dog along, especially when you see how much they enjoy rolling in something decidedly unsavory. Just make sure to keep an eye on them; you wouldn't want your furry friend to become the park's local celebrity by rolling in a puddle of mud while you're busy trying to take an Instagram-worthy photo.

If you're looking to dip your toes into Broomfield's cultural scene, you're in for a treat. The Broomfield Auditorium hosts a variety of performances, from concerts to plays, showcasing local talent that can sometimes rival Broadway. You might find yourself at a community theater production that, while charming, may leave you questioning the interpretation of Shakespeare. "To be or not to be" might just become "To read or not to read the program." Either way, it's an experience that's bound to leave you chuckling.

Let's not forget about the Broomfield Library, which is not just a place for books but also a community hub that offers classes, workshops, and events. Picture a place where toddlers are learning the ABCs while retirees are perfecting their knitting skills, all under one roof. It's a beautiful thing until you realize you've accidentally walked into a heated debate about the best way to brew coffee, leaving you wondering if you've become a contestant on a reality show about home brewing.

If outdoor sports are more your style, Broomfield is home to some fantastic facilities. The Broomfield Bay Aquatic Park is a splashy wonderland, complete with water slides and lazy rivers that will make you feel like a kid again—until you realize you're surrounded by children who can navigate the slides with the grace of Olympic athletes. You'll soon find yourself contemplating whether that last hot dog was a good idea as you brave the twisty slides and narrowly avoid a collision with a cannonballing six-year-old.

For those who prefer their recreation on solid ground, Broomfield offers a variety of golf courses. Picture manicured greens and fairways that could make even the most dedicated couch potato consider taking up the sport. Whether you're a seasoned pro or a newcomer who just wants to swing a club while trying not to embarrass yourself, there's a course for you. Just be prepared for the inevitable "helpful" advice from your friends, who will no doubt remind you that golf is 90% mental while they consistently hit the ball into the next county.

As the sun sets, Broomfield's culinary scene beckons. The town boasts an eclectic mix of eateries that cater to all tastes. From classic American diners serving burgers that are taller than your toddler to trendy restaurants that make kale salad look like a five-star meal, you won't go hungry here. And of course, no meal is complete without dessert. Make sure to swing by one of the local ice cream shops where you can get scoops so generous they could rival a small mountain range. Just remember, if you attempt to eat a sundae the size of your head, you may want to check if there are any medical facilities nearby.

If you're in the mood for a little local flavor, keep an eye out for food festivals. Broomfield hosts a variety of events throughout the year, including a farmers market that brings together local produce, crafts, and the kind of gossip that only small towns can provide. You might overhear heated discussions about the best tomato variety or the secret ingredient that makes the perfect salsa, while silently judging your own sad grocery store tomatoes. But if there aren't any food festivals happening when you visit, check out the classy 5280 Burger Bar or the casual Old Man Bar. One has blow-your-mind burgers, and the other - out of this world smoked WINGS!

As you mingle with locals and sample various treats, you'll likely find that Broomfield is a town filled with friendly faces and an uncanny ability to make everyone feel like family—whether you want to or not. There's a sense of community here that's palpable, even if it occasionally feels like everyone knows a little too much about each other. It's not uncommon to overhear conversations that would make you wonder if you've just stepped into a soap opera.

For a slice of history, check out the Broomfield Depot Museum. This quaint museum offers a glimpse into the town's past, showcasing artifacts from the days when Broomfield was just a tiny farming community. You might find yourself marveling at old photographs while trying to figure out how people managed to live without smartphones and streaming services. It's a fun trip down memory lane, though it may leave you wondering how those folks survived without their daily dose of cat videos.

As the day winds down, you can kick back in one of Broomfield's parks, where families gather for picnics and neighbors catch up on the latest gossip. Just be prepared for the occasional spontaneous game of frisbee or soccer, where everyone suddenly becomes an athlete, and you may find yourself awkwardly trying to fit in.

In the end, Broomfield, Colorado, is a place where small-town charm meets suburban convenience. It's a town that offers a little bit of everything—from shopping and dining to outdoor fun and cultural experiences. Whether you're exploring the parks, indulging in local cuisine, or simply enjoying the company of friendly neighbors, Broomfield is a town that embraces its quirks and leaves you with a smile. So grab your sense of humor and your appetite for adventure, because Broomfield might just become that unexpected friend you never knew you needed.

Brush

Brush, Colorado, a charming little town that feels like the last hidden gem on the treasure map of Colorado. Founded in the 1880s, Brush was originally a rail stop and quickly transformed into a thriving community, fueled by agriculture and a serious dose of small-town spirit. If you're looking for a place where everyone knows your name and your business, this is it. But fear not; it's the good kind of nosiness, where people genuinely care, not the kind that gets you a starring role in a reality show.

When you roll into Brush, the first thing that hits you is the small-town vibe. You'll be greeted by a town center that looks like it was plucked straight from a postcard, complete with a main street that's probably shorter than your last grocery list. Picture cozy shops that seem to sell everything from antique knickknacks to the kind of homemade jams that could make you rethink your commitment to store-bought. You can even grab a coffee from a local café that feels like stepping into someone's living room—if that living room had an espresso machine and a lot of cats.

Brush is a town that embraces its agricultural roots, and you can't talk about the place without mentioning its signature event: the Brush Rodeo. This annual rodeo is a spectacular display of cowboy skills, complete with barrel racing, bull riding, and enough cowboy hats to make you feel like you've wandered into a Western film set. It's the kind of event where you can enjoy the thrill of watching cowboys wrestle steers while also being entertained by the rodeo clown who somehow manages to steal the show. Just be careful; one minute you're watching a rider go for the gold, and the next, you're trying to decipher the difference between a steer and a heifer—without Google.

But rodeos aren't the only form of entertainment in Brush. If you're in the mood for something a little less dusty, check out the local parks, which offer a delightful array of outdoor activities. The City Park is a prime spot for picnicking, playing frisbee, or contemplating the mysteries of life while watching ducks waddle around. Just be prepared for the occasional family reunion that feels like a mini carnival, complete with overzealous potato sack races and a barbecue that could put any backyard cookout to shame.

For those who prefer more structured fun, the Brush Area Community Center is a hub of activity where you can find everything from fitness classes to community events. This is the place to go if you want to sweat it out in Zumba while also potentially learning the latest gossip about who brought the best potato salad to the last potluck. It's a no-judgment zone where everyone is there to have a good time, even if your "good time" looks suspiciously like trying to remember the last time you actually exercised.

Let's not overlook the culinary scene in Brush, which is a delightful mix of classic American fare and local flavor. The local diners serve up dishes that could make any heart happy, from burgers that are a meal unto themselves to breakfast plates that might as well be a food pyramid. You can enjoy a hearty meal while surrounded by friendly faces who will likely comment on how your food looks better than theirs—a classic small-town trait. Just don't get caught in a debate over who has the best pie in town; it could escalate into a full-blown bake-off.

For those craving a little history, the Brush Historical Museum is a hidden treasure that will take you on a journey through the town's past. You can learn about the early settlers, the railroads, and how this quaint town evolved over the years. Just be prepared for the occasional overly enthusiastic guide who might dive deep into the lore of the local quilt club, complete with a slideshow. It's a delightful way to spend an afternoon—if you can manage to keep your eyes open during the 20-minute overview of the 1978 Brush Potato Festival.

Speaking of festivals, Brush hosts a variety of community events throughout the year, each one more entertaining than the last. The annual Potato Festival is a crowd favorite, celebrating the humble spud with parades, games, and enough potato dishes to make you reconsider your stance on carbs. Who knew you could have a potato cannon contest right alongside the "Best Potato Salad" competition? It's the kind of event that leaves you questioning why you don't eat more potatoes on a regular basis while simultaneously trying to figure out how to sneak some of those festival fries into your bag for later.

As the sun sets, Brush doesn't slow down. The nightlife may not be as bustling as in larger cities, but you'll find cozy bars where locals gather to share stories and enjoy a cold drink. Picture a place where everyone knows each other, and the bartender is likely to slide you a drink with a side of unsolicited life advice. Just remember, no matter how many "just one more drink" promises you make, you'll still have to navigate that charmingly short main street back to your hotel without getting lost.

If you're in the mood for a little friendly competition, check out the local bowling alley. This is where you can witness true sportsmanship as friends and families come together to compete for the coveted title of "Bowling Champion"—an honor that's highly regarded in Brush. You can expect plenty of laughter, some friendly trash talk, and an impressive array of bowling shirts that might make you wish you had brought your own. Just be cautious of the "bowlers' diet," which often consists of nachos and soda in varying sizes, all while desperately trying to keep score without losing track of who is winning.

Brush, Colorado, is a town that encapsulates the spirit of small-town America. With its charming streets, rich history, and vibrant community, it offers a unique blend of entertainment and warmth that's hard to resist. Whether you're enjoying the rodeo, exploring the parks, or diving into the local culinary scene, Brush is a place that feels like home—if home were a lively gathering of friends and family enjoying every moment together. So grab your cowboy hat and your appetite for fun, because in Brush, every day is a *brush* with joy!

Buena Vista

Buena Vista, Colorado, is like that charming friend who always has the best stories and somehow manages to turn every outing into an adventure. Nestled in the heart of the Rockies, this small town, with a population that might be smaller than your high school graduating class, offers breathtaking views, thrilling activities, and enough quirky charm to make you feel right at home—or at least like you're in the middle of a sitcom.

The town's name, which means "good view" in Spanish, is not just a clever marketing tactic. As you drive into Buena Vista, you'll find yourself surrounded by stunning mountain vistas that might just make you weep with joy—or envy if you're stuck behind someone taking a selfie. The majestic Collegiate Peaks loom overhead, and you'll soon realize you've stumbled into a place that could double as a postcard for every hiking enthusiast's dreams. Just be careful not to stare too long; you don't want to accidentally drive off the road while admiring the scenery.

Buena Vista is also known as the "whitewater capital of Colorado," which is a fancy way of saying it has more river rapids than your local water park has slides. The Arkansas River runs through town, providing the perfect backdrop for a thrilling day of rafting. Just imagine yourself bobbing along the rapids, screaming with joy—or sheer terror—while your guide effortlessly maneuvers the raft like a pro. The best part? You get to say you've "conquered" the river, even if you spent most of the time clinging to the side like a scared cat in a bath.

If you're not quite ready to brave the wild waters, there are plenty of more serene options to enjoy the river. You can try kayaking or paddleboarding, which sounds relaxing until you realize that both activities involve a fair amount of coordination—something that can be tricky when you're still adjusting to the altitude. You might find yourself laughing as you paddle in circles, all while wondering if your balance was a skill you accidentally left behind in your last life.

For those who prefer keeping their feet on solid ground, Buena Vista is a hiker's paradise. With trails that range from "this is a nice stroll" to "are we trying to summon a higher power?" there's something for everyone. One of the most popular hikes is the Collegiate Peaks Trail, which offers sweeping views and enough elevation gain to make you feel like a mountain goat. Just be sure to pack plenty of snacks; you'll need the energy to keep up with all the "I swear it's just around the corner" comments from your hiking buddies.

Speaking of snacks, let's talk about the local dining scene. Buena Vista has a surprisingly vibrant food culture, considering its size. You can indulge in everything from hearty burgers to gourmet pizza, and if you're lucky, you might even stumble upon a food truck festival. Imagine biting into a taco so good you contemplate moving to Colorado just to eat it every day. Local breweries and distilleries also make sure you're well-hydrated after a long day of outdoor shenanigans. After all, what's better than a cold craft beer enjoyed on a sunny patio while you reminisce about your epic adventure on the river?

Probably nothing, unless you're counting the moments when you awkwardly try to explain to locals why you mispronounced "Buena Vista" as "Byoona Vista."

Now, let's not overlook the town's history, which is rich enough to make you feel like you're in a Western movie. Founded in the mid-1800s during the Colorado Gold Rush, Buena Vista has seen its fair share of boom and bust. The old buildings in the downtown area are like time capsules, offering a glimpse into the past. You can wander through the streets, marveling at the preserved architecture and imagining what life was like for those early settlers. Just be careful not to touch anything; you wouldn't want to accidentally activate a curse from the Gold Rush days that makes you unreasonably bad at poker.

If you're lucky enough to visit during one of the town's many festivals, you're in for a treat. The annual BV Heritage Festival celebrates the rich culture and history of the area, complete with music, art, and food that makes you question why you ever thought store-bought salsa was acceptable. It's the kind of event where you can dance like nobody's watching while simultaneously trying to impress someone with your newfound knowledge of local history.

As night falls, Buena Vista transforms into a cozy haven. You can unwind at one of the local bars, where the atmosphere is as inviting as the drinks are strong. Picture yourself sipping a cocktail while engaged in deep conversations about life, love, and why you didn't take that last hike seriously. The locals are friendly and eager to share stories about their adventures, often punctuated with laughter and a healthy dose of humility—unless they're talking about their river rafting triumphs, in which case, prepare for the exaggerated tales.

If you're feeling adventurous but need a break from the outdoor activities, you can check out the local shops that offer a variety of unique gifts, handmade crafts, and—of course—plenty of outdoor gear. You can buy that expensive jacket you'll swear you'll wear on all your future adventures, even if it's currently hanging in your closet next to your gym membership card.

For the more adventurous souls, consider a visit to the nearby ghost towns. Exploring these abandoned places feels like stepping into a real-life video game, complete with mysterious histories and the occasional eerie sound that makes you question your life choices. Who doesn't want to stumble upon an old mining camp and imagine what life was like for those who lived there? Just remember to stay in groups; you wouldn't want to be the star of your own horror movie.

Buena Vista, Colorado, is a delightful mix of outdoor adventure, rich history, and small-town charm. Whether you're paddling down the Arkansas River, hiking through stunning landscapes, or indulging in delicious local cuisine, there's something for everyone to enjoy. So grab your sense of adventure and your favorite pair of hiking boots, because Buena Vista is ready to offer you a river of good times that you won't soon forget.

Burlington

Burlington, Colorado, is a town that embodies the spirit of the American West with the kind of charm that could make even a tumbleweed feel at home. Located on the eastern plains, Burlington boasts a population that might be smaller than a high school reunion but is brimming with stories, quirky attractions, and the kind of hospitality that makes you question if you've accidentally wandered into a Hallmark movie.

Founded in the late 1800s, Burlington began as a railroad town. It quickly developed into a key stop for travelers making their way west. As you stroll through the downtown area, you'll see remnants of its rich history, like the historic train depot that feels like it could still be used for a quick getaway if only time travel were real. Just imagine standing there, gazing at a train that will never arrive while trying to figure out which direction to take for the best Instagram shot of the local scenery. Spoiler alert: it's mostly flat.

Now, let's talk about the scenery, or lack thereof. Burlington is surrounded by miles of open plains that stretch out as far as the eye can see. This means you get to enjoy an uninterrupted view of the sky, which is great if you've ever wanted to feel like a character in a Western film—minus the dramatic soundtrack. The sunsets are legendary, though. You can expect colors that could inspire a painter to quit their day job and devote their life to capturing the ever-changing sky. Just be sure to bring your camera—those Instagram followers need to see your flatland art appreciation.

When it comes to activities, Burlington knows how to keep things interesting. For starters, the Kit Carson County Carousel is a must-visit. Built in the 1920s, this charming carousel features hand-carved wooden animals that have more personality than most people you meet on a Monday morning. You can ride these whimsical creatures while pretending to be a kid again, if only for a few minutes. Just be careful not to let the nostalgia turn into a full-blown existential crisis about adulthood and responsibilities.

After the carousel, you might want to check out the Old Town Museum, a treasure trove of local history. This place is like a time capsule that transports you back to the days when life was simpler and the biggest concern was whether or not your horse was well-fed. You can wander through old schoolhouses, blacksmith shops, and even a fully stocked general store that might make you feel like you've walked into a scene from Little House on the Prairie. Just don't get too carried away imagining yourself as Laura Ingalls Wilder—you might find yourself considering a life of farming and churning butter.

For outdoor enthusiasts, Burlington offers the stunning Bonny Lake State Park, which is great for camping, fishing, and pretending you're the next Bear Grylls. The park features beautiful trails that are perfect for hiking, though you might want to pack extra water. The last thing you need is to be that person who runs out of steam halfway through a leisurely stroll and has to be rescued by a passing motorist. Fishing at the lake is a relaxing way to spend an afternoon—just don't be surprised if you leave with more sunburn than fish.

Burlington is also home to the annual Burlington Rodeo, which is an event that brings the community together like a family reunion but with more horses and less awkward small talk about who's still single. The rodeo features everything from bull riding to barrel racing, and it's the perfect place to unleash your inner cowboy or cowgirl. Be prepared for plenty of cheering, shouting, and the occasional "hold my beer" moment. You might even pick up some rodeo lingo along the way, which will come in handy for those late-night debates about who the real cowboy is.

When it comes to dining, Burlington offers a selection of local eateries that range from cozy diners to a few surprising gems. You can feast on classic American fare, including burgers and fries that could rival anything you'd find in a big city. Don't forget to sample some local favorites, like the iconic green chili that packs a punch stronger than a bull rider's grip. Just be sure to check the spice level first; you wouldn't want to end up with a mouth on fire and no way to cool it down except with a gallon of milk from the nearest convenience store.

And speaking of convenience stores, Burlington has a thriving collection of local shops where you can buy everything from quirky souvenirs to practical items you never knew you needed. You can peruse through aisles of items that may range from cowboy hats to an astonishing number of potato chips flavors. You might even find that perfect gift for Aunt Edna who still insists on sending you knitted sweaters every Christmas.

As the sun sets and the stars begin to twinkle, Burlington's nightlife springs to life—if by "nightlife" you mean a few local bars and plenty of opportunities to swap stories with fellow adventurers. You can find a cozy bar where the bartender knows everyone by name and the drinks are as strong as the locals' accents. Expect to hear tales of fishing trips gone wrong and the occasional ghost story about the local haunted hotel. Just don't bring up politics unless you want to see a lively debate erupt faster than you can say "flatlands."

Burlington, Colorado, may not have the flashiest attractions or the highest mountains, but what it lacks in elevation, it more than makes up for in charm and character. With a rich history, friendly locals, and an array of activities that will keep you entertained, Burlington is the kind of place where you can truly embrace the simplicity of life. So grab your cowboy hat, prepare for some flat terrain, and get ready to make some unforgettable memories in this delightful corner of the Centennial State.

Byers

Byers, Colorado, is the kind of town that could easily slip under the radar if you're not paying attention. Nestled in the eastern plains, it's got that classic small-town vibe where the population is so intimate that you might just end up getting roped into the annual pie-eating contest by a neighbor you've never met. Founded in the late 1800s, Byers started as a railroad stop, which means it's always been about connections—both on the tracks and in the community.

If you roll into Byers, the first thing you'll notice is the wide-open spaces that stretch out in every direction, making it perfect for those who enjoy staring into the horizon as they contemplate life's big questions, like "Why is my GPS taking me here?" The main street might not be bustling with shops and cafés, but you can be sure that the few establishments that are open have more personality than a reality TV star.

One of the town's best features is the Byers Historical Society Museum. Now, before you start yawning, let me assure you this isn't your grandma's museum—unless your grandma happens to be an avid collector of local artifacts and the occasional piece of taxidermy. The museum houses a charming collection of memorabilia that tells the story of the town and its residents over the years. You can wander through rooms filled with old photographs, farming equipment, and tools that look like they were used in a survival reality show. There's even a section dedicated to local legends, which means you might find out why everyone in town refuses to speak about the "Mysterious Incident of '87" or who really won that fabled potato sack race.

Once you've soaked up the history, you might want to check out some outdoor activities. Byers has access to plenty of open land, making it ideal for hiking, biking, or just standing still and wondering how a town this small can have so many prairie dogs. It's the perfect spot for those who appreciate the great outdoors without the distractions of heavy foot traffic or the sound of a thousand tourists taking selfies. Just be sure to pack your bug spray because those prairie mosquitoes can be as persistent as a toddler asking for candy.

When you need to refuel after your outdoor adventures, there's the local diner—a haven for hearty meals that could satisfy even the most ravenous appetites. The food is classic American fare, served with a side of small-town gossip. You can enjoy a burger the size of your face while eavesdropping on conversations about who won last week's county fair or the latest shenanigans at the local high school football game. Don't forget to save room for dessert; the pie here could make you reconsider your entire life's philosophy on baked goods.

Now, let's talk about the annual events that keep the spirit of community alive in Byers. The Byers Rodeo is a highlight of the summer, where locals gather to watch everything from bull riding to barrel racing. It's like a giant family reunion, except the uncles are on horses, and everyone's cheering like it's the Super Bowl. It's a chance to witness a spectacle of skill, strength, and just a hint of chaos, especially when the clown inevitably steals the show with his antics.

The town is also home to the annual Harvest Festival, which celebrates the local agriculture and gives everyone a reason to indulge in too much corn on the cob. Expect to see everything from pie contests to live music that you might either love or question your life choices over. It's the kind of event where you can try to balance a giant pumpkin on your head while contemplating the meaning of life—or just hoping nobody catches that on camera.

For those looking to get a little artsy, check out local galleries and studios that showcase the work of Byers' talented residents. You'll find everything from paintings that might make you feel cultured to sculptures that could prompt an existential crisis. Just remember to nod appreciatively at things you don't understand, because pretending to appreciate art is half the fun.

As the sun sets, Byers doesn't exactly become a nightlife hotspot, but you can find a local watering hole where the drinks are cold, and the stories are warm. This is where the magic happens—people gathering to swap tales of their adventures or misadventures in this quirky little town. You might overhear stories about the legendary fishing trip that went awry or the time someone mistakenly thought they could herd cattle on a bicycle.

Byers, Colorado, is a small town with a big heart and a history that could fill a novel—or at least a charming short story. With its friendly atmosphere, engaging museums, and community events that bring everyone together, it's a place where you can truly appreciate the beauty of simplicity. So grab your cowboy hat, take a stroll down main street, and embrace the quirky charm that Byers has to offer. You might just leave with a smile, a full belly, and the feeling that you've been part of something special, even if it was just for a little while.

Calhan

Calhan, Colorado, is the kind of place that can leave you wondering how a small town can pack so much character into a few square miles. Nestled in El Paso County, this charming hamlet has a rich history, quirky attractions, and enough local flair to keep even the most jaded traveler entertained. Founded in the late 1800s, Calhan was initially a stop on the railroad and has managed to maintain its small-town charm despite the ever-encroaching reach of modern life.

As you meander through Calhan, you might be surprised to discover that it's home to a handful of historical gems. The Calhan Historical Society Museum is a must-see, showcasing the town's past with exhibits that range from the ordinary to the utterly bizarre. Picture this: artifacts that date back to the days of cowboys and pioneers, mixed with curiosities like a collection of vintage lawn gnomes that could easily star in their own horror movie. You can spend hours wandering through the museum, trying to decipher whether that dusty old hat belonged to a local legend or just some guy named Earl who really loved gardening.

One of the most intriguing aspects of Calhan is its deep-rooted connection to agriculture. The town celebrates its farming heritage with annual events like the Calhan Harvest Festival, which is essentially a giant love letter to all things corn, pumpkins, and whatever else farmers can grow in these parts. Expect to see a parade of tractors that look like they were hand-painted by an enthusiastic art student, alongside stalls overflowing with produce that will make you question why you ever bought grocery store vegetables.

If you're feeling adventurous, check out the local rodeo, which is a highlight of the summer. Picture cowboys and cowgirls strutting their stuff, competing in everything from barrel racing to bull riding. It's like watching a live-action Western movie, complete with all the drama and excitement. Just be sure to keep an eye out for the clowns—those guys are masters of slapstick humor and could easily be mistaken for stand-up comedians if the whole rodeo thing doesn't work out.

As you explore Calhan, you might want to stop by the town's parks, which are surprisingly lovely given the town's small size. The parks are ideal for picnics, leisurely strolls, or pondering the mysteries of life, like why you decided to wear those shoes when you knew you'd be walking on gravel. The kids will love the playgrounds, and you might just find yourself reliving your glory days on the swings—if you can still manage to get your legs up without dislocating something.

No trip to Calhan would be complete without visiting the nearby Paint Mines Interpretive Park. This hidden treasure features stunning geological formations that look like nature's own abstract art exhibit. The vibrant colors and unique shapes of the clay formations will leave you in awe—just don't be surprised if you find yourself channeling your inner artist and contemplating a career change. After all, if Mother Nature can create masterpieces, why can't you?

For the history buffs, Calhan also has a handful of historic buildings, including the old schoolhouse that looks like it could have been straight out of Little House on the Prairie. You can almost hear the faint echoes of children's laughter and the occasional reprimand from a stern teacher. Imagine the stories these walls could tell—like that one time a kid tried to trade his lunch for a golden ticket to a candy factory.

As evening descends, the town takes on a different character. Local diners and cafes offer hearty meals that are guaranteed to hit the spot after a day of exploring. Picture yourself indulging in comfort food so delicious that you might momentarily forget about any diet plans you had made earlier that week. The conversation flows as freely as the coffee, and you'll likely find yourself swapping stories with locals who seem to know everyone in town—including that one guy who always brings a llama to the Harvest Festival for reasons nobody quite understands.

One of the quirkiest things about Calhan is its status as a bit of a hub for local art. The town is home to a surprising number of artists, which means you'll encounter unique sculptures and murals that brighten up the streets. Strolling through Calhan is like walking through an art gallery where the exhibits are free, and the explanations are often just as colorful as the pieces themselves. You might even find a sculpture made entirely of recycled materials that looks so good, you'll start to wonder if you can convince your friends that you're an avant-garde artist yourself.

And let's not forget the annual Calhan Rodeo, which is an event that practically transforms the town into a mini Wild West festival. Picture cowboys, cowgirls, and a smattering of enthusiastic spectators decked out in their best denim, all gathering to watch the excitement unfold. Whether you're there for the bull riding or the fried dough, the rodeo is an experience that sums up the heart and soul of this town—pure, unfiltered fun with a generous side of laughter.

Calhan, Colorado, may not be the biggest name on the map, but it's bursting with history, charm, and enough quirky attractions to make it a destination in its own right. From its vibrant arts scene to the annual festivals that unite the community, Calhan is a town where you can truly appreciate the simple joys of life. So grab your camera, prepare your taste buds, and get ready to immerse yourself in the delightful eccentricity that is Calhan. You might just leave with a few good stories and a deeper appreciation for the beauty of small-town living.

Canon City

Canon City, Colorado, is a town that wears its history like a badge of honor and throws in a dash of absurdity for good measure. Nestled in the heart of the Royal Gorge region, Canon City is often overshadowed by its more glamorous neighbors but boasts enough charm and quirkiness to keep you entertained for hours—or at least until the next meal.

Founded in the 1850s, Canon City sprang up during the gold rush, with dreams of striking it rich and riding off into the sunset. While most of the gold miners ended up with more dust in their pockets than riches, Canon City flourished into a bustling hub of activity. If you stroll through the downtown area, you'll notice buildings that date back to the early days, standing as testaments to the town's rugged past. These structures tell tales of pioneers who believed in the American Dream—primarily that they could build a town where the food was plentiful, the beers were cold, and the Wi-Fi was as slow as a mule in a marathon.

One of the standout attractions in Canon City is the Royal Gorge Bridge, which claims the title of one of the highest suspension bridges in the world. As you step onto this towering marvel, you might feel like you've been catapulted into an action movie—only instead of dodging bullets, you're navigating tourists and their phones as they try to capture the perfect selfie with the canyon below. Don't look down unless you want to be reminded that your fear of heights is still very much alive.

While you're in the area, make sure to check out the Royal Gorge Route Railroad. This scenic train ride takes you through breathtaking landscapes that make you question your life choices—specifically, why you ever thought you could hike it all on foot. The train has been around since the late 1800s, providing a leisurely way to soak in the scenery while enjoying a snack that's far more enjoyable than a granola bar. Just be careful when you open your window for a picture; the gust of wind may turn your hair into a modern art installation.

If museums are your thing, you're in luck! Canon City has a few that are bound to pique your interest. The Museum of Colorado Prisons is a must-visit, showcasing the history of the correctional system in the state. Yes, that's right—nothing says "good times" quite like learning about prisons. Here, you can explore the stories of infamous criminals and the architectural marvels of the prisons themselves. You might even walk through a cell and feel an inexplicable urge to break into a dramatic monologue about freedom and justice. Just remember, you're still in a museum, not an audition.

Next up is the Canon City Area Heritage Center, where you can dive deeper into the rich tapestry of local history. Expect to see artifacts, photographs, and exhibits that recount the town's evolution from a dusty gold rush outpost to the charming community it is today. It's the perfect place to unleash your inner history buff while pretending you have the stamina to read every plaque—an endeavor best approached with a snack in hand.

For the outdoor enthusiasts, Canon City offers plenty of activities to get your adrenaline pumping. White-water rafting on the Arkansas River is a thrilling experience that combines the joy of splashing in cold water with the terror of realizing you're in charge of a raft. Fear not, though; guides are usually present to ensure that you don't end up as part of the scenery. If you manage to survive without losing any gear, consider it a win and treat yourself to a burger afterward—you'll deserve it.

When you're ready to refuel, Canon City's dining scene has plenty to offer. From casual diners serving up hearty breakfasts that could double as an entire day's worth of calories to charming eateries with local flair, you'll find something to satisfy your cravings. The locally sourced ingredients might make you feel like a farm-to-table connoisseur, even if your idea of gourmet is a frozen pizza.

Don't miss the annual events that take place in Canon City, like the Royal Gorge White Water Festival. It's a chance to celebrate everything water-related, complete with races, food trucks, and more excitement than a barrel full of monkeys. You'll find yourself caught up in the festivities, cheering on competitors as they navigate rapids while you contemplate your own life choices from the safety of dry land.

As night falls, Canon City has a quaint nightlife scene that invites you to kick back and unwind. Local bars offer a friendly atmosphere where you can sip on a craft beer or a cocktail while trading stories with locals who have lived through all sorts of adventures. Just be prepared for them to share tales of the time they tried to build a raft out of pool noodles and ended up with a rather soggy disaster instead.

Canon City, Colorado, is a delightful mix of history, adventure, and quirky charm. From stunning natural beauty to fascinating museums, it's a place where you can explore the past while indulging in the present. So grab your camera, prepare for laughter, and get ready to discover all the wonders this hidden gem has to offer. You might leave with a few good stories, some questionable selfies, and a newfound appreciation for small-town life—along with a firm belief that you could definitely survive a rafting trip, as long as someone else is steering the boat.

Carbondale

Nestled between the stunning peaks of the Rockies, Carbondale, Colorado, is the kind of town that feels like it could double as a movie set for a quirky indie film. With a population that hovers around the small-but-mighty mark, Carbondale boasts a blend of outdoor adventure, artsy vibes, and the kind of charm that might just make you rethink your life choices—especially if your last choice was to live in a big city.

Founded in the late 19th century, Carbondale originally came into being thanks to coal mining, which made it the hottest place to be—literally, since mining can get a bit toasty. The town quickly attracted folks looking to strike it rich and get a tan in the process. Although the mining industry has long since passed its peak, the spirit of innovation still runs deep, and that's evident in the eclectic mix of residents you'll find wandering the streets.

The first stop on your whimsical adventure should be the Carbondale Historical Society and Museum. Here, you'll find exhibits that chronicle the town's quirky past, including everything from its mining origins to its evolution into a hub for artists and outdoor enthusiasts. The museum is like a time capsule that holds treasures from the past, including photographs, artifacts, and possibly a taxidermy squirrel that was someone's beloved pet. It's a place where you can get lost in time while also trying to figure out if that old tool on display was used for mining or was just a really early version of a blender.

Once you've soaked in enough history to make your head spin, it's time to head outdoors. Carbondale is located at the confluence of the Crystal River and the Roaring Fork River, making it a playground for those who prefer their adventures to include a little bit of water. Grab a kayak or a paddleboard and hit the rivers, where you can experience the thrill of gliding over the water—just don't forget to practice your "I totally meant to fall in" face before you set off.

If you're feeling more landlocked, there are miles of hiking and biking trails that offer breathtaking views and a chance to contemplate life's biggest questions, like "Why did I think I could wear these shoes for hiking?" The trails range from leisurely strolls to "I need a nap just thinking about it." Don't be surprised if you encounter the occasional deer or mountain goat; they're basically the unofficial welcoming committee.

Carbondale is also known for its vibrant arts scene, which means you'll find galleries and studios filled with work from local artists. The town embraces creativity like a cozy blanket on a chilly night. You might stumble upon an art show featuring everything from abstract paintings to sculptures made from recycled bicycle parts—because who doesn't want a conversation starter that involves a broken bike?

If you're in town during the summer, be sure to check out the Carbondale Mountain Fair. This annual festival is like a giant celebration of all things local, featuring arts and crafts, food vendors, and live music. You'll find yourself weaving through booths filled with handmade goods, sipping on local brews, and listening to bands that will either make you dance or make you question your taste in music. It's a perfect opportunity to test your ability to hold a drink while dodging excited children running around with balloon animals.

Speaking of food, Carbondale has a delightful dining scene that rivals larger cities. You can savor everything from gourmet burgers to artisanal pizzas, and yes, there's even a place that serves an unbelievable amount of craft beer. If you're feeling adventurous, try the local green chili—just be prepared for the heat to remind you why you should always read the fine print on the menu.

For a touch of local culture, don't miss the historic Crystal Theater. This charming venue is the heart of the local performing arts scene and offers everything from indie films to live performances. It's the kind of place where you can cozy up with a tub of popcorn and feel like you're part of a community, even if you're just there to enjoy a film about a cat that saves the world.

As the sun begins to set over the majestic mountains, you might find yourself wandering into one of Carbondale's local bars. Here, you can enjoy live music, share stories with friendly locals, and perhaps engage in a spirited debate about whether the town's biggest claim to fame is its amazing views or the annual chili cook-off. Spoiler alert: the cook-off might just win that battle.

In conclusion, Carbondale, Colorado, is a delightful blend of history, outdoor adventure, and artistic charm. From its quirky museums to its stunning landscapes, there's no shortage of things to see and do. So grab your hiking boots, prepare your taste buds for a culinary journey, and get ready to experience the whimsical charm that is Carbondale. You might just leave with a renewed appreciation for small-town life—and a few too many local craft beers under your belt, of course.

Castle Rock

Nestled between Denver and Colorado Springs, Castle Rock is a town that could easily be mistaken for the setting of a feel-good movie about a small town overcoming quirky odds. With its iconic rock formation that looks suspiciously like a castle—hence the name—you might expect to find knights in shining armor instead of friendly locals sipping coffee and discussing the weather. But fear not, because Castle Rock has plenty to offer, including history, unique attractions, and a heaping side of humor.

The town was founded in the mid-1800s, originally serving as a supply hub for gold miners heading to the booming camps in the mountains. Picture rugged prospectors frantically rushing to strike it rich while debating the merits of different pickaxes. As the gold rush fizzled, Castle Rock evolved into a charming community that decided to forgo the gold for a more stable economy based on hospitality and small-town charm—kind of like deciding to settle for a cozy cottage instead of a mansion on the hill.

One of the best places to kick off your Castle Rock experience is the Castle Rock Historical Society and Museum. This hidden gem is like stepping into your quirky great aunt's attic, filled with artifacts and memorabilia that tell the story of the town. You'll find everything from old photographs to documents that make you question how anyone managed to survive without smartphones. If you're lucky, you might even catch a glimpse of the town's original founding documents—though they're probably written in that fancy script that makes you feel like you need a degree in archaeology just to decipher "we the people."

After getting your history fix, head over to the iconic Castle Rock itself. This towering monolith isn't just a pretty sight; it's a chance to stretch your legs and embrace your inner mountain goat. The hike to the top is short but steep enough to remind you that your New Year's resolution to "get fit" was a great idea—last January. Once you reach the summit, you're rewarded with a view that makes the effort worth it. Just don't forget to take a selfie, because nothing says "I was here" like a poorly framed shot of yourself with a majestic backdrop.

If you're looking for more ways to enjoy the great outdoors, Castle Rock has you covered. The town boasts an impressive network of trails, parks, and open spaces that will make any nature enthusiast giddy with excitement. You can bike, hike, or even run if you're feeling particularly ambitious—or trying to outrun that second helping of dessert you just had. The trails range from leisurely walks that are perfect for pondering life's big questions to heart-pumping adventures that will have you gasping for air faster than you can say "I should have trained more."

For those who prefer a more leisurely approach to exploration, check out the local art scene. Castle Rock is home to several galleries and public art installations that add a splash of color to the town. You'll find everything from murals that seem to leap off the walls to sculptures that challenge the very notion of what "art" is. Wander through the streets and take in the creativity that thrives here—it's like walking through a living Pinterest board where the only thing missing is the "Pin It" button.

When hunger strikes, Castle Rock's dining scene is ready to satisfy your cravings. From cozy cafes serving gourmet sandwiches to trendy eateries specializing in locally sourced dishes, you'll find something to please every palate. Don't miss the chance to try a local brew; the craft beer scene is strong here, with breweries that treat hops like the sacred treasure they are. Just remember to pace yourself—nobody wants to be that person who has to ask for a ride home after one too many tastings.

As evening approaches, the town comes alive with events and entertainment. The Castle Rock Music Festival is an annual highlight, featuring local bands and a community vibe that will make you want to dance—whether you're a skilled performer or someone who once took a dance class and promptly forgot everything. It's a celebration of local talent that brings the community together, so grab a lawn chair, kick back, and enjoy the show. You might even find yourself inspired to pick up a guitar—just be prepared for your friends to politely decline any offers for a duet.

And let's not forget about the Castle Rock Outlets, where retail therapy is a legitimate form of self-care. With a plethora of shops, you can score deals on everything from clothing to home goods, proving that shopping is not only a pastime but a sport. Just make sure to wear comfortable shoes; the thrill of the hunt can lead to some serious mileage on your pedometer.

Castle Rock, Colorado, is a delightful mix of history, outdoor adventure, and quirky charm. With its stunning rock formations, local art scene, and lively community events, this town offers a little something for everyone. So pack your sense of humor, lace up your hiking boots, and prepare for a journey through a place where the past meets the present, and laughter is always around the corner. You might just leave with a few good stories, a belly full of local treats, and a newfound appreciation for the unique magic that small towns can offer.

Cedaredge

Cedaredge, Colorado, is a little slice of heaven that proudly sits at the base of the stunning Grand Mesa. Known for its apples and a sense of humor that could fill a bushel basket, this town combines outdoor beauty with small-town quirks that make it a delightful destination. Founded in the late 1800s, Cedaredge started as a ranching community but soon pivoted to become the apple capital of Colorado. Yes, that's right—this town has more apples than you can shake a stick at, and they're not afraid to flaunt it.

Let's dive into the history first, because nothing says "let's have a good time" like a little historical context. Cedaredge was originally settled by those brave pioneers who thought, "Why not move to a place that gets cold enough to freeze your nose off?" They were drawn by the promise of fertile land and the hope that they wouldn't have to share their apples with anyone. Fast forward to today, and you'll find that those apples have turned into a source of pride, leading to the annual Cedaredge Applefest. This event is basically the Super Bowl for apple lovers, complete with everything from apple pie eating contests to a parade that may or may not feature someone dressed as a giant apple. If you've never seen a float adorned with apples, you haven't truly lived.

Now, let's talk museums. While Cedaredge may not have the Louvre, it does have the Cedaredge Area Historical Society and Museum. This charming little spot is a treasure trove of local history that's just the right mix of fascinating and "did they really keep that?" Inside, you'll find artifacts that showcase the town's rich agricultural past, including vintage farming tools that look like they could double as medieval torture devices. The museum also hosts rotating exhibits, which means there's always something new to gawk at, like the time they displayed a collection of old apple crates. Yes, you read that right—apple crates! If you thought you could escape the apple theme, think again.

Once you've absorbed all the history and maybe even cracked a few jokes about apple puns, it's time to explore the great outdoors. Cedaredge is surrounded by the Grand Mesa, which boasts the largest flat-top mountain in the world. Hiking trails wind through stunning landscapes that are perfect for those who enjoy pretending they're in a nature documentary while trying to catch their breath. Whether you choose a leisurely walk or a heart-pounding hike, don't forget to pack a snack. You never know when you might encounter a chipmunk who thinks it's entitled to your granola bar.

In the winter, Cedaredge transforms into a snowy wonderland that's perfect for skiing and snowshoeing. The nearby ski areas offer powdery slopes that will make even the most seasoned skiers feel like they're gliding through a fairy tale—until they inevitably wipe out, of course. You can also enjoy cross-country skiing, which is basically like running without the shame of being in public while you're gasping for air.

If you're feeling particularly adventurous, head over to the nearby Vega State Park, where fishing, boating, and camping await. You might just find yourself casting a line while contemplating life's mysteries, like why anyone would want to go back to a cubicle after experiencing this much freedom. Just be wary of the fish; they can be surprisingly cunning when it comes to avoiding bait.

No visit to Cedaredge would be complete without indulging in the local dining scene. Restaurants here take pride in using fresh, local ingredients—especially apples, of course. You can find everything from apple cider donuts that will make you question your commitment to "healthy eating" to hearty meals that will fuel your adventures. Don't miss the chance to try a dish that incorporates apples in unexpected ways; you'll leave with a taste of the town that you won't soon forget.

As evening descends, the Cedaredge nightlife kicks into gear, albeit at a pace that won't leave you feeling overwhelmed. There are cozy bars where you can sip on a craft beer brewed with local apples, all while exchanging stories with friendly locals who seem to have a never-ending supply of tall tales. Just be prepared for the inevitable debate over which apple variety reigns supreme; the tension can get thick enough to slice with a... well, an apple slicer.

Cedaredge, Colorado, is a delightful blend of history, outdoor adventure, and whimsical charm. With its rich agricultural heritage, stunning landscapes, and a town spirit that embraces humor and community, this apple-centric paradise is sure to leave you with a smile. So grab your hiking boots, put on your favorite apple-themed shirt, and prepare to enjoy all that this quirky town has to offer. You might leave with a few funny stories, a new appreciation for apples, and perhaps even a desire to start your own apple-themed float for next year's Applefest parade.

Center

Center, Colorado, is a tiny town with a name that suggests it's the very epicenter of everything fabulous in the universe. Spoiler alert: it's not quite that grand, but it's certainly a charming spot that offers a unique blend of history, quirky attractions, and a dose of small-town hospitality that might just surprise you. Nestled in the San Luis Valley, Center is a place where the elevation is high and so are the expectations for a good time—even if you have to lower them just a tad.

Founded in the early 20th century, Center was originally established as a railroad town, popping up faster than you can say "locomotive." The name was chosen to reflect its position in the valley, making it the "center" of local commerce. Today, that sense of center-ness might be a little overblown, but the town does have its own unique charm, which is like a cozy blanket on a chilly day—if that blanket were made of hay and had a few cow hairs stuck to it.

One of the first stops on your adventure through Center should be the local museum. While it may not rival the Smithsonian, the Center Historical Society Museum is a treasure trove of local lore. Here, you can explore exhibits that highlight the town's agricultural roots, including an impressive collection of farming tools that may or may not have been used in ancient rituals. You'll find old photographs that capture the essence of life in the early 1900s, when the biggest concern was whether the horse would make it to the next haystack before getting sidetracked by an enticing patch of grass.

The museum is also home to a few bizarre artifacts that you'll want to see just for the "What on Earth is that?" factor. From antique farming equipment to a taxidermied animal or two, you can't help but feel a sense of nostalgia mixed with a pinch of confusion as you wander the exhibits. If you're lucky, the curator might even share a story or two about the town's history, complete with embellishments that would make any good storyteller proud.

Once you've soaked in the history, it's time to embrace the great outdoors. Center is surrounded by the breathtaking beauty of the San Luis Valley, which means there are ample opportunities for hiking, fishing, and possibly getting lost in nature—though hopefully not in the kind of way that ends with you trying to communicate with squirrels. Whether you're trekking through the mountains or casting a line into one of the nearby rivers, just remember to pack a snack. It's important to maintain your strength when you're trying to negotiate a peace treaty with a particularly aggressive chipmunk.

Speaking of fishing, the area is home to some fantastic fishing spots, where you can try your luck at catching the elusive trout. Just be prepared for the locals to have some strong opinions about your fishing techniques. They'll likely regale you with tales of the "big one" that got away while secretly judging your bait choice. You might even hear whispers of the legendary fish that has somehow managed to evade capture for decades—a true local myth that rivals Bigfoot in its elusive nature.

Now, let's not forget about the annual festivities. Center has a community spirit that shines bright, and the town hosts events that bring everyone together, including the Center Harvest Festival. This celebration of all things agricultural includes games, food vendors, and the kind of local pride that makes you want to buy a cowboy hat and join in on the festivities. Just be prepared for the smell of fried food and the inevitable pie-eating contest that will have you questioning your life choices—and possibly your waistline.

For those looking for a taste of local cuisine, you won't be disappointed. Center offers a selection of eateries that serve everything from classic American diner fare to dishes that feature local ingredients. If you find yourself craving a burger, you can indulge in one that's been cooked to perfection, topped with all the fixings. Just make sure you have a good appetite because these burgers are not for the faint of heart. You might even want to consider a workout plan afterward, unless you're planning to roll home.

As the sun sets over the mountains, the nightlife in Center might not be the bustling scene of a big city, but it's definitely got its own vibe. You can find local bars where the atmosphere is as relaxed as a Sunday morning, perfect for unwinding after a day of exploration. Don't be surprised if the bartender knows everyone's name and maybe even their life story—small towns have a way of fostering a sense of community that you won't find in larger cities. Just remember that in a place this small, gossip travels faster than you can order a drink.

Center, Colorado, is a charming little town that packs a punch when it comes to history, outdoor adventure, and community spirit. With its unique museums, stunning natural beauty, and a sense of humor that rivals the best stand-up comedians, this town is a delightful place to explore. So grab your hiking boots, your fishing pole, and your appetite for adventure, and get ready to enjoy all the quirks and charms that Center has to offer. You might just find yourself leaving with a new appreciation for small-town life and a few good stories to tell—if you can remember them after all those burgers and local brews.

Central City

Nestled in the Rocky Mountains, Central City, Colorado, is a town that feels like it jumped straight out of a Wild West movie, complete with saloons, miners, and the occasional ghost story to keep things interesting. Established during the gold rush of the mid-1800s, this town was once a bustling hub of activity, where hopeful prospectors traded pickaxes for dreams of striking it rich. Spoiler alert: most didn't strike it rich, but they did strike up a lot of interesting stories, many of which probably included a few tall tales about the ones that got away.

Central City was originally founded in 1859 and quickly became known as "the richest square mile on Earth." That's right—this little town was rolling in gold, at least until it wasn't. Mining operations boomed, and the town swelled with folks who thought they'd find fortune faster than they could say "gold digger." Sadly, as the gold veins ran dry, so did the town's population, leading to a decline that would have made even the most optimistic prospector shake their head in disbelief.

Now, before you think this town is just a ghost of its former self, let me assure you that Central City has had quite the comeback. It reinvented itself as a gambling haven, attracting those with dreams of hitting the jackpot instead of striking gold. It's as if the town said, "Why dig for gold when you can roll the dice and hope for the best?" Today, the streets are lined with casinos that make you feel like you've stepped into a scene from a heist movie—without the actual heist, of course. Just don't forget to check your pockets before leaving; those chips have a way of multiplying like rabbits when you're not paying attention.

One of the highlights of Central City is the Central City Opera House, which dates back to 1878 and is as charming as it is historic. This is not just a venue for highbrow performances; it's a place where you can catch opera, musicals, and the occasional production that leaves you wondering what you just witnessed. The opera house itself looks like it could house a ghost or two, and you can almost hear the spirits of past performers singing their hearts out—or perhaps just groaning at the current state of musical theater. If you're lucky, you might even catch a production that makes you laugh so hard you forget that you were just a few minutes ago wondering why you decided to come to an opera in the first place.

For a deeper dive into the town's history, visit the Gilpin County Museum. This gem of a museum features exhibits that take you on a journey through the town's past, showcasing everything from mining tools to photographs of the gold rush days. You'll see artifacts that might make you wonder how people ever lived without smartphones, like an old-fashioned washing machine that looks suspiciously like a medieval torture device. As you wander through the exhibits, you'll find yourself laughing at the ridiculousness of some of the historical relics and pondering how far we've come—like how we've traded in gold for internet likes.

When it comes to outdoor activities, Central City has its fair share of options. The nearby mountains are perfect for hiking, biking, and whatever other "-ing" activities you can dream up. You could spend hours getting lost in the breathtaking scenery—or you might just find yourself lost in a more literal sense. Don't be surprised if you end up asking a friendly squirrel for directions; they tend to know their way around better than most tourists.

If you're feeling adventurous, try your hand at the Central City Ghost Tour. As the sun sets, the ghosts of miners past come out to play, and you'll be led through the town to hear tales of hauntings, tragedies, and the occasional bad luck that seems to follow miners like a persistent shadow. The guides are usually well-versed in the art of storytelling, complete with dramatic flair that might just convince you that the town is, indeed, haunted by the spirits of those who failed to strike it rich. It's like a history lesson, a horror movie, and a comedy show all rolled into one.

As for dining, Central City offers a mix of local eateries that cater to every taste bud. Whether you're in the mood for a hearty burger, a light salad, or something in between, you'll find options that will fill your belly and perhaps leave you contemplating your life choices. Don't miss out on the local delicacies that often include dishes featuring ingredients sourced from the surrounding mountains. Just be prepared for the inevitable food coma that follows; the food here has a way of sneaking up on you when you least expect it.

When night falls, the casinos come alive, and the sound of slot machines fills the air like the sweet music of hope and despair. The thrill of gambling in Central City is palpable, with bright lights and excited chatter that makes you feel like you're at the center of it all. Just remember to set a budget—otherwise, you might find yourself trading your prized possession for another roll of the dice. You can enjoy live music, comedy shows, and the thrill of the game, all while trying to keep your dignity intact.

Central City, Colorado, is a delightful mix of history, culture, and modern-day shenanigans. With its rich mining heritage, quirky museums, and vibrant gambling scene, this town has something for everyone. So grab your sense of humor, your appetite for adventure, and your lucky rabbit's foot, and prepare to experience all the charm and absurdity that Central City has to offer. You might just leave with some golden memories of your own—minus the actual gold, of course.

Cheraw

Nestled snugly in the plains of southeastern Colorado, Cheraw is a tiny town with a history as rich as a double chocolate cake. Founded in the late 1800s, Cheraw was initially a hub for cattle ranching, and those ranching roots run deep, like the wells that water the local grasses. It's a place where the air is filled with the faint scent of sagebrush and aspirations of ranchers hoping to strike it big—though most were just trying to avoid being struck by a particularly feisty cow.

Cheraw was established as a stop along the Santa Fe Trail, a route that played a significant role in the early trade days. Imagine pioneers rolling through with covered wagons and dreams of wealth, only to find themselves sidetracked by the nearest watering hole—much like how you might be sidetracked by a donut shop if you were on a quest for enlightenment. The town eventually became a bustling agricultural community, with farmers and ranchers working hard to make the most of the fertile land. The motto here might as well be "If you can't beat 'em, grow hay!"

One of the highlights of Cheraw is the Cheraw Historical Museum, a quaint little spot that showcases the town's rich history. As you wander through, you'll encounter exhibits that look like they've time-traveled from the 19th century, including old farm equipment that might make you question how anyone ever got any work done without modern technology. You can see everything from vintage tractors that probably needed a prayer and a good luck charm to operate, to photographs of townsfolk who seem to be trying to channel their inner cowboy.

The museum also boasts an impressive collection of local artifacts, including things like old school desks and dusty books that have survived more than a century of "don't touch that!" This place is so filled with history that you might start to feel like you've been teleported back to a time when Wi-Fi was just a figment of someone's imagination. If you listen closely, you might even hear echoes of children's laughter from decades past—or perhaps just the wind whistling through the open windows.

For outdoor enthusiasts, Cheraw is a dream come true. The surrounding area offers beautiful landscapes that are perfect for hiking, fishing, and simply pretending you're in a Western movie. You can trek through the nearby grasslands and breathe in the fresh air—just be careful to avoid any tumbleweeds that seem intent on making you their next victim. The region is also home to several reservoirs and lakes, where you can fish for trout and enjoy a peaceful afternoon. Just make sure to bring your own snacks; the fish won't offer you a sandwich anytime soon.

Now, let's talk about the local cuisine. Cheraw may not be a culinary capital, but that doesn't mean you'll go hungry. You can find classic diner fare served with a side of genuine small-town hospitality. Picture burgers so big they require a strategic approach, and pies so good they could make even the most dedicated dieter crumble. Don't miss the chance to try some of the local specialties; you might discover that nothing beats a slice of homemade apple pie after a long day of exploring.

If you're in the mood for some festivities, Cheraw hosts a variety of community events that reflect the town's friendly spirit. The annual Cheraw Heritage Days is a celebration that brings the community together for a weekend of food, fun, and maybe even a few cowpoke competitions. Expect everything from a barbecue cook-off to good old-fashioned games that might leave you feeling like a kid again—especially when it comes to the three-legged races that usually result in some spectacular tumbles.

When the sun sets, Cheraw transforms into a quiet, starry wonderland. With minimal light pollution, you can enjoy a stargazing experience that feels like something out of a romance movie. Just imagine lying on a blanket, gazing up at the stars, and wondering if that bright object in the sky is a star or just a really ambitious satellite. The locals may tell you tales of constellations that involve everything from cows to cowboys, so be prepared for some storytelling that might just put your astronomy knowledge to shame.

If you're looking for a more laid-back evening, find a cozy spot to relax with a local brew or a glass of wine from one of the nearby wineries. Cheraw may not be a bustling metropolis, but the quiet evenings are perfect for reflection—or for creating your own adventure stories that may or may not involve heroic cattle drives.

Cheraw, Colorado, may be small, but it's packed with history, charm, and a dose of rustic whimsy that keeps things interesting. With its rich agricultural heritage, friendly locals, and opportunities for outdoor adventure, this little town is a hidden gem just waiting to be explored. So, grab your sense of humor, your appetite for hearty meals, and perhaps a good pair of walking shoes, and prepare for a delightful journey through the land of cattle, history, and a surprisingly vibrant community spirit. You might just leave with some golden memories and a newfound appreciation for small-town life—and maybe even a recipe for that infamous apple pie.

Cheyenne Wells

Cheyenne Wells, Colorado, is a town that embodies the spirit of the Wild West while also embracing a charm that's as refreshing as a cold drink on a hot summer day. Nestled in the eastern plains, Cheyenne Wells has a history that reads like a classic Western novel, filled with cowboys, cattle, and more dust than you could shake a broom at. Founded in the late 19th century, this little gem emerged as a vital railroad hub, connecting the dots between various trading routes. Imagine the scene: pioneers in their covered wagons, a few wayward cattle, and the occasional tumbleweed rolling through, all while someone yells, "Yeehaw!"—because that's how things went down in the Old West.

The town was named after the Cheyenne people and, yes, the wells that were dug to provide much-needed water in this arid landscape. It was a true frontier town where survival hinged on ingenuity, a little luck, and possibly a well-timed cowboy hat. As the railroad expanded, so did Cheyenne Wells, attracting settlers looking for a fresh start, a good plot of land, or a good excuse to wear boots. The golden days of the cattle drives were not far behind, with ranchers dreaming of striking it rich and occasionally losing a few hats to the wind.

Today, the Cheyenne Wells Historical Society Museum is your portal to the past. Inside, you'll find exhibits that cover everything from the town's founding to the quirks of daily life in a small town. This museum is like stepping into your eccentric great-aunt's attic, filled with relics that leave you wondering about their stories. You'll see antique farming equipment that looks suspiciously like it could double as medieval torture devices and photographs of townsfolk from yesteryear who seem to have mastered the art of serious faces. Seriously, if you want to learn how to look intense while holding a pitchfork, these photos are your guide.

While you're in the museum, take a moment to admire the displays that celebrate local culture and history. You might find a section dedicated to the legendary cowboys who roamed these plains, complete with tales of daring escapades and questionable fashion choices. The stories are often accompanied by artifacts, like saddles that could probably use a good cleaning and boots that have seen more dust than the average sneeze.

If you're feeling adventurous, venture outdoors for some fresh air and wide-open spaces. Cheyenne Wells is surrounded by stunning landscapes that are perfect for hiking, fishing, and the occasional daydream about what it would be like to live off the land. The nearby rivers and lakes provide ample opportunities to cast a line and catch a fish that will likely end up being more "tall tale" than dinner. Just remember, the fish are usually smarter than they look, and they definitely know how to play hard to get.

For those who prefer a taste of local flavor, Cheyenne Wells offers dining options that will satisfy your appetite after a long day of exploring. You can find classic American diners serving hearty breakfasts, lunch specials, and enough pie to make any grandmother proud. Don't miss out on the chance to sample a slice of homemade pie; it's a rite of passage in these parts, and you might even find yourself fighting off a sugar coma afterward.

As the sun begins to set, the nightlife in Cheyenne Wells offers a unique twist. While you won't find fancy nightclubs or bustling bars, what you will find is a sense of community that is hard to beat. The locals love to gather at the local watering holes, sharing stories that often blend truth and exaggeration like a fine cocktail. You can enjoy live music, trivia nights, or just a good old-fashioned game of cards. It's a chance to kick back and laugh, especially when someone inevitably starts telling a tall tale about "the one that got away" in fishing or a heroic horseback ride into the sunset.

If you're feeling particularly brave, join in on a local event like the Cheyenne Wells Rodeo. The rodeo is a beloved tradition that showcases the skills of cowboys and cowgirls, from roping to barrel racing. It's like a circus but with more dirt, fewer clowns, and a lot more cowboy hats. Watching the competitors is a thrilling experience, and you'll find yourself cheering louder than you ever thought possible while trying not to get trampled by an enthusiastic bull. Just be sure to wear your best pair of boots—style matters, even in rodeos.

As you stroll through Cheyenne Wells, you might notice the people here have a certain resilience and humor that's hard to find elsewhere. The locals are friendly, eager to share stories, and more than willing to lend a hand—just don't ask them to help you find a Wi-Fi signal. In a place like this, the internet is about as reliable as a goldfish at a cat convention.

Cheyenne Wells, Colorado, is a delightful blend of history, culture, and small-town charm. With its rich past, engaging museums, and a community spirit that invites you to relax and enjoy life, this town proves that sometimes the best adventures can be found in the simplest places. So grab your sense of humor, a hearty appetite, and maybe a pair of boots that are ready to take on anything, and prepare for an unforgettable experience. You might leave with a smile on your face, a few good stories, and perhaps a newfound appreciation for the wild and wacky world of small-town life.

Clifton

Nestled comfortably between the more famous towns of Grand Junction and Fruita, Clifton, Colorado, is like that quirky relative everyone loves to visit but doesn't quite know how to explain at family gatherings. Founded in the late 19th century, Clifton started as a humble agricultural community, where the only hustle was figuring out how to get the cows to stop trying to eat the laundry. It blossomed into a quaint town that retains its charm while looking suspiciously like it's still waiting for its big break on reality TV.

The story of Clifton begins in the 1880s when settlers flocked to the area in search of fertile land and fresh opportunities. They planted roots, literally and figuratively, cultivating crops and starting businesses that still serve the community today. Imagine farmers trying to make a living while dodging the occasional tumbleweed and negotiating with their cows over who gets the best patch of grass. If cows could talk, they'd probably tell stories about how they should've gotten a cut of the profits from the local cheese factory.

One of the standout attractions in Clifton is the Clifton Historical Museum. This charming establishment is a treasure trove of artifacts that tell the tale of this quirky little town. As you stroll through the museum, you might find yourself contemplating how many things you can identify without googling—spoiler alert: it's not many. From antique farming equipment that looks like it could double as medieval torture devices to photographs of local families who seem to have mastered the art of the serious pose, the museum is like a walk through a time capsule with a sense of humor.

The exhibits cover everything from the town's founding to more recent history, featuring displays that make you wonder if the previous owners of the artifacts were just a little too fond of plaid. The museum staff, who are just as colorful as the exhibits, are often eager to share stories about the town's history that may or may not include embellishments worthy of a Hollywood script.

For those with a penchant for the outdoors, Clifton offers a variety of activities that can turn any ordinary day into an adventure. The nearby Colorado River provides a scenic backdrop for fishing, kayaking, or simply contemplating life's mysteries—like why the ice cream truck always shows up when you're not home. You can spend an afternoon casting a line, hoping to catch something bigger than your last excuse for skipping the gym.

If you're not in the mood for water activities, how about a stroll through the lovely parks that dot the town? There are green spaces that invite you to lay back, gaze at the clouds, and ponder the meaning of life, or at least why your phone won't stop buzzing. The parks are perfect for family picnics, where you can enjoy the classic sandwich-and-chips combo while dodging the occasional squirrel that looks way too interested in your potato chips.

Clifton's culinary scene is worth a mention, especially if you enjoy classic diner fare served with a side of small-town charm. You can find local diners and cafes that whip up hearty breakfasts, juicy burgers, and milkshakes that are so thick they should come with a warning label. If you're lucky, you might even stumble upon a restaurant that has a "secret menu" item—a mythical concept that could very well just be a rumor spread by a particularly imaginative local.

As the sun sets and the stars start to twinkle, the nightlife in Clifton takes on a different vibe. While it may not resemble the bustling scenes of bigger cities, the local bars and hangouts are perfect for enjoying a cold drink and swapping stories with the friendly locals. You might hear tales of fishing exploits or debates about who makes the best chili—definitely a topic that can stir up some passionate discussions.

One of the highlights of the social calendar is the annual Clifton Community Day, a celebration that brings the town together for food, fun, and festivities. Picture a gathering where the kids are running around, adults are enjoying homemade treats, and everyone is debating which local baked goods deserve a blue ribbon. It's the kind of event where you can meet your neighbors, sample every dessert within reach, and leave with enough sugar in your system to fuel a small rocket.

If you're looking for unique shopping experiences, don't miss the local boutiques and shops that offer everything from handmade crafts to questionable knick-knacks. You never know when you might find that perfect conversation starter—like a ceramic cat wearing a sombrero or a t-shirt proclaiming "I survived Clifton."

Clifton is also conveniently located near some of Colorado's breathtaking natural attractions. A short drive away, you'll find stunning views, hiking trails, and the kind of scenery that makes you wonder if you've accidentally walked onto a movie set. Take a hike in the nearby Bookcliff Mountains, where the views are so spectacular you might just start contemplating a second career as an Instagram influencer.

Clifton is a delightful mix of history, quirky charm, and small-town hospitality. It's a place where you can embrace the simplicity of life while enjoying the little things that make each day special. Whether you're exploring the historical museum, enjoying the local cuisine, or simply taking in the beautiful scenery, there's always something to appreciate in this under-the-radar town. So, put on your cowboy hat, grab a slice of pie, and get ready for a delightful adventure in Cheyenne Wells. You might just find that sometimes the best journeys are the ones that lead you to unexpected places, like a small town where everyone knows everyone and the stories are as colorful as the landscape itself.

Coal Creek

In the heart of Colorado, nestled between the mountains and an alarming number of places with "coal" in their name, lies Coal Creek. If you've ever found yourself wondering what it would be like to live in a town with a name that sounds like a minor character from a Western film, this is your chance. The history of Coal Creek reads like a tale of ambition, hard work, and a touch of "why did we think this was a good idea?"

The town's origins trace back to the late 1800s, when coal was all the rage. Picture miners in dusty hats digging into the earth, convinced they were on the brink of striking it rich while simultaneously ensuring that the phrase "dirty work" would take on a whole new meaning. Coal Creek was no different; it sprang up as a hub for coal mining, serving the ever-hungry appetite of a nation enamored with steam engines, toasty homes, and the sheer audacity of sticking a mine in the middle of a mountain. If you think about it, what could go wrong?

Fast forward to today, and Coal Creek is a place where the remnants of its mining past still linger in the air, occasionally mixing with the scent of something that might be a BBQ or just the local diner cooking its famous "mystery meat" special. The Coal Creek Historical Society Museum is a must-see—if only to fully appreciate how far technology has come since the days when miners communicated through grunts and hand gestures. Here, you'll find artifacts that tell the story of the town's coal mining history, such as old tools that look like they've survived at least three apocalypses and photographs of miners posing like they're in a 1950s family portrait, complete with solemn expressions that say, "We've just unearthed a rock that weighs more than our collective dreams."

The museum isn't just a walk down memory lane; it's a chance to see how things used to be done. There are displays of coal samples that look suspiciously like lumps of burnt cake and a whole section dedicated to the various hats worn by miners. Who knew headwear could be so dangerous? You might leave the museum with a newfound respect for the humble hard hat and a burning desire to never take a job that requires it.

Now, let's talk about the outdoors, because Coal Creek has some nature to offer. The surrounding areas are prime for hiking, which is great if you enjoy sweating profusely while contemplating life decisions. The local trails vary from "I might die" to "I definitely should have brought more water." Keep an eye out for wildlife—if you're lucky, you might spot deer or even the elusive mountain goat, who probably looks at hikers and thinks, "You call this a challenge?"

For dining, Coal Creek has a couple of local eateries that could generously be described as "character-filled." The diner is a local favorite, serving up everything from pancakes that could double as frisbees to burgers that might make you question the meaning of "fresh." Just be careful when ordering the daily special; you might receive something that is best enjoyed while trying to remember if you had breakfast three days ago. The decor is charmingly retro, with a mixture of old posters and tables that seem to have witnessed more family arguments than any therapist.

But what about the best things to see and do? Coal Creek is known for its outdoor activities. The town's proximity to the mountains makes it a good base for some serious adventuring. You can hike, bike, or simply sit and contemplate the existential dread of life while surrounded by nature. If you're feeling particularly adventurous, you could also try rock climbing—just be prepared to yell "Oh, dear!" as you slip and hope for the best.

As for the worst things to do, let's address the infamous Coal Creek's Annual "Coal Dust Festival." Yes, that's a real thing, and yes, it's exactly what it sounds like. Picture a celebration of all things coal, complete with games that involve attempting to shove as much dust in your lungs as possible. Sure, there are activities for kids, but one glance at the dunk tank filled with "mystery water" should be enough to make any parent rethink their life choices. If you love the idea of celebrating coal while simultaneously considering the long-term effects on your lungs, this festival might just be for you.

But fret not; if the festival isn't your speed, you could always take a leisurely drive through the scenic byways surrounding the town. This is a great way to enjoy the beauty of Colorado while avoiding the madness of the festival. Just be careful not to drive too fast; you might miss the one and only "World's Largest Coal Shovel" attraction. Yes, it's as thrilling as it sounds—almost as exciting as watching paint dry but with more rust.

Coal Creek also has a few local events throughout the year that might catch your interest, like the "Rock Collectors' Gathering," which is precisely what it sounds like. A bunch of folks gather to show off their rock collections, leading to spirited discussions about the relative merits of quartz versus granite. It's the kind of event where you might find your enthusiasm waning as someone passionately debates the unique qualities of a rock you can't even pronounce.

As night falls, Coal Creek takes on a different ambiance. With limited nightlife options, your choices typically consist of gathering around a campfire or attempting to identify constellations while someone inevitably talks about the time they got lost in the woods for three days.

Coal Creek, Colorado, is a small town rich in history and charm. It may not be bustling with activities or attractions, but it boasts a unique character that can only come from a place with deep coal roots. Whether you're wandering through the historical museum, tackling the local hiking trails, or trying to decipher the diner's daily special, you'll find yourself wrapped up in the quirky, small-town atmosphere. Just remember to pack your sense of humor and a good appetite for adventure—because in Coal Creek, life is as unpredictable as the weather, and just as dusty.

Collbran

Nestled in a picturesque valley surrounded by the Grand Mesa and the flanking hills that would make even a goat feel insecure, Collbran is a town that could easily serve as the set for a sitcom about small-town life. With a population that hovers around the number of people you might invite to a slightly awkward family reunion, Collbran packs a punch with its charm, quirky history, and a dash of "what were they thinking?"

Founded in the late 1800s, Collbran emerged as a hub for agriculture and ranching. The original settlers probably thought they were striking gold, only to realize they were really just hitting fertile soil and a serious amount of cow dung. The town's history is rich with tales of hardy pioneers who tamed the wild west with grit, determination, and the kind of stubbornness that could make a mule jealous. They cultivated crops, raised livestock, and established the kind of community spirit that only comes from enduring extreme weather and the occasional raucous town meeting about the best flavor of ice cream.

One of the first things you might want to do in Collbran is check out the Collbran Historical Museum. It's not the Louvre, but it has its charm. The museum features artifacts from the town's agricultural roots, including tools that look like they were designed by someone who definitely failed shop class. You'll find old photographs that show off the town's vintage outfits—think suspenders, hats, and expressions that say, "We took a long time getting ready for this photo." The museum staff is often eager to share stories, some of which may have been embellished over the years, especially when it comes to the local legends involving a certain cow named Bessie who allegedly saved the town from a stampede by simply being too lazy to move.

Now, if you're hoping for a bit of outdoor adventure, Collbran has you covered—literally. The surrounding Grand Mesa National Forest is perfect for hiking, biking, and getting lost in nature. The trails can be breathtaking, but don't forget to pack a good sense of direction, as it's easy to wander off and find yourself wondering if that rustling in the bushes is a bear or just your imagination running wild after too many energy bars.

For those who prefer their adventures a bit more structured, there's the Collbran Community Center, which might not sound exciting but hosts a range of activities. You might find yourself taking a pottery class or learning how to line dance—an experience that will make you grateful for the invention of the two left feet. The community center is also home to various events throughout the year, including the infamous "Collbran Potato Festival." Yes, you read that right. A festival dedicated to potatoes, because what could be more thrilling than celebrating a vegetable? It's an event that brings the community together, not just to admire potatoes but to engage in potato sack races, which might make you question your life choices while trying to balance on a burlap sack.

When it comes to dining, Collbran is a mixed bag. The local diner serves up meals that are hearty enough to put hair on your chest, but you might want to double-check what's in the daily special before diving in. The owner prides themselves on their unique approach to cooking—"if it's not questionable, we don't serve it." You can enjoy classic diner fare while sitting on booths that are probably older than some of the locals. Just be cautious about ordering the "mystery meat" special; it's best left uninvestigated.

As for nightlife, let's just say that if you're looking for a vibrant club scene, you might want to recalibrate your expectations. After sundown, the highlight is often sitting around a fire pit, swapping stories about the day's adventures or trying to remember where you left your keys after the last county fair. It's not quite Las Vegas, but the town does know how to have fun—mostly by organizing game nights at the community center where bingo can become a high-stakes affair.

If you're seeking the worst things to do in Collbran, it's easy to start with the annual "We're Not Lost" Hiking Challenge. It's a lighthearted event that invites locals to test their navigation skills by seeing who can get lost the fastest. Participants often return with wild tales of encounters with other hikers who also got lost, forming impromptu support groups that meet for coffee and commiseration. Then there's the "Wildlife Viewing Tour," which can sometimes lead to awkward situations where you discover you're just staring at a rock that looks like a bear. But hey, at least it's a good story to tell at dinner!

Collbran also has a few quirky local events that deserve a mention. The "Unicorn Rides" might sound enchanting, but it's really just a local farmer who thought it would be funny to paint a goat white and attach a horn. Kids love it, and adults chuckle while secretly wondering if they've finally stepped into a surrealist painting.

As for shopping, the local general store is a delightful mishmash of everyday essentials and oddities that might make you question the concept of consumerism. Want a vintage toy from the 90s? Check. How about a bottle of soda from 1998? Why not? The store has a unique way of showcasing items that didn't quite make the cut for mainstream retail. You might leave with a souvenir that has "you'll never guess where I got this" written all over it.

Collbran, Colorado, may not be the first destination that pops into your head when dreaming of a getaway, but it's a place rich with history, charm, and a plethora of activities that range from delightful to downright peculiar. Whether you're exploring the historical museum, participating in the Potato Festival, or attempting to navigate the wilderness, you're sure to leave with some unforgettable memories—and possibly a potato or two. Just remember, life in Collbran is a little like a mixed bag of trail mix: you never know if you'll get the sweet chocolate or the questionable nut. But isn't that what makes it fun?

Colorado City

Colorado City, Colorado, is a place where history meets the present in a way that can only be described as "interesting." Nestled near the foothills of the Rocky Mountains, this small town has a history as colorful as the local flora, which often looks like it's been painted by a five-year-old who just discovered watercolors.

Originally founded in the late 1800s, Colorado City was once a bustling hub during the gold rush. Prospectors flocked to the area with dreams of striking it rich and an uncanny ability to believe that gold was just lying around waiting to be picked up like fallen leaves. This was a time when the air was filled with the smell of optimism—and probably a fair amount of unwashed miners. The town grew rapidly, fueled by hope, hard work, and a few too many claims of "I swear, I saw gold glinting over there!"

As you stroll through Colorado City today, you might notice that it has a charm that's part historical relic, part "why did I come here again?" The local museum is a must-visit if you're interested in the eccentricities of small-town life. Housed in a building that could easily be mistaken for a large barn, the museum features a collection of artifacts that tell the tale of the town's past. Expect to see items like old mining tools that look like they belong in a horror movie and photographs of people who clearly didn't know how to smile. The highlight is a section dedicated to the various gold rush scams that took place—after all, what's history without a little trickery?

One of the more bizarre displays includes a section on "Notable Residents" which features a variety of portraits and biographies. You might find names that sound like they could double as characters in a low-budget Western film. There's "Old Man Jenkins," famous for his claims of having the largest gold nugget that turned out to be a rock he painted gold. His fame didn't last long, but the story lives on as a warning to anyone thinking of going into the rock-painting business.

For outdoor enthusiasts, Colorado City offers access to some lovely trails, but be warned: the scenery is so beautiful that you may find yourself lost in thought—or just plain lost. Hiking up the nearby foothills can lead to some breathtaking views, provided you don't trip over your own enthusiasm. The trails are well marked, but there's always that one spot where the signs mysteriously disappear, leading you to question your life choices and your sense of direction.

When it comes to dining, Colorado City has a few local spots that can only be described as "unique." There's a diner that serves up meals that could generously be categorized as "nostalgic." The menu features dishes that your grandmother might have made, but with the caveat that she may have had a few too many glasses of sweet tea. The "special of the day" is often an adventure in itself—think meatloaf that could probably win a wrestling match against you and mashed potatoes that seem to have been made during the last ice age.

And then there's the annual "Colorado City Potato Festival." Yes, a festival dedicated to potatoes—because why not? The event features everything from potato sack races to a cooking competition that would make even Gordon Ramsay weep. Attendees can participate in a "potato peel-off," which is exactly what it sounds like and might make you question how you spent your Saturday.

As for the worst things to do in Colorado City, you might want to steer clear of the "Ghost Tours." These excursions promise spooky encounters with spirits from the town's mining days, but the only thing that might haunt you is the lingering smell of stale popcorn from the last town fair. Those who have braved the tour often report more laughter than screams, as the stories tend to meander into tales about the "ghost" who turned out to be a raccoon rummaging through trash cans.

Shopping in Colorado City is an experience unto itself. The local shops are a delightful blend of arts and crafts that might make you wonder who thought that hand-painted rocks were a good idea. You can find everything from bizarre knickknacks that are perfect for making your friends question your taste to handmade soap that smells like a field of flowers that was just visited by a herd of cows. If you're lucky, you might even come across a shop selling "authentic" Native American artifacts, which may or may not have been made in someone's garage last weekend.

If nightlife is what you seek, prepare yourself for a serene evening. The local bar has karaoke nights where you can belt out your best rendition of "Sweet Caroline," while the rest of the patrons politely applaud—or engage in a spirited debate about who sings it better. The vibe is casual, and the drinks are strong enough that you might find yourself thinking you're a lot better than you actually are.

Colorado City, Colorado, is a quirky little town filled with character and charm that will leave you with a mix of laughter and bewilderment. From its rich history to its oddball events, there's something for everyone—even if that something is merely the realization that not every town can be a bustling metropolis. Whether you're exploring the historical museum, savoring a questionable meal at the diner, or participating in potato-themed competitions, you'll surely have stories to tell. Just remember, in Colorado City, the adventures are as plentiful as the oddities, and that's exactly how they like it.

Colorado Springs

Colorado Springs, Colorado, is a town that wears its history like a badge of honor, or perhaps more like an oversized belt buckle that's just a bit too tight. Founded in the 1870s, this city has transformed from a dusty outpost into a hub of outdoor enthusiasts, tourists, and those who are just desperately seeking an Instagram-worthy backdrop. The local motto could easily be, "Why just climb a mountain when you can pay to take a picture with one?"

The history of Colorado Springs is as colorful as its stunning sunsets, which might explain why residents have such a fondness for hiking. The city was established by General William Jackson Palmer, a Union Army officer with a vision for a place that would become the Mecca for fresh air, good coffee, and an unending supply of outdoor activities. Palmer must have had a strong affinity for mountains because he sure picked a good spot—Pikes Peak looms majestically nearby, as if saying, "Look at me! I'm taller than you!"

One of the first things on your Colorado Springs checklist should be the Colorado Springs Pioneers Museum. This gem of a museum offers an extensive collection of artifacts and exhibits that chronicle the city's history, from its Native American roots to the modern-day caffeine-fueled tech boom. The exhibits are curated with such flair that even a mannequin dressed in pioneer garb could evoke a chuckle. Just try not to stare too long; you might end up wondering if that mannequin is judging your life choices.

If you're feeling particularly adventurous, head over to the Garden of the Gods. This stunning park is like Mother Nature's art installation, showcasing towering sandstone rock formations that could easily double as the backdrop for a low-budget sci-fi movie. Here, you can hike, rock climb, or simply engage in existential pondering while trying to comprehend how the rocks managed to look so majestic while you're still struggling to get your morning coffee to actually brew.

For those looking for a taste of the weird and wonderful, the Manitou Cliff Dwellings are a must-see. These ancient dwellings, built by the Ancestral Puebloans, were relocated here and are about as close to time travel as you're going to get without a DeLorean. Walking through the dwellings gives you a sense of what life might have been like for the early inhabitants, minus the Wi-Fi and artisan coffee shops. You might leave wondering how they survived without a solid breakfast burrito.

On the culinary front, Colorado Springs offers a variety of dining options that range from upscale eateries to places that serve burgers that are basically works of art. The local food scene has embraced everything from craft beer to farm-to-table dining, which is great unless you're the person who just wants a good old-fashioned slice of pizza without quinoa on it. Fear not! The pizza joints in town are more than willing to oblige.

Let's not forget the annual Pikes Peak Ascent, a race that challenges participants to run up a mountain. Yes, you read that right—people actually pay to run uphill, voluntarily. Watching this event is like witnessing a live-action version of "Survivor," where people question their sanity as they trudge up the trail. The finish line is at the summit, and if you make it, you'll be rewarded with the breathtaking view and the overwhelming sense of accomplishment—along with a side of "why did I think this was a good idea?"

But not everything in Colorado Springs is sunshine and scenic views. For the worst things to do, let's talk about the local ghost tours. They promise spine-tingling encounters with the supernatural, but many participants leave more amused than frightened. The only spirits you might encounter are those that are a bit too friendly and eager to share their life stories, which can feel less like a haunting and more like an awkward chat with that one neighbor who doesn't realize you're trying to leave the party.

Another contender for the "worst things to do" title is the Cheyenne Mountain Zoo. Now, before you send me a strongly worded letter, hear me out. The zoo is perched on a mountainside, which means it's not only home to an array of exotic animals but also a relentless uphill trek that feels like an Olympic event. By the time you reach the giraffes, you may have convinced yourself that you're training for a marathon—or just desperately in need of a snack.

Shopping in Colorado Springs is an experience that runs the gamut from delightful to downright bizarre. The local shops often feature artisanal goods, ranging from handmade soaps that promise to make you smell like a wildflower meadow to stores filled with crystals that may or may not have mystical properties. Just be wary of the shops selling "genuine" Native American artifacts; some items might have been made during last week's craft fair rather than in a traditional setting.

As for nightlife, Colorado Springs doesn't exactly boast a booming club scene. Instead, you can find cozy bars where locals gather to sip craft beers and discuss the latest Pikes Peak gossip. Karaoke nights are a thing, where you can belt out your rendition of "Livin' on a Prayer" while half the bar pretends to cheer you on. It's a low-key affair, where the best stories come from the "what happened last weekend" discussions that often spiral into hilarity.

Colorado Springs is a city filled with charm, quirky history, and a landscape that could make a postcard jealous. From the grandeur of the mountains to the delightfully odd attractions, there's something for everyone—unless you're looking for a wild nightlife scene or a serious ghost encounter. You'll leave with stories, laughter, and maybe a newfound appreciation for the art of running uphill voluntarily. And who knows? You might just find yourself standing atop Pikes Peak, pondering life's mysteries while surrounded by a sea of awe-inspiring mountains. Just don't forget to bring snacks—trust me, you'll need them.

Commerce City

Commerce City, Colorado, is a place that thrives on the kind of energy you can only find where urban grit meets suburban charm. Founded in the 1850s, this city is often overshadowed by its flashier neighbors, like Denver, but trust me, Commerce City has its own special brand of quirky that makes it worth a visit—if you're into that sort of thing.

Originally known for its agricultural roots, Commerce City sprang up along the banks of the South Platte River. Picture early settlers, hats firmly in place, trying to cultivate the land while wondering why the water tasted like it had come straight from a used paint can. The city's growth really kicked into gear with the arrival of the railroad, which promised new opportunities and, of course, a whole lot of rickety train whistles in the middle of the night.

Fast forward to today, and you'll find a vibrant community that's not afraid to flaunt its industrial past. The city is home to the famous Rocky Mountain Arsenal National Wildlife Refuge, which, as its name suggests, has a slightly confusing mix of wildlife and a history tied to the military. It's like if Bambi decided to have a sit-down with a retired general. You can explore the refuge, spotting bison and deer, while imagining the time when this area was filled with munitions and the occasional top-secret government project. Nature has truly taken back the land, and it's not shy about it.

If museums are your jam, you might want to check out the Commerce City Historical Society Museum. It's a charming little place filled with artifacts that represent the city's history—think dusty old photographs, vintage farming tools, and the occasional piece of memorabilia that raises more questions than answers. The museum is like a time capsule that transports you back to a simpler time when people didn't have to worry about smartphones, social media, or what filter to use on their breakfast burrito pics. Just remember to watch out for the docents; they love to share stories, and once they get going, you might find yourself lost in a tale about a cow that once roamed the streets—yes, that's a real story.

Now, let's talk about the best things to see and do in Commerce City. First up is Dick's Sporting Goods Park, home to the Colorado Rapids soccer team. This place is like a mecca for soccer fans and a hotbed for tailgating enthusiasts. Imagine people grilling burgers and sipping drinks while trying to convince you that soccer is the most exciting sport on the planet. The atmosphere is electric, especially when the Rapids score, and fans erupt in cheers that could probably be heard all the way in Denver. Just make sure to bring your sense of humor; if you're new to soccer, you might spend a good chunk of the game trying to figure out why people are so excited about a tie.

If you're feeling particularly adventurous, check out the local parks. Prairie Gateway Park offers walking trails that will take you through open spaces where you can contemplate life's big questions—like why you decided to wear flip-flops in a place that has actual dirt paths. The park is great for picnicking, as long as you don't mind sharing your sandwich with the local wildlife. Just know that the squirrels are not shy; they've clearly done their research on how to win you over with adorable antics while plotting to steal your food.

On the flip side, the worst things to do in Commerce City could be a bit of a surprise. Let's start with the local dining scene. While there are some decent spots, you might stumble upon a restaurant that has clearly not seen a health inspection since the last ice age. Sure, it has character, but that character might include a suspiciously unkempt bathroom and a menu that looks like it was printed in 1987. Eating there could either be a rite of passage or a brave choice that leads to regrettable decisions later. Choose wisely.

Another contender for the worst is the ghost tours—yes, they exist. While the concept is enticing, the reality might leave you wondering if the only ghosts around are the spirits of people who couldn't get out fast enough. The stories told during these tours tend to lack the spine-chilling effect they promise. Instead, you may find yourself chuckling at the overly dramatic reenactments or listening to guides who seem more interested in their own acting careers than in the actual history of the area.

Shopping in Commerce City can be a mixed bag. You might find yourself in a local shop that proudly sells everything from kitschy souvenirs to inexplicably random items, like "authentic" Native American dream catchers that were clearly made in someone's garage. You can never have too many of those, right? Just be prepared to sift through the treasures and trash—after all, what's a small-town shopping experience without a few eye-rolls and laughs?

When it comes to nightlife, don't expect any booming nightclubs. The local scene is more about laid-back bars where you can enjoy a drink with the locals who may or may not have deep-rooted opinions about how the city should be run. Karaoke nights can get particularly lively, with enthusiastic participants belting out classics while the rest of the crowd debates whether it's "The Best Song Ever" or just "Another Song That's Okay."

Commerce City is a patchwork of history, quirks, and community spirit. From its rich past to its oddball attractions, it offers a unique blend of experiences that can range from the charmingly delightful to the bewilderingly bizarre. Whether you're hiking the trails, enjoying a soccer game, or dodging the occasional rogue squirrel, you're sure to have stories to tell—if only to ensure that someone else gets to hear about that time you tried to find the best restaurant in a city known for its dive bars. So, pack your bags, bring your sense of humor, and dive headfirst into the delightful oddities that Commerce City has to offer.

Cortez

Cortez, Colorado, is a town that's like the quirky friend you didn't know you needed—filled with charm, history, and just a hint of unpredictability. Nestled near the Four Corners, where Colorado, Utah, Arizona, and New Mexico meet, Cortez is a gateway to adventure, or at least a good excuse to step outside your comfort zone. Founded in the late 1800s, this place has been serving up a rich blend of Native American culture, Old West history, and the kind of weird roadside attractions that make you question your life choices.

The history of Cortez is as colorful as the sunsets over the mesas. Originally settled by the Ute and Navajo tribes, this area was later "discovered" by European settlers who apparently thought the place needed more folks trying to make a living in a desert. The town itself was named after the Spanish Conquistador Hernán Cortés, which is a bit ironic since he was more interested in gold and glory than in enjoying a scenic view of Mesa Verde. But hey, naming rights are hard to come by.

Mesa Verde National Park is one of the top attractions nearby, showcasing the impressive cliff dwellings of the Ancestral Puebloans. Visiting Mesa Verde is like stepping into a history book, except this one is filled with actual ancient structures rather than just dusty pages. Here, you can hike, tour, and contemplate how those ancient peoples managed to build entire communities in the cliffs while you struggle to put together an IKEA bookshelf. The park is breathtaking, but beware of the occasional chipmunk that has clearly been trained in the art of theft; if you bring snacks, expect to negotiate with nature.

Back in Cortez, the Cortez Cultural Center is a must-see, especially if you're a fan of local art, history, and a whole lot of cultural exhibits that may or may not require you to brush up on your anthropology knowledge. You might wander through the museum thinking you'll see ancient artifacts, and you will, but you'll also likely stumble upon exhibits about local contemporary artists, which could lead to existential musings about your own artistic abilities. Spoiler alert: you probably won't come out feeling like a genius.

For those looking to dive deeper into the history, the Anasazi Heritage Center is the perfect spot. This place is like a crash course in everything you didn't know you needed to know about the ancient inhabitants of the area. It features archaeological exhibits that could make even Indiana Jones nod in approval. You'll leave with a newfound appreciation for those who lived here long before we had Wi-Fi or avocado toast.

Now, let's get to the good stuff—the best things to do in Cortez. First up is the great outdoors. The surrounding area is a playground for hiking, biking, and outdoor mischief. You can hit the nearby trails, where the scenery is stunning and the chances of running into a bear are slim but thrilling enough to keep you on your toes. Just remember: bears don't like selfies, so keep your distance.

If you're in the mood for a good old-fashioned farm-to-table experience, Cortez has a few eateries that will satisfy your cravings. The local dining scene often features dishes made from ingredients sourced from the surrounding farms. Picture yourself biting into a burger that's so fresh it might have mooed at you earlier in the day. Just be prepared for the inevitable debate about whether it's better to eat locally or if you're really just trying to impress your friends on social media.

Now, for the worst things to do—Cortez has its share of oddities that might leave you scratching your head. Take the local thrift stores, for example. You can find some of the most bizarre items, like that one stuffed animal that looks like it might be from a long-forgotten horror movie. They're treasures, of course, but only if you appreciate the kind of "unique" that could either make or break your home décor.

Cortez also has a few questionable roadside attractions that you might want to approach with caution. There's a giant rubber band ball somewhere in town, a fitting tribute to the local commitment to collecting the things that absolutely no one else cares about. It's the kind of place where you take a picture just to say you've seen it, but deep down you're really just trying to figure out how you ended up here.

When it comes to nightlife, Cortez is a bit like that quiet kid in school—mostly chill but occasionally surprising. There are a few local bars where you can grab a drink and share stories with friendly locals. Just be prepared for the possibility that one of them might insist on showing you their extensive collection of bottle caps or trying to convince you that they once wrestled a mountain lion. Either way, you'll leave with some colorful tales.

Cortez, Colorado, is a delightful mix of history, culture, and outdoor fun, with just enough quirks to keep things interesting. From the ancient cliff dwellings to the cultural exhibits and the various bizarre attractions, you'll find a little bit of everything here. Sure, there may be some questionable dining choices and thrift store treasures that leave you pondering your life choices, but that's all part of the adventure. So pack your bags, grab your sense of humor, and dive into the wonderfully weird world of Cortez—you might just find it's more entertaining than you ever imagined.

Craig

Craig, Colorado, is the kind of place that feels like a secret whispered among a handful of adventurous souls. Nestled in the northwest corner of the state, this small town has a history that's as colorful as a patchwork quilt made by someone who's really into tie-dye. Originally established as a railroad town in the late 1800s, Craig was named after a Scottish settler, which gives you a sense of the town's commitment to being as welcoming as a Scottish pub—minus the bagpipes, of course.

The history here is rich and, at times, a bit quirky. Craig was built on the backs of coal miners and ranchers, leading to a culture that appreciates hard work and knows how to throw a good barbecue. You might find it hard to believe, but this town was once the center of Colorado's coal mining industry, producing enough coal to fuel a small army—though probably not one that would win a battle with a sandwich.

One of the top attractions in Craig is the Museum of Northwest Colorado. If you ever wanted to dive into the weird and wonderful history of the area, this is the place to do it. Picture yourself walking through a treasure trove of artifacts, including everything from cowboy gear to Native American pottery. You'll find exhibits that could make you question your own life choices, like the time you thought it was a good idea to wear flip-flops in the snow. The museum also has a special section dedicated to the history of the area's coal mining, which could make you rethink your career choices—unless you really enjoy spreadsheets and fluorescent lighting.

If you're looking for the great outdoors, Craig is your ticket to adventure. The Yampa River runs through the town, providing ample opportunities for fishing, kayaking, and floating lazily down the river while pretending you're in a nature documentary. Just be careful not to look too relaxed; the local ducks might start demanding your snacks. The river is lined with trails that are perfect for hiking or biking, and if you're lucky, you might spot some wildlife that isn't just the usual deer and rabbits. Think along the lines of "Did that bear just look at me?" kinds of moments.

Now, let's get into the best things to see and do in Craig. If you're feeling brave, take a short drive to the nearby Elkhead Reservoir. It's a picturesque spot where you can fish for trout, boat, or simply enjoy the stunning views. Just remember to pack snacks, because if the fish aren't biting, your mood might depend on those cheesy puffs you stashed away in your bag.

If you happen to be in Craig during the summer, you can't miss the annual Moffat County Fair. This event is a celebration of all things local, with rodeo events, livestock shows, and competitions that will make you question if your pet hamster could win a ribbon. The fair has that delightful small-town charm, complete with cotton candy, questionable rides, and the kind of people-watching that could provide material for a lifetime of comedy routines.

On the flip side, let's talk about the worst things to do in Craig, which can sometimes feel like a rite of passage. First, there's the local fast-food scene. You might find a few chain restaurants that could give you nostalgia for your high school lunch line, but the options can leave a lot to be desired. If you're feeling adventurous, try the local diner that boasts a "unique" menu. You might end up with a burger that looks more like modern art than food. And let's not even mention the milkshakes that have a suspiciously thick consistency. Is it ice cream or is it a dessert that could double as construction material? The world may never know.

Then there's the nightlife. If you're expecting a hopping club scene, prepare yourself for a letdown. The local watering holes tend to close early, leaving you with just enough time to sip your drink and contemplate life's big questions, like why the jukebox hasn't played "Free Bird" yet. If you're lucky, you might catch a local band playing in a dive bar, but be prepared for music that could either charm you or make you question your life choices yet again. You might end up listening to an enthusiastic rendition of "Achy Breaky Heart" performed by a guy who seems to think he's a modern-day Billy Ray Cyrus.

Shopping in Craig can also be an adventure. There are a few local shops that sell everything from Western wear to odd trinkets that might leave you scratching your head. If you've ever wanted a cowboy hat made from material that looks like it came straight from a clearance bin, you're in luck! Just be sure to check for any suspicious stains; the last thing you want is to bring home a hat with a history you didn't sign up for.

In terms of accommodations, the hotels in Craig tend to lean toward the charmingly outdated, with decor that hasn't been updated since the last time the town experienced a mining boom. If you're not careful, you might end up in a room that feels like a time capsule, complete with floral wallpaper and a TV that probably still uses dials. On the bright side, you'll get a fantastic night's sleep, mostly due to the sheer amount of nostalgia floating around.

To wrap it all up, Craig, Colorado, is a hidden gem filled with a history that could entertain even the most seasoned traveler. Whether you're exploring the Museum of Northwest Colorado, casting a line in the Yampa River, or trying to decipher the menu at the local diner, you're bound to have a story to tell. Sure, there are some questionable dining choices and a nightlife scene that might leave you longing for the excitement of your living room, but that's all part of the charm. Embrace the weirdness, enjoy the quirks, and maybe grab a cowboy hat along the way—you never know when it might come in handy.

Crawford

Crawford, Colorado, is the kind of place that has perfected the art of being charmingly unassuming. Tucked away in the northwestern part of the state, this small town is so quaint that you might think the entire population is just a bunch of friendly squirrels trying to convince you to stay. Founded in the late 1800s, Crawford was originally a hub for cattle ranchers and settlers drawn to the promise of fertile land. Today, it's a delightful mix of old Western history, breathtaking scenery, and a few quirks that could make even the most seasoned traveler raise an eyebrow.

The history of Crawford is like a classic cowboy movie—full of rugged individuals, dusty trails, and a few unexpected plot twists. It was named after the nearby Crawford Gulch, which was as appealing to early settlers as a bottomless bag of chips at a party. The town's main claim to fame is its proximity to the Black Canyon of the Gunnison National Park, which is both a mouthful and a sight to behold. Imagine standing on the edge of a cliff and feeling as small as a speck of dust in the grand scheme of nature. Just try not to think about how the last person to lean over that edge might have had a less-than-pleasant experience.

One of the highlights of Crawford is the local museum, which is a must-visit for anyone who enjoys learning about the past without the pressure of actually doing anything productive. The Crawford Area Historical Society operates a quaint little museum that showcases artifacts from the area's rich history. You'll find everything from farming equipment to old photographs that might make you question your own family's sense of fashion. Who knew that oversized hats and suspenders were once considered cutting-edge style? As you wander through the exhibits, you might even feel a sense of kinship with the pioneers who settled here—after all, they were brave enough to face the unknown while you're just trying to navigate your way through the world of online shopping.

If you're looking for outdoor activities, Crawford doesn't disappoint. The surrounding landscape is like a giant playground for those who enjoy hiking, biking, and possibly getting lost in nature. The nearby Black Canyon of the Gunnison National Park is a stunner, with sheer cliffs that drop dramatically into the river below. It's a place where you can hike, camp, and contemplate life choices while marveling at the beauty of the natural world. Just remember to keep an eye out for the occasional deer that seems to have more confidence than you do—those animals have a knack for posing dramatically against the stunning backdrop.

For those who enjoy fishing, the area is home to some excellent spots where you can cast a line and try to catch dinner. Just be warned: the fish in these waters are not only smarter than they look, but they also have an uncanny ability to sense desperation. You might end up spending hours trying to catch a fish, only to realize they've all gathered for a collective laugh at your expense. Don't be surprised if you end up telling your friends about "the one that got away" when, in reality, it was just a particularly crafty trout.

Now, let's dive into the best things to do in Crawford. If you're in the mood for a little local flavor, check out the annual Crawford Heritage Days festival. It's a celebration of all things Crawford, complete with food, crafts, and enough small-town charm to make even the most hardened city dweller crack a smile. Expect local vendors selling handmade goods that you never knew you needed but can't resist. You'll find everything from homemade jams to handcrafted pottery, all while trying not to trip over your own excitement.

For those with a sense of adventure, consider taking a scenic drive through the surrounding countryside. The views are enough to make you want to roll down the windows, blast some country music, and embrace your inner cowboy. Just keep an eye out for wildlife; you might spot an elk or two strutting their stuff like they own the place.

As for the worst things to do in Crawford, let's not sugarcoat it: the dining options can be hit or miss. While there are a few local spots that serve up hearty meals, you may stumble upon a diner that seems like it hasn't changed its menu since the Eisenhower administration. You might find yourself staring at a plate of mystery meat that could double as an art project. The desserts, however, might be worth the risk, as they often come with a side of local gossip that could entertain you for hours.

Shopping in Crawford can also be an adventure. The local stores have that delightful small-town charm, but they might also have a few items that make you question your choices. If you're lucky, you might find a vintage cowboy hat that's seen better days, or a T-shirt that says "I love Crawford" but is suspiciously faded. You'll leave with something unique, even if it's just a funny story about what you almost bought.

When it comes to accommodations, expect a mix of quaint bed-and-breakfasts and rustic motels. The charm of staying in a place where the furniture looks like it's been lovingly curated from various yard sales can't be overstated. You might even find yourself in a room decorated with antiques that make you feel like you've stepped into your grandmother's attic. Just remember to check under the bed for any lingering spirits of the past—they might be just as curious about you as you are about them.

For my money, Crawford, Colorado, is a delightful blend of history, nature, and quirky small-town charm. From the fascinating local museum to the stunning landscapes of the Black Canyon, there's plenty to see and do. Whether you're enjoying the local festivities or trying your hand at fishing (with varying degrees of success), you'll find that Crawford is a place where the adventure is as unpredictable as the menu at the local diner. So grab your sense of humor, your cowboy hat, and get ready to explore this hidden gem—you might just find that the journey is more entertaining than the destination.

Creede

Creede, Colorado, is a town that looks like it was plucked straight from a postcard featuring a dream vacation. Nestled in the heart of the San Juan Mountains, this former silver mining town has a history as colorful as its mountain vistas. Founded in the late 1800s during a silver rush that made miners richer than your average lottery winner, Creede was once a bustling hub where dreams and delusions went hand in hand. The town's main street was once lined with saloons and shops catering to miners who believed they were about to strike it rich—because what's better than spending your hard-earned fortune on whiskey and questionable life choices?

As you wander through Creede today, you might feel like you've stepped into a time machine that only goes back to the 19th century. The buildings, many of which are preserved as historical landmarks, give off a vibe that screams, "I once hosted a rowdy poker game!" You might even find yourself half-expecting a cowboy to stroll by, tipping his hat and offering you a piece of sage advice about life and cattle.

One of the most intriguing spots in Creede is the Creede Historical Museum. This museum is a treasure trove of artifacts, showcasing everything from mining equipment to photographs that could make you cringe at your own fashion choices. The walls are lined with relics that tell the story of the town's rough-and-tumble past. Here, you'll learn about the legendary silver mine known as the "Last Chance Mine." Rumor has it that the name was fitting, as many miners thought it would be their last chance at prosperity—though they probably could have used a good financial advisor.

For outdoor enthusiasts, Creede is a paradise. Surrounded by the stunning San Juan Mountains, there's no shortage of hiking trails that could make you feel like you're in a nature documentary, complete with dramatic music and a voiceover about your impressive endurance. You might even encounter a marmot or two who seem completely unfazed by your presence. Just remember to bring a snack; those little guys have a way of making you feel like you're sharing your lunch with a bunch of furry thieves.

If you're looking to catch a glimpse of the local wildlife, the nearby Rio Grande National Forest is a great spot for fishing, camping, and contemplating the meaning of life while staring into the abyss of a peaceful lake. Just make sure to bring a sturdy fishing pole—there's nothing quite like the thrill of catching a trout, especially when you're pretending to be a professional angler in the middle of a vacation.

Now, let's talk about the best things to do in Creede. If you're in town during the summer, make sure to catch the annual Creede Arts Festival. This delightful event showcases local artists, musicians, and food vendors, turning the town into a vibrant celebration of creativity. You'll find everything from handcrafted jewelry to paintings that make you question your own artistic skills. Plus, there's often live music, which means you can enjoy a good jam session while stuffing your face with food truck tacos.

Just don't forget to grab a few pieces of art that you'll inevitably have to explain to your friends later, like, "Yes, that giant metal sculpture of a chicken is a conversation starter."

For those who prefer a bit of action, consider a visit to the Creede Repertory Theatre. This intimate theater is known for its productions that could rival anything you've seen on Broadway—if Broadway were located in a former silver mining town. From musicals to dramas, the talent on stage is impressive, and the performances often leave you laughing, crying, or wondering why you didn't pursue a career in theater yourself. Just be prepared for the occasional plot twist that feels more like a soap opera than a highbrow production.

However, not everything in Creede is sunshine and rainbows. The local dining scene can be a mixed bag. You might find a cozy café that serves up comfort food that feels like a warm hug after a long day, or you could stumble into a restaurant that seems to have borrowed its menu from a time capsule. Ever wanted to try a casserole that could double as a doorstop? You might get your chance. The key is to follow the local advice and stick to the places that come highly recommended—because no one wants to spend their vacation in a culinary nightmare.

Shopping in Creede can also be an adventure. The local shops are filled with unique items that range from hand-knit scarves to quirky souvenirs that you didn't know you needed until you saw them. However, you might also encounter a few stores that have that charmingly dusty vibe, with items that look like they've been sitting on the shelves since the town's heyday. You might leave with a knickknack that you'll swear has a backstory, even if it's just a ceramic cow with an unsettling expression.

When it comes to accommodations, expect a mix of rustic cabins and quaint inns. Some places will make you feel like you've stepped into a cozy cabin in the woods, while others might remind you of a time when "vintage" was just another word for "slightly worn." Whichever you choose, you'll likely have a fantastic view of the mountains, as long as you don't mind the occasional spider lurking in the corners.

In general, Creede, Colorado, is a gem nestled in the mountains, offering a delightful blend of history, natural beauty, and small-town charm. From the fascinating historical museum to the vibrant arts scene, there's plenty to see and do. Just keep an open mind about the dining options and embrace the quirky vibe of this former mining town. Whether you're hiking, fishing, or simply enjoying the artistic endeavors of the locals, Creede promises an experience that's as memorable as it is entertaining. So pack your sense of adventure and prepare for a journey that might just include a few unexpected plot twists—because when you're in Creede, anything can happen.

Crested Butte

Crested Butte, Colorado, (or as my friend Dan used to call it, Crusty Butt) is like the quirky cousin of Aspen who shows up at family gatherings wearing mismatched socks and talking about how they're living their best life in a yurt. Nestled high in the Rockies, this mountain town has managed to keep its charm while attracting a blend of outdoor enthusiasts, artists, and a few people who just got lost on their way to the next big ski resort. Founded in the late 1800s as a mining town, Crested Butte has since transformed into a haven for those who enjoy fresh air, breathtaking views, and more outdoor activities than you can shake a snow shovel at.

Let's dive into the history. Crested Butte was originally a mining camp that thrived on silver and coal. Picture a bunch of miners with more grit than grooming, frantically digging for treasure while avoiding the occasional avalanche. The town's name supposedly comes from a local peak that resembles a "butte"—which is just a fancy term for a hill that's too lazy to be a mountain. As the mining industry waned, the town's real fortune turned out to be its stunning scenery, leading to a shift towards tourism. Today, it's hard to believe this charming place was once the Wild West—now it's more of a Wild Best, where the biggest concern is whether to hike or bike that day.

If you find yourself in Crested Butte, a visit to the Crested Butte Mountain Heritage Museum is an absolute must. Here, you can immerse yourself in the town's colorful past. The museum is filled with artifacts that could make you feel like you've stumbled upon the world's most interesting garage sale. There are old mining tools, photographs of bewildered miners who clearly didn't know how to smile, and even exhibits on the local flora and fauna. It's like a history lesson, but without the boring lecture. The highlight might be the "How to Survive an Avalanche" display, which, ironically, is located right next to the section on the history of skiing.

Speaking of skiing, if you're in Crested Butte during winter, you're in for a treat. The slopes here are legendary, attracting skiers and snowboarders from all over the world. However, there's a distinct chance that you'll spend more time falling down the mountain than actually skiing. There's something about the thin air that makes your legs feel like jelly, and by the end of the day, you might look less like a skilled skier and more like a confused penguin. If you're lucky, you'll make it to the bottom without losing a ski—or your dignity.

When the snow melts, the town transforms into a lush paradise for hikers and mountain bikers. The trails around Crested Butte are like a buffet for outdoor lovers. You can choose from easy strolls that leave you feeling like a weekend warrior or grueling hikes that will have you questioning all of your life choices. Don't forget to bring your camera, because every turn reveals a view that will make you feel like you're in a postcard, even if your hair is sticking up like you just survived a wind tunnel.

Now, let's talk about the best things to do in Crested Butte. If you're a fan of art and creativity, the town is home to an impressive art scene. Local galleries feature works that range from the breathtaking to the bizarre. You might come across a sculpture made entirely of recycled ski gear, or a painting that looks suspiciously like a five-year-old's finger painting. Either way, you'll leave with a story—or at least a new appreciation for creative interpretations of "mountain life."

One of the most popular events in Crested Butte is the annual Wildflower Festival, which is basically an Instagram influencer's dream come true. Imagine fields of colorful wildflowers, local artisans selling handmade goods, and people taking way too many selfies with flowers that probably have names longer than their own. It's the kind of event where you can wear your brightest outfit and feel completely normal—until you realize everyone else is in hiking gear and you just stand out like a sore thumb.

But let's not gloss over the less glamorous aspects of Crested Butte. The dining scene, while often delightful, can sometimes feel like a culinary game show where the secret ingredient is confusion. You might find a restaurant that specializes in "fusion cuisine," which usually means someone tried to make tacos with quinoa and kale. Sure, it's healthy, but it might leave you longing for a simple burger. Just remember, if a dish has more syllables in its name than you have dollars in your wallet, it's probably best to skip it.

Shopping in Crested Butte can also be a mixed bag. The local shops have a unique charm, selling everything from outdoor gear to funky souvenirs. You might find a T-shirt that says "I survived the Wildflower Festival," or a mug that looks like it survived a battle with a mountain goat. The prices can be a little steep, but hey, who doesn't want to pay extra for a mug that proclaims their love for overpriced coffee?

As for accommodations, you'll find a range of options from rustic cabins to upscale lodges. Some places might have that homey feel, while others will make you feel like you've accidentally wandered into a Pinterest board. Just keep in mind that if you're staying somewhere that advertises "rustic charm," it might also mean "no Wi-Fi and questionable plumbing." It's all part of the adventure!

Crested Butte, Colorado, is a delightful mix of history, breathtaking landscapes, and quirky charm. Whether you're exploring the local museum, hitting the slopes, or sipping a latte while contemplating your next hike, there's never a dull moment. Just remember to embrace the unexpected, because in Crested Butte, life is an adventure—complete with wildflowers, penguin-like skiing, and a few culinary surprises along the way. So grab your sense of humor and get ready to experience all that this mountain town has to offer, including the inevitable mishaps that will make for the best stories later.

Cripple Creek

Cripple Creek, Colorado, is a town that wears its history like a miner's helmet—proudly and a little dusty. Nestled high in the Rockies, this former gold rush boomtown has transformed from a rowdy mining hub into a quirky destination that offers a mix of old-time charm and the occasional casino. Founded in the late 1800s after the discovery of gold, Cripple Creek quickly attracted dreamers, schemers, and anyone hoping to strike it rich faster than you can say "pickaxe."

Once upon a time, Cripple Creek was bustling with prospectors who believed that gold was just waiting to be scooped up like a scoop of ice cream. The town's streets were filled with saloons, gambling halls, and a few establishments that probably shouldn't have been classified as "family-friendly." It was a wild place where fortunes were made and lost faster than you can lose a game of poker against a guy named "Lucky." Today, remnants of that rowdy past can still be seen, but thankfully the "wild" part is more of a charming memory than a daily reality.

If you're keen on history, the Cripple Creek Heritage Center is a must-visit. This gem of a museum offers a deep dive into the town's past, with exhibits that make you feel like you've walked onto the set of a Western movie. There are artifacts that range from mining tools to old photographs of men with mustaches that could rival any current hipster trend. You'll learn about the infamous "Cripple Creek Strike" of 1894, which was less about protesting bad working conditions and more about miners trying to figure out who had the best poker face. Just be careful not to get too absorbed; you might find yourself planning your next career as a gold prospector.

One of the best ways to experience the town's mining heritage is by taking a ride on the Cripple Creek & Victor Narrow Gauge Railroad. This delightful little train chugs through the mountains, giving you views that will make you feel like you're in a postcard. Just don't get too comfortable; the seats are about as spacious as a sardine can, and you'll likely spend half the ride dodging elbows while trying to capture the perfect selfie. The guide will regale you with stories of the town's wild past, and you might even learn a few mining terms that you can impress your friends with later—because nothing says "fun" like casually dropping "lode" into conversation.

Now, let's talk about the highlights of Creede, which include more than just history. The local casinos might make you think you've stumbled into a scene from a low-budget film. Picture this: bright lights, the sounds of slot machines, and the distant echo of someone shouting "Bingo!" You'll find everything from poker tables to themed slots, because what's better than spinning a wheel adorned with cartoonish characters while hoping to hit the jackpot? Just remember to set a budget, or you might end up with a pocket full of regret and a compulsion to sell your possessions to finance your next gambling spree.

For those who prefer their excitement without the risk of losing a week's pay, the surrounding natural beauty offers a plethora of outdoor activities. Hiking trails abound, and you can find paths that range from leisurely strolls to grueling hikes that make you question your life choices. One popular trail is the iconic "Gold Camp Road," which, despite its name, has a far greater chance of revealing stunning views than actual gold. Just keep an eye out for wildlife; you might spot a deer or, if you're lucky, a bear who looks just as confused as you are.

Now, let's not forget the culinary landscape. Cripple Creek boasts a few local eateries that are worth exploring. You might stumble upon a diner that serves up breakfast so hearty that you'll wonder if they've secretly partnered with a local farm to keep the livestock industry alive. But beware, because not all culinary experiences are created equal. You might find a restaurant that claims to specialize in "local cuisine," which usually translates to "we bought the ingredients yesterday and hope for the best." Just remember to check reviews before committing to a meal that could very well become a conversation piece for years to come.

If you're a fan of live entertainment, the historic Cripple Creek District Museum sometimes hosts events that make you feel like you've stepped back in time. Picture yourself in a dimly lit room, sipping on a drink while watching a local production of something that may or may not have been written in the 1800s. You might witness a reenactment of a miner's life, complete with dialogue that sounds suspiciously like it was pulled from a textbook. But who doesn't love a little dramatic flair with their history?

When it comes to accommodations, you'll find options ranging from cozy inns to hotels that resemble a slightly worn version of what you'd expect from a Vegas getaway. You may encounter a place that boasts "historic charm," which is code for "you might hear creaking noises that could either be the building settling or a ghost that's taken a liking to your snoring." Just remember that staying in Cripple Creek adds a layer of authenticity to your visit—there's nothing quite like waking up to the sound of a train whistle and a glimpse of the mountains outside your window.

Dacono

Dacono, Colorado, is the kind of place where you might think, "Wow, I didn't even know I needed a trip to a small town that sounds like a character from a cheesy sci-fi movie." Nestled in Weld County, Dacono is often overshadowed by its larger neighbors, but it has its own unique charm that's just waiting to be discovered—if you know where to look and can handle the occasional tumbleweed rolling by.

The town was officially established in the late 1800s and has since transformed from a sleepy little spot into a community with a personality that can only be described as "endearingly quirky." Dacono's name is derived from "Dakota," a nod to the area's early settlers who likely thought they were a lot more creative than they actually were. At some point, someone must have said, "Let's just add an 'o' at the end!" And voilà, Dacono was born. The town is primarily residential, which means it's perfect for those looking to escape the hustle and bustle—provided you find the hustle and bustle to be overrated.

One of the first stops on your journey should be the Dacono Community Center. This is not just a building; it's a hub of activity where everything from yoga classes to bingo nights happens. You could join a line dancing class that will have you kicking up your heels—quite literally—or attempt to channel your inner Picasso at an art class that's definitely more about fun than fine art. Just be prepared for the strong possibility that your masterpiece will end up looking like something a toddler might have produced. Still, the community center is the heart of Dacono, where friendships are forged over shared interests and questionable craft projects.

If you're interested in history—and not just the "I watched a documentary on Netflix" kind—Dacono has a few historical nuggets worth exploring. The Dacono History Museum might be smaller than your living room, but it's packed with local artifacts that tell the story of the town's humble beginnings. Here you can marvel at exhibits that feature everything from mining equipment to old photographs of residents who definitely had a flair for the dramatic. It's the kind of museum where you can learn about the town's early days while feeling slightly jealous of how much cooler people dressed back in the day.

For a taste of local flavor, don't miss out on a visit to Dacono's restaurants. While you won't find Michelin-starred establishments here, you'll discover a few diners that serve food as comforting as a warm hug. You might encounter a place that claims to have the "best breakfast burrito in Colorado," which may or may not come with a side of overinflated expectations. But hey, who doesn't love a meal that could double as a doorstop? On the other hand, you might end up at a fast-food chain that offers a value menu so extensive it feels like a high-stakes game of "What Do I Even Want?"

Nature enthusiasts will be pleased to find that Dacono is close to several parks. The Dacono Park is a local favorite, complete with a playground that could either be a child's paradise or a slightly concerning hazard zone. There's nothing quite like watching kids run around while you sip your coffee and wonder how many times you're going to have to untangle your own legs from the swing set. The park is also an excellent place for a leisurely stroll—if you enjoy the smell of grass and the sounds of children screaming.

Let's talk about the best—and worst—things to see in Dacono. On the one hand, there's the annual Dacono BBQ Festival, a culinary extravaganza where local grill masters battle it out for barbecue supremacy. Imagine the smells of smoky meats wafting through the air while you try to decide between brisket and ribs. On the flip side, there's the infamous "art installation" in the town square, which looks suspiciously like a collection of discarded lawn ornaments. It's the kind of art that makes you question not just your aesthetic preferences but your entire life trajectory. "Why am I here? What does it all mean?" You'll ponder while staring at a flamingo that appears to be contemplating its own existence.

For outdoor lovers, the surrounding areas offer a plethora of hiking and biking trails. You might set out on a grand adventure only to find yourself lost in a field of wildflowers, realizing that your navigation skills are worse than you thought. Fortunately, you can usually find your way back by following the sound of other hikers who look far more competent than you. The trails vary in difficulty, ranging from "I just want to stretch my legs" to "Why did I think this was a good idea?"

Shopping in Dacono is an experience all its own. You won't find a bustling mall, but there are local shops that cater to the unique needs of the community. Expect to see a mix of thrift stores that hold hidden gems alongside boutiques selling everything from hand-knitted socks to local honey. If you're lucky, you might stumble upon an antique store that makes you feel like you've entered a time capsule—or a hoarder's dream. Just be prepared to ask yourself if you really need a vintage typewriter that may or may not still work.

If you're staying overnight, the accommodations range from cozy motels to charming bed-and-breakfasts. You might end up in a place that offers complimentary breakfast, where the options are as varied as the guests. Expect everything from cereal to homemade pastries, though you may want to avoid the "mystery casserole" that sits mysteriously on the buffet.

Dacono, Colorado, may not be on the top of everyone's travel itinerary, but it has its quirks and charm that make it a hidden gem in the Centennial State. Whether you're exploring the local history, indulging in BBQ, or enjoying the great outdoors, there's an undeniable sense of community here that makes every visit feel like a gathering of old friends—even if you're just passing through. So grab your sense of humor and a healthy dose of curiosity, and embark on an adventure that promises to be both entertaining and maybe just a little bewildering. After all, in Dacono, you never know what you'll find—or what you might accidentally step in along the way.

De Beque

De Beque, Colorado, is a small town that might just be the best-kept secret in the state. Nestled along the Colorado River, it's the kind of place where the scenery is so beautiful that even the tumbleweeds seem to be on vacation. Founded in the late 19th century, De Beque started as a rail stop and quickly grew into a hub for coal mining and agriculture. If you're picturing a wild west town full of cowboys, you're not too far off—except that the cowboys here are likely just trying to figure out how to keep their hats from blowing away in the wind.

One of the first things to do in De Beque is to visit the De Beque Town Hall. Now, you might think, "Town Hall? How thrilling!" But hold on to your hats because this isn't just any boring government building. It's a quaint little place that showcases the community's history. You'll find old photographs that capture the town's essence, including images of early settlers who probably thought their main challenge was staying awake during long meetings. If you're lucky, you might even catch a glimpse of local officials having a serious discussion about whether the annual barbecue should feature ribs or brisket. Spoiler alert: it's always a heated debate.

If you fancy yourself a history buff, the De Beque History Museum is worth a stop. This delightful little museum might not be the Louvre, but it has its own charm. You can learn about everything from the coal mining era to the town's founding families. The exhibits are arranged with all the enthusiasm of a group project that someone forgot to finish, but that just adds to the quaintness. You might find yourself giggling at artifacts that seem completely irrelevant today, like a collection of ancient tools that look like they were designed for a game of medieval torture rather than mining.

Nature lovers, rejoice! De Beque is surrounded by stunning landscapes that are perfect for hiking, biking, and probably getting lost. The De Beque Canyon is a local favorite. Picture this: you're hiking along a beautiful trail, the sun is shining, and suddenly you realize you've wandered off the path and are now face-to-face with a cactus that clearly has a vendetta against you. The canyon is stunning, and the views make it worth the adventure—even if the adventure involves a lot of yelling at nature for not providing clear directions.

Now, let's talk food. De Beque isn't exactly a culinary hot spot, but you might be surprised by the local dining options. You could end up in a diner that has a menu so extensive it looks like a novel—except it's mostly just variations of burgers and fries. The locals will tell you that the "special sauce" is a closely guarded secret, which probably means it's ketchup mixed with something unidentifiable. It's the kind of place where the waitstaff remembers your name because, let's be honest, there aren't that many customers. Expect hearty meals that make you feel like you're about to hibernate for the winter.

If you're a fan of festivals, De Beque hosts a few events throughout the year. The annual De Beque Community Festival is a colorful explosion of local culture featuring everything from live music to craft booths that sell handmade items—like that questionable dreamcatcher you bought at the last minute. The festival atmosphere is thick with laughter, and the only real danger comes from overindulging in funnel cakes. Just try not to trip over the person selling tie-dye T-shirts while you're trying to navigate your way through a sea of enthusiastic locals.

Let's not ignore the fact that De Beque is also home to some interesting wildlife. While hiking or driving around, you might spot deer, rabbits, and the occasional prairie dog who looks suspiciously like he's plotting world domination. If you've never seen a prairie dog up close, you'll be delighted by their cheeky antics as they pop in and out of their burrows. It's like they're playing a never-ending game of peekaboo with you, and you can't help but root for them as if they were the underdogs of the animal kingdom.

For those seeking a bit of adventure beyond the local sights, De Beque is conveniently located near some of Colorado's more well-known attractions. You could take a day trip to Grand Junction, where the landscape shifts from serene plains to dramatic red rock formations. Just don't forget your camera; you'll want proof that you made it out of De Beque without losing your sanity—though some might argue that sanity is overrated.

As for accommodations, your options in De Beque might be limited, but that just adds to the charm. You might find yourself in a cozy motel that offers complimentary breakfast, which usually consists of a "mystery meat" that could be sausage or a failed science experiment. The rooms might not have all the modern amenities you're used to, but they do come with a certain rustic charm—read: a slight musty smell that reminds you of your grandma's attic. Just keep the windows open to let in that crisp mountain air.

In summary, De Beque, Colorado, is a hidden gem that packs a punch of history, nature, and quirky local charm. From the delightful little museum to the jaw-dropping canyon views, there's plenty to see and do—even if some of it involves a questionable dining experience or two. Embrace the town's eccentricities, grab a plate of whatever the diner is serving, and take in the beauty of a place that feels like it's straight out of a charming indie film. Whether you leave with a new appreciation for small-town life or just a funny story about a prairie dog encounter, one thing's for sure: De Beque is a place you won't forget—if only because you might still be trying to find your way back to the main road.

Deer Trail

Deer Trail, Colorado, is the kind of place where you might feel like you've stumbled into a time warp—a delightful blend of cowboy culture and quirky Americana. Founded in 1869, this small town is known for its storied history, which might sound impressive until you realize that most of it revolves around the local bar and a few infamous prairie dog races. Yes, you read that right. Prairie dog races. If that doesn't get your heart racing, then perhaps you should check your pulse.

Historically, Deer Trail was a railroad town, which means it was once bustling with activity. Now, it's more like a quiet little corner of Colorado where everyone knows your name—because there are only about 500 of you living there. The local lore claims that the town is the birthplace of the world's first rodeo, but let's be honest, the most exciting thing to happen in Deer Trail lately was when the local diner finally upgraded its coffee machine from the 1980s.

If you're keen on diving into the local history, the Deer Trail Historical Society is your best bet. This place could easily be mistaken for a community garage sale that accidentally turned into a museum. You'll find old photographs, dusty artifacts, and a lovely collection of historical memorabilia, including the first official cowpoke hat and a range of items that appear to have been rescued from the set of a low-budget Western. You might even stumble across an exhibit dedicated to the town's famous prairie dog races—because what better way to celebrate your heritage than with the speedy little critters that seem to dominate the local consciousness?

Speaking of museums, if you're into roadside attractions, Deer Trail doesn't disappoint. The Deer Trail UFO Watchtower is a must-visit for those with a fascination for extraterrestrials—or those who simply enjoy a good laugh. This unique attraction offers a chance to sit in a structure that looks like it was assembled from parts scavenged from an old shed. It's adorned with all sorts of alien paraphernalia, making it a haven for conspiracy theorists and bored tourists alike. Just try not to trip over the alien cutouts while you're pondering whether the next "unidentified flying object" will be a UFO or just another local farmer's drone.

Once you've soaked in all that rich history, you'll likely feel the urge to sample some local cuisine. The Deer Trail Diner is the place to be—if you want to experience food that has a "rustic" charm. The diner has all the staples: burgers, fries, and breakfast served all day. Just be prepared to see the daily specials written on a chalkboard that looks like it hasn't been updated since the invention of the wheel. The "mystery meat" might be the best thing on the menu, depending on how adventurous you're feeling. Locals swear by the burgers, claiming they're "the best in town," which is a title that might not carry much weight when you consider the competition is a taco truck that rolls through once a month.

For those seeking outdoor adventure, Deer Trail has its fair share of natural beauty. The surrounding plains are perfect for a leisurely hike, although you might find yourself dodging the occasional tumbleweed or trying to figure out which direction the wind is blowing. If you're lucky, you might even spot a deer—or at least something that vaguely resembles a deer from a distance, which could just as easily be a large dog. The area is also popular for hunting, so if you're into that sort of thing, bring your gear and keep an eye out for those elusive critters. Just remember: it's all fun and games until someone mistakes you for a deer.

As for local events, the Deer Trail Rodeo is a highlight of the year. Picture this: cowboys, cowgirls, and lots of dusty hats. If you've ever wanted to witness the excitement of a local rodeo where the biggest star might just be the announcer's mustache, this is your chance. The rodeo typically features all the classic events, like bull riding and barrel racing. Just don't be surprised if half the competitors are doing it for bragging rights rather than any real glory. And if you're wondering about the prizes, let's just say a handmade trophy could end up being more impressive than the prize money.

For a little slice of Americana, don't forget to check out the Deer Trail Town Hall. It's not just a place for government meetings—it's also a hub for community events and local gossip. You can catch up on who's won the latest prairie dog race, who's been spotted at the diner, and whether the rumors about a new UFO sighting are true. The Town Hall is where the magic happens, including the occasional heated debate about whether to have a potluck or just order pizza. It's the kind of place where you might find yourself laughing at the sheer absurdity of it all while trying to figure out how you ended up in a town where the main attraction is its quirky charm.

For accommodations, Deer Trail isn't exactly teeming with hotels. You might find yourself in a cozy little motel that has more character than some of the exhibits at the historical society. Think retro décor and perhaps an unintentional homage to the '70s. Don't be surprised if the Wi-Fi password is scrawled on a sticky note next to the reception desk, and remember that the continental breakfast might consist of coffee and the odd donut that has been around since the dawn of time. Still, it's all part of the experience, right?

Del Norte

Del Norte, Colorado, is a charming little town that might just feel like the universe's way of saying, "Here's a cozy spot for people who love nature and don't mind a good dose of small-town oddity." Founded in 1871, Del Norte was originally a railroad town, and while the trains have long since departed, the spirit of the Wild West lingers like that last stubborn tumbleweed rolling down Main Street.

The town's name literally means "the last" in Spanish, which is fitting because you might feel like you've arrived at the end of the line—both geographically and culturally. If you're looking for a place that embraces its history while simultaneously having no idea what to do with it, you've hit the jackpot. Del Norte's historical society might not boast a lot of glitzy exhibits, but it does have a collection of artifacts that could be described as "collectibles" if you squint hard enough and drink enough coffee.

Speaking of coffee, let's talk about the local diner. This beloved establishment has the kind of menu that would make even the most adventurous eater think twice. You've got your standard diner fare—burgers, fries, and pie—but if you're feeling bold, you can try the "Daily Special," which is as mysterious as it sounds. Rumor has it that the special is just whatever the chef found in the fridge that morning. One time, it was a questionable casserole that locals now refer to as "that one thing we never talk about."

When it comes to museums, Del Norte has a small but mighty one. The Del Norte Museum offers a peek into the town's past, showcasing everything from Native American artifacts to mining tools. It's like stepping into your great-grandparents' attic, only less dusty and with fewer questionable family secrets. You might even discover some old photographs that illustrate how fashion trends have changed—or haven't changed—over the decades. The museum does a fine job of making history as exciting as watching paint dry, but hey, it's history, and it's free. Plus, the museum's volunteers are more than eager to share stories, some of which may or may not have been embellished over the years.

Now, if you're seeking outdoor activities, you're in luck. Del Norte is surrounded by stunning mountains and the Rio Grande River, which is perfect for fishing, rafting, or just yelling at the fish for being smarter than you. The river might be great for water sports, but the local mosquitoes seem to think you're the main course, so pack some bug spray and maybe a full suit of armor.

And let's not forget about the Del Norte Depot, which is a historic building that looks like it just walked out of a Western film. Here, you can imagine cowboys tying up their horses while they grab a soda, but don't expect any actual trains. Instead, you'll find a charming space that serves as a gathering point for local events, or as the town's best-kept secret for a very, very quiet afternoon.

Now, as for events, the annual Del Norte Rodeo is a highlight that no one seems to miss—mainly because it's the only rodeo within a hundred miles. The rodeo features all the classic events: bull riding, barrel racing, and the occasional cowpoke who seems to have entered more for the free hot dogs than any real rodeo ambition. If you've ever wanted to see a local cowboy try to wrangle a calf while simultaneously explaining the finer points of fishing, this is your moment.

As you stroll through the town, be on the lookout for the famous Del Norte Welcome Sign, which is rumored to have seen more wear and tear than the average road sign. It serves as a reminder that while you're in this quirky little town, you may never really know what's around the corner. It could be a charming café, a random yard sale where everything is slightly more confusing than it needs to be, or a gathering of locals discussing the merits of different types of ranch dressing.

On the subject of ranch dressing, the local cuisine is a delightful medley of hearty comfort food that'll either make you feel right at home or question your life choices. Try the local burritos that have been known to cause spontaneous dance parties due to their sheer deliciousness. Just be careful not to challenge a local to a burrito-eating contest unless you're prepared to lose—miserably.

For those seeking a night out, you might think you'd find a bustling nightlife scene, but you'll quickly discover that "nightlife" in Del Norte often consists of a few folks gathered around a bonfire, sharing stories that range from the bizarre to the completely unbelievable. You could hear tales of a mysterious ghost that roams the outskirts of town or legends about a giant catfish lurking in the Rio Grande. The best part? The locals are friendly and will likely invite you to share in their folklore, which could be as entertaining as anything you'll find in the museum.

As the day winds down, you can take a quiet walk down Main Street, which, at any given moment, feels like the set of a low-budget Western film—minus the soundtrack. The old buildings, the distant mountains, and the almost palpable air of nostalgia create a picturesque scene. Just watch out for the occasional cowboy hat-wearing local who may still be riding around on horseback, looking for a good place to tie up for a soda.

Delta

Delta, Colorado, is a town that proudly wears its history like a badge of honor—one that's slightly faded and maybe even a little crooked. Established in 1881, Delta was originally a bustling hub for the railroad, but nowadays, it feels more like the kind of place where you'd stop for gas, stretch your legs, and ponder your life choices while staring at a wall of various potato chip flavors.

As you meander through Delta, you might wonder if you've accidentally entered a time warp. The historic downtown area is like stepping into a living museum, but without the helpful signs or enthusiastic tour guides. Instead, you get charming old buildings that look like they were last painted during the Carter administration. These structures have stood the test of time, which is impressive considering they seem to have faced every element known to man—rain, snow, and what can only be described as a freak hailstorm that happened in July.

When it comes to museums, Delta has the Delta County Historical Society Museum, which houses artifacts and exhibits that tell the town's story. Picture this: old farming equipment, vintage photographs, and an assortment of items that could make you question why anyone ever thought to keep them. The museum's mission seems to be to answer the question, "What on earth did we do with our time before Netflix?" You'll find displays that include everything from old-fashioned tools to a collection of hats that looks suspiciously like a local garage sale exploded. If you're lucky, you might even catch a volunteer giving a tour and embellishing every story with a flair that could rival a Broadway production. "And here we have the plow that was used in the great potato famine of 1903… or was it 1904? Regardless, it's definitely old."

For those who fancy the great outdoors, Delta is nestled between the gorgeous Grand Mesa and the stunning Gunnison River, providing endless opportunities for outdoor adventures—assuming you're equipped with a strong sense of direction and maybe a GPS. Hiking, fishing, and camping await you, and the best part is that you'll be doing it surrounded by locals who seem to take outdoor activities as seriously as they take their morning coffee. Be prepared to engage in conversations that may include fishing stories that sound suspiciously like tall tales, complete with exaggerated fish sizes that could rival the Loch Ness Monster.

If you're more of a cultural connoisseur, the Delta Center for the Arts is a must-see. This place hosts everything from art shows to musical performances, and the experience is akin to finding a hidden gem in a vast wilderness—if that gem were run by very enthusiastic volunteers who sometimes forget how to turn on the lights. If you're lucky, you might catch a local talent show that will leave you wondering how many of those acts actually made it to rehearsal.

As for local cuisine, Delta's dining scene is nothing if not varied. From quaint diners serving up greasy spoon specials to more upscale establishments attempting to be the "next big thing" in Colorado cuisine, you're in for a treat—or a trial, depending on your palate. The local burger joint might have the audacity to boast "the best burgers in Colorado," which is likely said with a straight face by someone who has never ventured outside the state lines. Just be cautious with the "secret sauce"—some say it's a family recipe, while others suspect it's just ketchup and mystery.

And let's not forget the great Delta County Fair, which happens every summer and feels like a rite of passage for locals and visitors alike. This annual event has everything you'd expect from a county fair: livestock shows, carnival rides, and deep-fried food items that defy the laws of physics. One year, a deep-fried Twinkie was declared the highlight of the fair, leading to discussions about whether it was a culinary masterpiece or an existential crisis on a plate. Either way, it's an experience that might leave you questioning your life choices—specifically, the one where you decided to try that suspiciously bright yellow corn dog.

As you explore, keep an eye out for the Delta Welcome Sign, which is definitely not the biggest or most elaborate welcome sign you've ever seen, but it certainly gets the job done. Locals may occasionally pose in front of it for social media posts, usually accompanied by captions like, "Living my best life in Delta!" This typically happens just before they dive into a platter of fried food at the fair.

For those craving nightlife, Delta's options are limited but have their own unique charm. There's a local bar that seems to be the epicenter of social activity, where the drink specials are as enticing as the regulars' stories. One minute, you're sipping a beer while listening to a debate about the best fishing spots; the next, you're neck-deep in a heated discussion about which season of "The Office" is the best.

Dillon

Dillon, Colorado, is a town that feels like it was crafted by someone who decided to put a ski resort, a beautiful lake, and a touch of Rocky Mountain charm into a blender, hit "puree," and called it a day. Nestled at the base of the majestic Tenmile Range, Dillon is the kind of place where the scenery is so stunning it could make you forget that you're surrounded by people who are just as likely to be wearing ski gear in July as they are flip-flops in January.

The history of Dillon is like a well-told joke: it has a punchline, but getting there takes a bit of a winding road. Founded in 1881, Dillon was initially a mining town, but like many Colorado towns, it soon realized that the real gold was in tourism. The town was moved in the 1960s to make way for the Dillon Reservoir, because nothing says "progress" like flooding a few buildings for a massive lake. Today, Dillon is home to a picturesque marina, which, let's be honest, is more fun to look at than to actually navigate on a sailboat, unless you enjoy doing donuts while desperately trying to look cool.

For museums, Dillon isn't exactly overflowing with options, but it does boast the Dillon Schoolhouse Museum. This charming little building might not have the extensive collections of bigger cities, but it has that "you can't judge a book by its cover" vibe. Inside, you'll find artifacts that make you question how people ever survived without Wi-Fi. Old desks, dusty textbooks, and a chalkboard that probably hasn't been used since "D" was the only grade you could get for effort tell the story of education before smartphones made kids smarter than their teachers.

If you're seeking something a bit more interactive, the Dillon Farmers Market is the place to be during the summer months. Picture this: a gathering of local farmers who are not just selling produce but also actively judging your choice of zucchini. "Oh, you picked that one? It's a little... small." You can wander through stalls filled with organic vegetables, artisanal cheeses, and honey so locally sourced that the bees practically have a personal brand. You'll inevitably end up engaging in a lively discussion about whether heirloom tomatoes are truly worth the extra two dollars or if it's just a fancy way of saying "slightly bruised."

Dillon is also home to the Dillon Amphitheater, a venue that seems to have been designed for people who enjoy both live music and breathtaking views—because what's better than jamming to your favorite band while contemplating the existential meaning of life with the mountains as your backdrop? If you're lucky, you might catch a concert where the opening act is an aspiring local musician who clearly forgot that there's a reason they aren't on the main stage of Coachella yet.

For outdoor enthusiasts, Dillon is a playground. Hiking, biking, and boating are practically national pastimes here. You could spend your days traipsing along the picturesque trails or trying to figure out how to not fall off your paddleboard. Just remember, if you take a spill into the frigid waters of Dillon Reservoir, the only thing you'll be doing more than swimming is apologizing to any nearby fish for ruining their peaceful day.

If you're feeling particularly brave, you can take a stroll around the town's ice skating rink in winter. It's a delightful experience—assuming you're willing to embrace the fact that you might end up on your backside more often than you'd like. Skating under twinkling lights while trying to avoid the toddler who has mastered the art of zooming past you like a figure skating prodigy is a challenge that builds character. Just remember to wear a helmet—because falling is inevitable, and dignity is overrated.

When it comes to dining, Dillon's culinary scene offers a mixed bag of experiences. From cozy coffee shops serving the kind of artisanal lattes that could make you feel like you're in a hipster paradise to diners that proudly serve everything on a menu that seems to be stuck in the '90s, you'll find plenty to fill your belly. One local gem is a spot known for its burgers, where the size of the patty is directly proportional to how adventurous you're feeling. "Sure, I'll have the 'Big Kahuna.' I'll just add a side of regret, please."

Now, let's talk about the winter sports scene. Dillon transforms into a ski mecca, with nearby resorts that offer everything from skiing to snowshoeing. It's a time when the town fills with adrenaline junkies who proudly display their latest gear while simultaneously trying to convince you that they didn't just spend the entire day face-planting down the slopes. For the less athletically inclined, there's always the option of sipping hot cocoa and watching fellow skiers wipe out while you enjoy a front-row seat to the chaos.

As for nightlife, Dillon may not be the party capital of Colorado, but it has a few hidden gems. Bars and taverns line the streets, each with their own vibe, where the locals gather to share tales of epic powder days and skiing adventures. Just be prepared for the occasional "did I ever tell you about the time I out-skiied an avalanche?" story that gets told a little too enthusiastically.

In summary, Dillon, Colorado, is a delightful blend of outdoor adventure, small-town charm, and quirky history that makes it a unique destination. While it may not have the hustle and bustle of bigger cities, it offers plenty of opportunities to laugh, explore, and enjoy a slower pace of life—one that occasionally involves a faceplant on the ice or a hilarious encounter at the farmers market. Whether you're navigating the waters of Dillon Reservoir or trying to decipher the menu at a local diner, you'll leave with stories that are more memorable than a fishing tale and experiences that make you appreciate the simple joys of life in the mountains. And who knows, maybe you'll even find a new favorite zucchini along the way.

Dinosaur

Dinosaur, Colorado, is not just a name; it's a state of mind. Nestled in the northwest corner of the state, it's the kind of town where people who love dinosaurs, fossils, and all things prehistoric gather, presumably because they can't get enough of things that are both gigantic and extinct—kind of like that high school friend who still talks about their glory days on the wrestling team.

The history of Dinosaur is as rich as the soil that once held the massive bones of the creatures that roamed these lands. Founded in the 1980s—yes, you read that right, the 1980s, when mullets and neon spandex were at their peak—Dinosaur was established primarily because someone thought, "Hey, why not capitalize on all these dino bones?" It's a town that understands its brand. You don't find a "Dinosaur" here; you find a whole theme park of them, complete with quirky roadside attractions that would make even the most serious paleontologist chuckle.

First stop, the Dinosaur National Monument. This isn't just any old park; it's where you can gaze at a wall of fossilized dinosaur bones, some dating back over 149 million years. It's like the world's oldest museum exhibit, only it's all outdoors, which means you can enjoy the fresh air while wondering how in the world you're supposed to explain to your kids why their favorite dinosaur is not available for selfies. "Sorry, kids, T. rex is busy—he's been extinct for a while now."

Now, for a taste of culture, head to the Dinosaur Community Center. This isn't just a random building filled with questionable taxidermy and old bowling trophies. It's where the local residents gather for events, meetings, and, yes, probably the occasional debate over who really won the Great T-Rex vs. Triceratops argument. The center doubles as a museum, featuring exhibits that highlight the town's dinosaur heritage, which often leads to fascinating discussions about the relative merits of velociraptors over, say, pterodactyls. If you ever wanted to see a heated argument over which dinosaur would win in a fight, this is the place to be.

When it comes to food, Dinosaur has a few culinary gems that will delight and confuse you in equal measure. There's the famous Chuckwagon Restaurant, where the menu might read like it was designed in a time capsule from the Wild West. You can feast on "Dino Burgers," which may or may not be made from actual dinosaur meat (spoiler alert: they're not). But hey, a burger is a burger, and if it comes with fries shaped like dinosaur footprints, who's complaining? You might find yourself pondering the existential question of whether you're actually consuming the meat of an animal that once roamed the Earth or just the result of a creative marketing strategy.

As you explore the town, keep an eye out for the "Dinosaur Tracks" on the road. No, they're not actual footprints left behind by ancient behemoths, but rather playful reminders that you're in a town dedicated to these magnificent creatures. Driving over them feels like you're part of an exclusive club where the initiation rites include not just a sense of humor but also a willingness to embrace your inner child. "Look, Mom, I'm driving on dinosaur tracks!" you'll shout, as if that's somehow a valid excuse for forgetting to stop at the red light.

For those seeking outdoor adventures, Dinosaur is surrounded by the stunning landscapes of the Utah border, which is basically nature's version of a high-definition movie. Hiking trails abound, and you can even go on fossil hunts—because nothing says "fun" quite like searching for ancient bones in the ground while trying not to trip over a rock or, worse, another dinosaur enthusiast who might steal your spotlight. Just make sure to wear sturdy shoes, as the last thing you want is to leave with a sprained ankle and a dinosaur bone that you didn't even find.

If you're feeling particularly brave, try your hand at some "dino-themed" crafts offered at local shops. From dino-shaped soap to ceramic dinosaurs that make you question the taste of whoever bought them, these activities are perfect for families looking to create "unique" souvenirs. You may walk away with a trinket that you swear looked better in the store, but hey, it'll serve as a conversation starter for years to come. "Oh, this? It's a ceramic T. rex. I bought it in a place called Dinosaur."

For those who enjoy the thrill of the hunt, don't miss the Dinosaur Yard Sale, which feels like an episode of "American Pickers" but with more plaid shirts and slightly less drama. Here, you can dig through piles of stuff ranging from vintage clothing to that one weird dino lamp that your cousin probably thought would be a good gift. Just remember to negotiate like a pro; this is no ordinary garage sale, and who knows, you might walk away with the deal of the century—a framed picture of a dinosaur doing yoga, for example.

As the sun sets over the vast Colorado landscape, don't forget to check out the local stargazing spots. With minimal light pollution, the night sky transforms into a celestial show of shooting stars and constellations. You'll find yourself debating which dinosaur would've had the best view. T. rex? Probably too busy trying to figure out how to scratch its own back. Pterodactyl? Definitely flying high enough to catch the best view, right before its wing cramp kicks in.

Dolores

Dolores, Colorado, is that charming little town you've never heard of but probably should have if you enjoy the idea of small-town quirks and outdoor adventures. Nestled in the heart of the San Juan Mountains, this place might be small, but it's got a personality bigger than a moose wearing a cowboy hat. Established in the late 1800s, Dolores started as a humble railroad town, but don't let that fool you; it's packed with enough history to keep any curious traveler entertained—provided they can stay awake past 8 PM.

Now, the town was named after the Dolores River, which flows nearby like it's trying to keep up with the gossip about how great it is to live here. Legend has it that the river got its name from some Spanish explorers who probably thought "Dolores" sounded more romantic than "Water That's Cold Enough to Freeze Your Toes Off." This little detail sets the stage for what you might expect from Dolores: a mix of history and natural beauty with just a hint of wild frontier spirit.

If you're feeling particularly adventurous, the Dolores River is the main attraction. You can raft down it, which is a surefire way to engage in that classic vacation pastime: "Will I survive this?" Whether you're an experienced rafter or someone who just thought "How hard could it be?" while watching a YouTube video, the river offers plenty of excitement. Just remember to keep your paddle in the water, unless you're trying to earn extra points for dramatic splashes that soak everyone around you. Rafting here is like playing a game of dodgeball, but instead of balls, you've got rocks, and instead of friends, you've got strangers desperately trying not to look like they're about to fall in.

For those who prefer to keep their feet dry and their sense of adventure in check, the Dolores Historical Museum is a must-visit. Housed in an old church, it's a delightful little trove of artifacts that showcase the town's past. You'll find everything from old photographs to mining tools, all meticulously organized by someone who clearly enjoys telling the story of Dolores more than anyone else does. The museum curator has probably spent a few too many hours contemplating the implications of a 1930s tin can found under a porch. "What did it contain? Was it beans? Were they good beans? Or were they the kind that make you question your life choices?"

Don't forget to check out the town's namesake, the Dolores River, at Joe Rowell Park. This park is the social hub where locals gather to swap stories, play frisbee, or engage in a spirited game of "Who Can Make the Best S'mores?" There's a picnic area that doubles as a gathering spot for families, couples, and maybe even a rogue bear or two looking for some leftover hot dogs. It's the perfect place to spend an afternoon contemplating the universe or just how to pronounce "Dolores" without sounding like you're about to recite poetry.

Now, when it comes to dining, Dolores doesn't disappoint. There are a few charming local eateries where you can fill your belly with some hearty food. One standout is the Dolores River Brewery. Here, you can sip on craft beer brewed right on site while contemplating the meaning of life—or at least the meaning of that weird aftertaste in the IPA you just ordered. The food is decent, and the atmosphere is casual, making it a favorite among locals who believe that any meal can be improved with the addition of fries and a side of laughter.

However, beware of the local legend: "The Great Spaghetti Incident." Apparently, it involved a dinner special that went awry, leaving half the town in a carb-induced coma. To this day, some residents still look at spaghetti with suspicion, eyeing it like it might spring back to life and throw a meatball at them. Just ask anyone at the brewery about it, and you'll get an animated story that will keep you entertained while you awkwardly twirl your own pasta, hoping it doesn't turn into a town-wide conspiracy theory.

As for outdoor activities, Dolores is surrounded by stunning landscapes just begging to be hiked, biked, or driven through in a convertible with the top down while you blast 80s music. The San Juan National Forest is practically next door, offering trails that range from "I might actually survive this" to "What was I thinking?" It's the perfect place to commune with nature—just don't forget the bug spray unless you want to discover the true meaning of "being eaten alive."

During the summer, Dolores hosts the annual Dolores River Festival, where you can enjoy live music, food vendors, and a strong sense of community that comes from gathering in a small town to celebrate the joy of, well, having a good time. This festival is like a family reunion where you hope no one brings up that one embarrassing story about you from ten years ago. Instead, it's all about fun, laughter, and the smell of nachos wafting through the air as locals engage in friendly competition over who can craft the best paper boat for the river race.

However, it's not all sunshine and local craft fairs. Dolores also has a reputation for being a bit sleepy. The "nightlife" in town is akin to watching paint dry—unless you're really into that sort of thing. As the sun sets, the streets get quieter than a library at midnight. If you're seeking vibrant nightlife, you might want to look elsewhere, unless your idea of a good time involves counting stars and critiquing the local wildlife.

Dove Creek

Dove Creek, Colorado, is a tiny gem nestled in the southwest corner of the state, known for its sagebrush, wide-open skies, and enough quirks to fill a book—if anyone had the time to write one in this sleepy little town. The population hovers around 700, which means that on any given day, you might see more deer than people. In fact, if you're ever lonely, just wander outside; there's a good chance you'll find a deer staring back at you, contemplating life's big questions. "Is that human going to feed me? Can I trust them? Why can't I fly?"

Historically, Dove Creek is famous for two things: its piñon nuts and a reputation for being the "Pinto Bean Capital of the World." That's right, if you've ever enjoyed a delicious pinto bean, it likely came from this area. The town's identity is wrapped up in these humble legumes, which is a rather impressive feat for a place so small that if you blink, you might miss it while driving by. To put things into perspective, the annual Pinto Bean Festival celebrates the town's culinary pride, complete with bean-themed games, cooking contests, and probably a very serious debate about the best way to prepare beans. Just don't bring any chickpeas to the festival unless you want to be shunned.

As you stroll through the town, you'll quickly discover that Dove Creek's charm is evident in its murals. Yes, murals. They're everywhere, depicting everything from local wildlife to historical scenes that likely made you ask, "Why didn't they just use a selfie stick?" One mural even shows the rich history of pinto beans, as if they were the Kardashians of the agricultural world. These works of art create a delightful backdrop for your social media posts, ensuring that your friends think you've wandered into some sort of quirky paradise.

The Dove Creek Historical Museum is a must-see, not just for its impressive collection of artifacts but also for the fact that it's about the size of a large living room. Here, you can admire local artifacts, photographs, and perhaps the world's smallest collection of pinto bean recipes. Just be prepared for the museum curator, who is likely to engage you in an intense discussion about the history of the bean. "Did you know that pinto beans were first introduced to this area in the early 1900s?" they might say, eyes gleaming with passion. "We're very proud of our beans here." And who could blame them? If you're known for producing the best beans in the world, you'd talk them up, too.

Now, if museums aren't your jam, fear not! Dove Creek has outdoor activities that will make you question why you ever thought city life was so exciting. Hiking trails weave through the nearby San Juan Mountains, where the views are breathtaking and the air is so fresh you might start singing about the hills being alive. Just make sure to wear good shoes because, let's be honest, it's less "romantic mountain stroll" and more "trying not to trip on rocks while wondering if you're lost."

The highlight of Dove Creek, of course, is the annual Pinto Bean Festival, which attracts visitors from all over. It's a spectacle of fun and food, and if you're lucky, you might catch a bean-eating contest where you can witness the sheer determination of people trying to consume as many beans as possible in under a minute. It's a sight that truly brings a tear to your eye—mainly from the overwhelming aroma of beans wafting through the air. Just be prepared for some serious gastrointestinal consequences; the aftermath is less "American Pie" and more "Where's the nearest bathroom?"

Dove Creek also offers some fascinating roadside attractions, such as the infamous "World's Largest Pinto Bean." This masterpiece of local pride isn't just a random bean plopped in the ground; it's a monument of sorts, a testament to the town's identity and dedication to all things bean-related. Be sure to take a selfie with this giant legume, as it's the kind of photo that will get you serious street cred among your friends. "Check it out! I'm bigger than a bean!"

As for dining options, Dove Creek may not boast a Michelin star, but it does have some great local spots where you can enjoy the culinary wonders of pinto beans. You can find burritos, chili, and, of course, bean-related dishes that will have you questioning every meal you ever had in a big city. One restaurant even offers a pinto bean soup that's allegedly been passed down through generations. Just be sure to ask about the family recipe; it's probably a closely guarded secret involving beans and a touch of "don't ask questions."

On the flip side, if you're looking for nightlife, you might be better off counting stars or getting to know the local deer population. After the sun goes down, Dove Creek quiets down faster than a teenager caught scrolling on their phone during a family dinner. There are no clubs or bars, just a few folks sitting on porches, sharing stories about the legendary pinto beans and perhaps keeping an eye on their gardens. It's peaceful, for sure, but don't expect anything wild unless you count the occasional raccoon rummaging through the trash.

Dove Creek, Colorado, is a unique blend of history, agriculture, and some of the friendliest folks you'll ever meet. Whether you're there for the beans, the murals, or the incredible mountain views, there's something delightfully offbeat about this small town. Just remember to appreciate the pinto beans while you're there because if you don't, you might find yourself in a very serious debate with a local. And trust me, you do not want to be on the wrong side of a bean argument in Dove Creek.

Durango

Durango, Colorado, is a charming town that feels like a slice of the Wild West plopped down in the middle of the Rockies, complete with mountains, history, and enough outdoor activities to make even the most committed couch potato rethink their life choices. Founded in 1880, Durango was a bustling hub for the mining industry, and today, it's known for its beautiful scenery and a vibrant downtown that has more character than a soap opera.

The first thing you might notice about Durango is its historic train. The Durango and Silverton Narrow Gauge Railroad is a must-see, if only for the sheer thrill of hopping on a train that looks like it was borrowed from a movie set. Seriously, if you see a cowboy with a lasso and a ten-gallon hat, don't be surprised. The ride takes you through some of the most breathtaking scenery you could imagine—unless, of course, you're imagining a beach. In which case, you might be in the wrong place entirely. As you chug along the tracks, the conductor will probably regale you with tales of the old days when trains were the only way to get around, and nobody had heard of Uber. If you're lucky, they might even toss in a few ghost stories about the old mining camps. Nothing like a little supernatural lore to spice up your ride.

Speaking of ghosts, Durango has its fair share of haunted locations, including the historic Strater Hotel, which claims to be home to several friendly spirits. You can spend the night there, but be warned: if you hear the sound of boots walking down the hall or feel an unexplained chill, it might just be the hotel staff practicing for their next Halloween party. Some guests say they've experienced strange happenings, but honestly, after a long day of exploring, it's probably just your mind playing tricks after too many of those delicious local brews. Remember to drink responsibly, or you might end up trying to argue with a ghost about the best way to brew a cup of coffee.

The downtown area is a delightful mix of shops, restaurants, and galleries that will make you feel like you've stepped back in time—if time had Wi-Fi and artisanal coffee shops. You can stroll along Main Avenue and pop into local boutiques that sell everything from handmade jewelry to quirky home décor that will make your friends question your taste. Be sure to check out the Animas River Trail, where you can walk off the calories you just consumed from that slice of local pie—because let's face it, if you don't indulge in dessert while in Durango, are you even doing it right?

Now, if you're looking for something a bit more educational, the Durango Discovery Museum is the place to be. It's the town's answer to "What do we do with all this history?" This hands-on museum offers a glimpse into the area's past through exhibits that would make any fourth-grader squeal with joy. There's something oddly satisfying about playing with interactive displays while pretending you're actually learning something. One moment, you're a history buff, and the next, you're knee-deep in a physics exhibit, trying to prove that you still have some knowledge left over from high school science class.

Outdoor enthusiasts will find themselves in paradise with Durango's stunning natural beauty. Hiking, biking, and white-water rafting are just the tip of the iceberg. If you're feeling particularly adventurous, you can try your hand at rock climbing or even go zip-lining over the Animas River. Just be prepared for the awkward moment when you realize that all your friends are far braver than you are and are already halfway up the mountain while you're still trying to figure out how to tie your shoelaces.

But let's not forget about the food scene. Durango has some seriously good eats that range from fancy dining to food trucks that will leave you wondering how you ever lived without a burrito the size of your face. Make sure to stop by local favorites like the Durango Diner, where the portions are generous, and the service is just the right mix of friendly and sassy. You might even find yourself bonding with the waitress over shared grievances about the state of the world, or at least the last political debate.

For those who enjoy a good brew, Durango boasts a thriving craft beer scene. You can hop from one brewery to another, tasting everything from IPAs to stouts while engaging in deep conversations about the merits of hops and malt. Just be sure to pace yourself; nobody wants to be the person who tries to order a pizza in the middle of the afternoon because they "forgot what it feels like to be hungry."

Now, let's talk about the worst things you might encounter in Durango. While it's a charming town, it has its fair share of quirks. For starters, be prepared for the occasional encounter with wildlife. Squirrels here seem to have developed a sense of entitlement, and if you're not careful, you might find yourself in a showdown over your lunch. There are also the local "mountain bikers," who navigate the trails with the kind of confidence that makes you question your entire life's choices. You'll see them flying past you, making you feel like you're standing still—even when you're actually just trying to catch your breath.

And let's not forget the weather. One minute it's sunny and beautiful, and the next, you're caught in a snowstorm that seemingly came out of nowhere. Be sure to pack layers, or you'll spend your day either sweating profusely or shivering uncontrollably, all while trying to maintain some semblance of dignity as you navigate the extremes.

Eads

Eads, Colorado, a gem nestled in the vast plains of Kiowa County, is the kind of place that makes you question your decision to visit. Founded in the 1880s and named after the railroad engineer who probably got tired of dealing with people, Eads is a small town that prides itself on having more tumbleweeds than residents. With a population that hovers around 1,000, you can bet that the locals know each other better than your family knows your embarrassing childhood stories.

As you roll into Eads, you'll immediately notice the wide-open spaces. And by wide-open, I mean you can literally see your future from here. The town is flat as a pancake, which is great for those who enjoy long, uninterrupted views of the horizon. Just don't forget your sunscreen because it can feel like you're standing in a giant frying pan during the summer months. You might even wonder if you've accidentally entered a parallel universe where shade is a myth.

The local history is a patchwork of Wild West tales and a few more recent developments. Eads was originally a stop for cattle drives, and while the cattle have long since moved on, the stories of cowboys, saloons, and the occasional bank heist live on. In fact, you might even hear a few ghost stories about the old days. It's rumored that if you listen closely at night, you can hear the faint sound of spurs clanging, which is just the local kids practicing their "cowboy" impressions after a few too many sodas.

Now, let's dive into the museums because what small town would be complete without them? The Kiowa County Historical Museum is the crown jewel of Eads. Here, you can learn about everything from local artifacts to the history of the railroads that helped shape the area. Expect displays that are probably dustier than the town itself. And if you're lucky, you might catch a glimpse of the museum curator, who likely has more stories than artifacts and might just be the last person to actually remember when things were "exciting" around here. The museum's motto might as well be, "Where the past comes to nap."

When it comes to activities, Eads has a charm that's as subtle as a sledgehammer. For starters, you can visit the local park, which boasts a playground that hasn't been updated since the last time someone used the phrase "groovy." The swings might feel a little rusty, but hey, a little danger never hurt anyone, right? Just be careful not to swing too high; you might end up launching into another dimension where people still wear bell-bottoms.

If you're feeling particularly adventurous, head over to the nearby terrain for some good old-fashioned hiking. The surrounding landscape is ideal for those who enjoy getting lost in the great outdoors—literally. It's so flat that even your GPS will throw up its hands in defeat. Make sure you bring plenty of water, a map, and maybe a flare gun, just in case. You never know when a rogue tumbleweed might whisk you off course.

For those who prefer indoor activities, you might find some excitement at the local library. Yes, that's right! The Eads Public Library, where the books are plentiful, and the Wi-Fi is free—if you can find a signal strong enough to support your Instagram scrolling. While you're there, don't hesitate to chat with the librarian, who has undoubtedly heard every conspiracy theory about the town and can give you the lowdown on which titles are the most "thrilling." Spoiler alert: it's probably not the history section.

If you're looking for culinary delights, you may want to adjust your expectations. The local diner serves up classic American fare, which means you can expect to see the same five items on every menu. Burgers, fries, milkshakes, and the ever-popular "mystery meat special." Don't ask what's in it, just order it and take your chances. After all, a little adventure in the realm of food can be just as thrilling as hiking, right?

But let's not ignore the worst things about Eads because, let's face it, every town has its quirks. The weather can change faster than a teenager's mood. One minute you're basking in the sun, and the next, you're caught in a surprise hailstorm that leaves you questioning every life choice leading to that moment. You might also encounter the local wildlife, which includes everything from prancing deer to the occasional fox that seems to judge you from a distance. "Look at that person with the camera," they'll think. "What are they doing in our neck of the woods?"

Let's not forget the town's infamous "Eads Days," an event that celebrates, well, Eads. There are parades, games, and food stands that make the county fair look like a Michelin-starred restaurant. Expect to see floats that could double as your neighbor's shed and pie-eating contests that leave you wondering if you'll ever eat dessert again. The only thing more entertaining than the festivities are the stories you'll hear about the folks who've been partaking in the festivities just a little too enthusiastically.

Eads, Colorado, is a town that might not be on everyone's bucket list, but it certainly has its charm. From the history that feels like a well-worn cowboy hat to the museums that could use a little more polish, Eads offers a quirky slice of Americana. Sure, you might not leave with your mind blown, but you'll definitely leave with a few good stories about a town that knows how to keep things interesting, even if it means embracing the oddity of life in the middle of nowhere. And who knows, you might just find that tumbleweed racing down the street is the most excitement you've had all week.

Eagle

Eagle, Colorado, is a place that has mastered the art of being both breathtakingly beautiful and amusingly uneventful. Nestled in the Vail Valley, this little gem could easily be mistaken for the world's largest postcard. Founded in the late 1800s, Eagle was originally a hub for mining, ranching, and probably the occasional cowboy duel. Today, it's a picturesque town where you can experience the beauty of the Rockies while wondering if there's actually anything to do aside from staring at mountains.

Let's start with the history, shall we? Eagle got its name because someone thought "Mountain Town #47" just didn't have the same ring to it. The area was originally inhabited by the Ute Indians, and they must have chuckled when they saw the settlers show up with their big dreams and even bigger hats. The town blossomed during the Gold Rush, but soon realized that mining was messy business. So, like any sensible place, it pivoted to a more leisurely lifestyle—cue the beautiful ski resorts and a complete shift in how locals define "hard work."

One of the main attractions in Eagle is the Eagle County Historical Museum. Picture it as a quaint little building where history goes to take a nap. You'll find artifacts from the town's mining days, complete with dust bunnies that might just qualify as historical relics themselves. The museum boasts everything from old mining tools to photographs of people who probably regretted wearing those outfits. It's the kind of place where you can marvel at how fashion has evolved—because let's face it, those old-timey hats deserve a comeback, if only for the laughs.

When you step into the museum, the first thing you'll notice is the overwhelming sense of quiet. It's like entering a library where everyone has decided to forget how to whisper. The curator, who probably knows every single detail about Eagle's history, may greet you with an enthusiasm reminiscent of someone who's just discovered coffee for the first time. "Did you know this town was once home to the largest gold nugget in the state?" they might say, eyes sparkling with excitement. Yes, we can see the spark; it's just overshadowed by the town's more recent claim to fame: being a peaceful getaway where the most drama you'll encounter is which flavor of ice cream to choose at the local parlor.

Speaking of ice cream, let's discuss the culinary scene in Eagle. If you're expecting Michelin-star dining, you might want to recalibrate your expectations. The local eateries serve up classic American fare, and you can find burgers and fries that would make your arteries sing. You'll feel right at home as you chow down on a burger that's approximately the size of your face, all while contemplating how your salad-eating days are behind you. And don't even get me started on the local coffee shop. It's a place where the coffee is strong, and the gossip is stronger. You'll hear about the latest mountain bike trails while pretending you didn't just struggle to figure out how to operate the espresso machine.

But let's not ignore the outdoor activities that Eagle touts with pride. If you enjoy skiing, hiking, and mountain biking, you're in for a treat. Eagle is surrounded by stunning landscapes that make you feel like you've stepped into a nature documentary. Just remember, while the scenery is gorgeous, the altitude can turn your casual hike into an aerobic nightmare. Don't be surprised if you find yourself gasping for breath halfway up a hill, wondering if that was really a mountain you just decided to conquer or simply a really large molehill.

One of the best-kept secrets in Eagle is the annual Eagle Outside Festival. It's a celebration of all things outdoorsy, with activities that range from stand-up paddleboarding to yoga classes where people attempt to balance on one leg while not thinking about how they just accidentally stepped in dog poop. Expect booths filled with locals trying to sell you everything from handcrafted jewelry to the latest in outdoor gear—because nothing says "I love nature" quite like $200 hiking boots that you'll only wear twice a year.

But not everything in Eagle is a walk in the park. Let's talk about the worst things to see and do, because every town has its quirks. First on the list: the local traffic. If you've ever been stuck behind a cow on a dirt road, you know the struggle. Eagle's traffic jams typically consist of a leisurely pace as a few cows amble their way to greener pastures, giving you plenty of time to contemplate your life choices. You'll sit there, engine idling, wondering if this is how nature intended it—stuck behind a cow while trying to get to the grocery store.

Another potential pitfall is the unpredictable weather. One moment you're basking in sunshine, and the next you're caught in a surprise snowstorm that leaves you questioning if you should have packed more than just sunscreen. You might even find yourself participating in the town's favorite sport: guessing whether the weather will cooperate with your outdoor plans or decide to throw a curveball just for fun.

Let's not forget the infamous Eagle Valley Library District, where silence is not only golden but the only option. If you dare to enter, prepare to tread lightly and avoid making any noise that might disturb the peace. The library is home to some of the most dedicated bookworms you'll ever encounter, who seem to believe that discussing the latest bestseller should be done in hushed tones, as if they're planning a secret mission.

Eagle, Colorado, is a town that blends beauty, history, and just a touch of absurdity. With its stunning scenery, charming museums, and outdoor activities galore, it's a place where you can experience the great outdoors while contemplating the oddities of life in a small town. Whether you're sipping coffee while watching the cows cross the road or finding yourself deep in conversation with the museum curator about the latest historical find, Eagle has a charm that can only be fully appreciated through laughter and a willingness to embrace its quirks. So, if you ever find yourself there, just remember: life is better with a side of humor, especially in a town where the most exciting thing may be watching the grass grow—or maybe that's just me.

Eaton

Eaton, Colorado, is a delightful little town that often finds itself overshadowed by its more flamboyant neighbors. Nestled in the northern part of the state, Eaton is like that dependable friend who always brings the chips to a party but never gets to choose the movie. Founded in the late 19th century, it was named after the local landowner, who probably thought "Eaton" was a much better idea than "The Place with the Cows." With its rich agricultural roots, Eaton has cultivated a reputation for being a peaceful, if not slightly quirky, slice of Americana.

The town's history is as colorful as its community events. Settled by farmers looking for fertile land, Eaton quickly became a hub for agriculture and, believe it or not, beet production. That's right—beets. The town may not have the glitz of the big cities, but it has its pride in those purple root vegetables. So, if you're wondering why beet-themed decor is a thing, it's because Eaton is ready to embrace its identity as "The Beet Capital of Colorado." Imagine the annual beet festival, where locals gather to discuss the merits of various beet recipes, all while sporting T-shirts that say, "I'm a BEET believer!"

Now, onto museums! You might think that in a town like Eaton, the museums would be sparse, but they're just hiding under a layer of beet juice. The Eaton Area Historical Society Museum is a small but mighty establishment that showcases the town's agricultural heritage. Inside, you'll find exhibits that include farming equipment so old it could probably be featured in a retirement home for rusty tools. Expect to see displays of life in the 1900s, complete with a charming little display about how people used to entertain themselves before Netflix and TikTok. Spoiler alert: it involved a lot of sitting around and hoping the crops didn't die.

The museum's curator, a delightful local character, is often seen guiding tours while wearing suspenders and a wide-brimmed hat, looking every bit like he just stepped out of a time machine from the 1950s. He'll regale you with stories of Eaton's founding fathers, who, rumor has it, had a passionate disagreement over the best way to cook beets. Visitors often leave feeling like they've just attended a quirky family reunion—minus the awkward small talk about everyone's latest ailments.

In terms of outdoor activities, Eaton's location provides some pretty scenic views, perfect for those Instagram posts that require a backdrop of mountains and greenery. You can stroll through parks that might feel more like a gathering place for squirrels than for people, but hey, it's a picturesque spot to have a picnic and contemplate life choices. Just don't be surprised if the local wildlife is more interested in your sandwich than you are.

One of the highlights in town is Eaton's annual Sweetheart Festival, where the community comes together to celebrate love and all things sweet. Think of it as a sugar-coated carnival of sorts, where you can indulge in baked goods that make your dentist's heart race. There's everything from pie-eating contests to a parade that features floats made entirely of cupcakes. It's a wonderland for the sweet-toothed, and it's hard to resist the allure of all that frosting. Just be careful, because after a few too many treats, you might find yourself thinking you're in a romantic comedy while trying to convince yourself that those beets really are good for you.

However, not everything in Eaton is as sweet as its festival. Let's talk about the less-than-stellar aspects of this charming town. First up, the local traffic situation. If you're expecting rush hour chaos, you'll be disappointed. In Eaton, rush hour consists of maybe two cars waiting behind a farmer's truck that's taking its sweet time. This can lead to some very passionate honking, which is basically just a friendly reminder that someone is mildly inconvenienced. It's hard to get too upset when you're stuck behind a truck loaded with freshly harvested beets, though—those roots have priorities!

Another interesting "attraction" is the infamous Eaton "Roundabout of Confusion." This roundabout is the pride and joy of local traffic engineers, who clearly got carried away with their love for circular intersections. Every year, tourists find themselves entering the roundabout, only to circle it like confused ducks trying to figure out which way to go. Locals have mastered the art of navigating it, but for outsiders, it can feel like you've stepped into a scene from "Alice in Wonderland," complete with a grinning Cheshire Cat urging you to "Take the second exit—no, the third one! Wait, what day is it?"

And let's not forget the local weather, which can be as unpredictable as a toddler with a sugar high. One minute you're basking in glorious sunshine, and the next you're caught in a surprise hailstorm that makes you question your life choices. It's the kind of weather that makes you wonder if Mother Nature has a vendetta against your plans. If you're planning a day out, just remember to bring a parka, a sunhat, and possibly a flotation device, because who knows what will happen next?

The local diner, while a staple for breakfast burritos and strong coffee, is also where dreams go to die—or at least where your waistline goes to expand. The portions are enormous, and the menu boasts items like "The Heartstopper"—a plate piled high with pancakes, bacon, and enough whipped cream to send your cardiologist into a fit. It's a place where you can find yourself in deep conversation with the waitstaff about the best ways to prepare beets, and you'll leave either completely satisfied or questioning all your dietary decisions.

Eckley

Eckley, Colorado, is a tiny dot on the map that many people have never heard of, and that's probably just how the residents like it. Nestled in Yuma County, this town has a history that could make even the most mundane road trip seem like a wild adventure—or at least a mildly interesting detour. Founded in the late 19th century, Eckley originally served as a bustling stopover for those heading west. Today, it's more of a "stop and wonder why" kind of place, where you can feel like you've stepped back in time to an era when the biggest excitement was getting a new mule.

Let's talk about the history of Eckley, which is about as colorful as a black-and-white film. Named after a local railroad official, the town blossomed in the late 1800s, thanks to its proximity to the railroad. The train brought in goods, settlers, and possibly an awkward number of singing cowboys who thought they could make it big. Over the years, the town has seen its fair share of ups and downs, much like your favorite roller coaster—if that coaster were made entirely of rusty nails and questionable engineering.

One of Eckley's most notable claims to fame is its place in the agricultural world. The town has a rich farming background, and you'll find locals who can tell you all about growing corn like it's a competitive sport. If there were awards for corn-growing, Eckley would probably have a trophy case filled with blue ribbons and possibly a giant ear of corn as the grand prize.

In terms of museums, Eckley isn't exactly overflowing with options. However, the Eckley Community Museum is a hidden gem that showcases the town's history and agricultural heritage. The museum is run by a lovely couple who are always ready to share stories that feel like they've been passed down through generations. The exhibits include farming tools so ancient they probably have their own social security numbers, and photographs of the town that make you wonder what hairstyles were really like in the 1920s. Spoiler alert: they were as questionable as you'd expect.

Visitors might find themselves wandering through the museum, nodding along as the curator passionately describes the significance of a plow that hasn't been used since the Great Depression. If you're lucky, you'll hear tales of the town's founding that will either make you laugh or convince you that life in the 1800s was one long episode of a reality show—without the cameras, of course.

For outdoor activities, Eckley has a few parks where you can spread a blanket, enjoy a picnic, and contemplate the complexities of life while being serenaded by the sound of crickets. There's not much in terms of organized fun, but you could always try your hand at some friendly corn tossing. Just be aware that if you throw it too far, you might start a turf war with a nearby cornfield that has dreams of its own.

Eckley's annual events are a delightful mix of tradition and small-town charm. The Harvest Festival is a highlight of the year, where locals gather to celebrate the fruits of their labor—literally. Expect a day filled with games that involve too many pies, corn mazes that are surprisingly easy to get lost in, and local crafts that could either be art or something your grandmother made after one too many glasses of sweet tea.

However, not everything in Eckley is as sweet as a piece of homemade apple pie. The town's biggest downside might be the "traffic." If you're imagining gridlock, you'd be mistaken. Here, "rush hour" is defined as the time it takes for two cars to cross paths, and that's only if one of them is a tractor. Getting stuck behind a tractor can feel like an Olympic sport in patience as you inch along at a thrilling speed of 2 miles per hour. This can lead to existential crises and deep philosophical debates about the meaning of life, or just a really awkward silence.

Another charming feature of Eckley is its unpredictable weather. One moment you're basking in the sun, and the next, a storm rolls in that seems to have taken a wrong turn at Albuquerque. It's the kind of place where you can experience all four seasons in a single day, so make sure to pack a parka, shorts, and possibly a flotation device—because who knows when it might rain?

Now let's not forget about the local diner, which serves up food that's comfortingly familiar yet slightly suspicious. The menu boasts items like the "Eckley Special," which is a heart attack on a plate, combining bacon, eggs, and enough grease to fuel a small car. It's the kind of meal that makes you question your life choices but is utterly irresistible at 2 a.m. when you've just spent the night in a corn maze and have convinced yourself that you deserve a reward.

The locals at the diner are a quirky bunch, always eager to strike up a conversation. You'll hear stories about the glory days of Eckley when the population boomed, and rumors about the mysterious ghost that supposedly haunts the old grain elevator. If you're brave enough to ask, you might even get the inside scoop on which local family has the best secret pie recipe. Just remember, it's best not to get involved in debates over whose cornbread is superior—those conversations can get heated faster than a chili cook-off.

In terms of nightlife, well, Eckley is pretty much a ghost town after dark. The streets might as well be rolled up tighter than a grandma's secret cookie recipe. If you're looking for vibrant nightlife, you'll need to set your sights on the nearest city. Here, the most exciting thing you'll find after sundown is the occasional coyote howling in the distance, or perhaps a raccoon that's taken an interest in your snacks.

To sum it all up, Eckley, Colorado, is a quirky little town that offers a slice of small-town life that you won't find in a guidebook. With its historical charm, occasional traffic jam behind a tractor, and festivals that celebrate everything from corn to community, Eckley stands out in its own peculiar way. It might not have the glitz and glamour of larger towns, but its uniqueness is what makes it special. So if you ever find yourself in Eckley, take a moment to embrace the quirks, savor the local pie, and consider the mystery of why anyone would want to grow beets in the first place.

Edwards

Edwards, Colorado, is that charming little nook nestled between Vail and Beaver Creek, which often feels like the quiet sibling who never quite gets the spotlight but has all the good stories. Founded in the 1870s, it started as a railroad stop—because who wouldn't want to hang out in a place with a name that sounds like a fancy law firm? Back then, it was mostly a hub for miners and ranchers, all looking to strike it rich or at least keep their livestock from wandering too far into the neighbor's backyard.

Today, Edwards has transformed into a vibrant community with a flair for outdoor sports and a unique knack for hosting events that can make even the most mundane Wednesday feel like a festival. But before we dive into the present-day shenanigans, let's take a stroll down memory lane and explore how Edwards came to be the place where "outdoor adventure" meets "why is my phone not getting service?"

The area was initially settled for its rich resources, which are the traditional gold, silver, and the occasional unfortunate decision to invest in a "surefire" mining venture. If you listen closely, you can almost hear the ghosts of miners debating whether they should have stuck to farming instead of chasing glitter. Today, the only thing glimmering in Edwards is the sun reflecting off the Vail River, which, spoiler alert, does not have any gold nuggets hiding in it.

For a glimpse into the town's history, the Edwards History Museum is a charming little spot that packs more nostalgia than a family reunion with your favorite distant cousin. Here, you'll find exhibits featuring old photographs of the town that will make you wonder how people ever lived without smartphones and Instagram filters. The curator, who is always eager to share tales of the "good old days," might even regale you with stories of how the first settlers celebrated a successful harvest. Hint: it involved way more potatoes than you'd expect.

Now, let's talk about the outdoor activities that Edwards has to offer, because if you didn't break a sweat while you were here, did you even visit Colorado? The area is a paradise for outdoor enthusiasts, with hiking trails that wind through stunning landscapes, making you question why you ever thought a couch was a valid substitute for nature. Edwards is surrounded by mountains that practically beg to be climbed, and rivers that tempt you to kayak—because nothing says "relaxation" like battling a current while trying not to capsize.

For the adventurous souls, there's the Vail Valley, where you can try your hand at mountain biking, skiing, or what locals like to call "extreme window shopping." Don't worry, though; the only danger you'll encounter is that of buying way too many overpriced souvenirs—like that artisan soap that smells like a lavender field and regret.

One of the best events in Edwards is the annual Edwards Arts Festival, where locals showcase their artistic talents and possibly some of the most bewildering sculptures you'll ever see. Think abstract art that looks like it was created during an impromptu game of charades with paint and random materials.

There's always live music, food vendors who serve everything from gourmet tacos to funnel cakes, and a healthy dose of people pretending to be more cultured than they really are.

If you're feeling particularly brave, make sure to visit the local brewery, which has become a staple in the community. Their craft beers are said to be the best in the valley—just don't ask how they came up with names like "Mountain Hops of Madness" or "Amber Avalanche." You might also encounter a few locals who will share stories that include a blend of bravado and "you had to be there" moments. Just be sure to smile and nod, even if they start discussing how they once wrestled a bear. (Spoiler: it was likely just a particularly bold raccoon.)

Of course, not everything in Edwards is sunshine and freshly brewed coffee. The winters can be brutal, turning this idyllic town into a snow globe of icy despair. Driving can feel like participating in a live-action version of Mario Kart, where the only power-up is your ability to slide gracefully into a snowbank. If you're not careful, you may find yourself in a snowdrift, contemplating the choices that led you to this moment. On the bright side, if you do get stuck, you'll have plenty of time to reflect on how your life choices led you to a mountain town instead of a tropical beach.

When it comes to food, Edwards has its fair share of eateries that range from quaint cafés to slightly overzealous fine dining. Don't be surprised if your plate arrives with a sprig of something that looks suspiciously like a weed. That's called "elevation dining," where the altitude adds flair to whatever you're eating. The local pizza joint is a favorite, known for its "mountain-sized" slices that are the perfect fuel for your next hike or, you know, just lounging around feeling like you've accomplished something for the day.

Let's not forget about the residents of Edwards, who are as colorful as the mountains that surround them. You'll find a mix of outdoor enthusiasts, artists, and maybe a few hermits who have perfected the art of living off the grid. They're a friendly bunch, always ready to share advice on the best hiking trails or where to find the biggest snowflakes. Just don't mention the last winter storm; it's a touchy subject for anyone still digging their car out.

Eldorado Springs

Eldorado Springs, Colorado, is the kind of place that sounds like a charming plot twist in a rom-com set in the Rockies, but trust me, it's even better than the script. Nestled just a hop, skip, and a caffeinated leap from Boulder, this tiny town is known for its natural mineral springs, making it feel like nature's version of a spa retreat—minus the overpriced facials and gossip about celebrities.

Historically, Eldorado Springs was established in the late 1800s, when settlers stumbled upon these bubbling springs and thought, "Hey, this could be the perfect place for a resort!" Little did they know, they were setting the stage for a town that would one day become the ultimate weekend getaway for people who love both relaxation and the occasional existential crisis while gazing into the water.

Now, if you think Eldorado Springs is all about serene landscapes and tranquil waters, think again. The town boasts a rich history that includes a variety of shenanigans. The original settlers, eager for a slice of the mineral-rich pie, built a hotel that quickly became a hot spot for those looking to soak away their worries—or at least pretend to while sipping on overly priced herbal tea. And if you believe the legends, some of those early guests were quite the characters, leaving behind tales of laughter, romance, and probably a fair share of misunderstandings involving sauna etiquette.

One of the best things to do in Eldorado Springs is visit the Eldorado Springs Pool. This isn't just any pool; it's fed by those famous mineral springs, which means you're literally swimming in nature's bubbly bathwater. Just be prepared for the occasional surprise from the local wildlife. You might find a duck paddling by, giving you the side-eye as if questioning your life choices. "What are you doing here, human? Can't you just waddle around like me?"

After your invigorating swim, it's time to take a hike. The area surrounding Eldorado Springs is a hiker's paradise, with trails that will make you feel like you're starring in your own nature documentary—complete with dramatic music and the occasional squirrel photobomb. The Eldorado Canyon State Park offers breathtaking views that will have you gasping in awe, but don't let that distract you from the fact that you might also be gasping because you're out of breath. It's all part of the experience.

For those interested in a little local culture, don't miss the Eldorado Springs Historic District. This quaint collection of buildings tells the story of the town's growth from a sleepy mineral springs getaway to a thriving community where the biggest debate is over which restaurant has the best nachos. Spoiler alert: it's all of them. The town has done a great job preserving its historic charm, and you can almost hear the whispers of the past, urging you to take a picture and post it online so everyone knows you're "living your best life" in Eldorado Springs.

As for museums, well, don't expect a sprawling art gallery filled with highbrow masterpieces. Instead, you'll find a charming little nod to the past at the Eldorado Springs Museum. Here, you can marvel at photographs and artifacts that chronicle the town's history. There's something oddly comforting about looking at sepia-toned photos of people who clearly had no idea what a smartphone was. It's a gentle reminder that while our gadgets may change, the quest for a good time and a refreshing drink remains timeless.

Now, let's talk food. The dining scene in Eldorado Springs is as varied as the hikers you'll encounter on the trails. You've got local cafes that serve up hearty breakfasts perfect for refueling after your early morning trek. Be sure to order the pancakes—fluffy clouds of goodness that will make you question every other pancake you've ever had. Then there's the charming little sandwich shop that prides itself on creating "the best sandwich in the universe." I didn't know we were in a galaxy far, far away, but if you're ever asked to choose between a BLT and a cosmic experience, just go with the sandwich. It's a safe bet.

As for the worst things to do in Eldorado Springs? Let's just say avoiding the hot springs in the middle of July is a good idea. If you think being boiled alive is a plot twist in a horror movie, just try sitting in 100-degree water while the sun blazes down. You'll question every decision that led you to this moment, especially when you see a perfectly content duck floating by, judging you for your poor life choices.

And then there's the weather. Ah, Colorado weather—where it can be sunny one moment and snowing the next. If you visit in spring, be prepared for a rollercoaster of temperatures that could make your head spin. You might leave the house in shorts and come back in snow pants. It's like nature is playing a prank on you, and you're just the punchline.

Despite its quirks, Eldorado Springs is the kind of place that stays in your heart long after you've left. It's a little slice of serenity amidst the hustle and bustle of modern life. Whether you're swimming in mineral springs, hiking through breathtaking landscapes, or simply enjoying a hearty meal while watching the sunset, you'll find a sense of peace that's as refreshing as the springs themselves.

Eldorado Springs, Colorado, might just be the perfect antidote to the chaos of everyday life. So grab your hiking boots, your sense of humor, and get ready to soak up everything this delightful town has to offer. Just remember to pack extra snacks for those hikes—you never know when a rogue squirrel might try to steal your trail mix.

Elizabeth

In the heart of Colorado lies Elizabeth, a town that feels like it was plucked straight from a Western movie set—complete with dusty roads and the faint sound of tumbleweeds rolling by. Established in the late 1800s, this charming little town has a history that could rival the plot of any low-budget indie film. Picture it: pioneers trekking through the wild, deciding that this would be the perfect spot to set up shop. Probably after a heated debate over which patch of land had the best view of the sunset.

In those early days, Elizabeth was a bustling stop for weary travelers, complete with a post office and a general store where everyone knew your name—mostly because they were all named something like "Bob" or "Maureen." Fast forward to today, and you'll find a community that has embraced its quaint charm while adding a sprinkle of modernity. Don't let the small-town vibe fool you; Elizabeth has an unexpected knack for surprising visitors.

One of the best things to do in Elizabeth is to visit the Elizabeth Historical Museum. Housed in an old church, this museum is the perfect place to immerse yourself in the town's storied past. You'll find artifacts that showcase everything from the town's founding to its quirky moments—like the time someone tried to host a chicken race and inadvertently turned it into a town-wide event. The museum's displays are like a time capsule, reminding you of a simpler era when people entertained themselves with farm animals and bad jokes instead of TikTok.

If you're in the mood for a bit of outdoor adventure, head over to the nearby Parker Jordan Centennial Open Space. This hidden gem offers a plethora of trails that will have you feeling like an intrepid explorer, or at least an adventurous hiker who forgot to bring water. The scenery is breathtaking, with views that will have you questioning why you ever thought a treadmill was sufficient exercise. Just remember, if you spot a deer staring at you, it's probably judging your life choices.

For those who prefer a more leisurely pace, the local parks in Elizabeth are perfect for picnicking. Grab a sandwich from one of the local delis and settle down under a tree. Just be careful not to attract the local squirrel population; these furry little thieves have a knack for snatching snacks faster than you can say "Where's my sandwich?"

As for dining options, Elizabeth has a handful of eateries that reflect the town's warm, welcoming spirit—or at least the spirit of its chefs. You might stumble upon a cozy diner that serves up breakfast all day. Here, the pancakes are larger than your head, and the coffee flows like a river. Be prepared for friendly banter from the staff, who might just become your best friends for the duration of your meal. Just remember to tip well; they're the real heroes behind your oversized plate of food.

Now, let's address the elephant in the room: the worst things about Elizabeth. First off, the weather can be as unpredictable as a cat on a hot tin roof. One minute you're basking in sunshine, and the next, you're caught in a sudden hailstorm. Always carry an umbrella and a good sense of humor; you never know when you'll need to improvise an impromptu rain dance.

Then there's the town's nightlife. If you're looking for a raging party scene, you might want to reconsider. Elizabeth is not exactly known for its clubs and late-night shenanigans. You'll find more excitement at the local coffee shop, where the biggest event is the weekly open mic night. Watch as local talents strut their stuff, from aspiring singers to poets who might need a bit more practice.

As for museums, there's the occasional quirky roadside attraction. One memorable site is the giant cowboy boot that serves as a landmark for visitors. You can't go wrong with a giant piece of footwear that feels like it's trying to escape the Wild West. It's a great photo op, and you can pretend you're a cowboy escaping the dangers of the modern world—like traffic and long grocery store lines.

Now, let's talk about festivals. Elizabeth hosts a number of small-town events throughout the year that are charming in their own right. The annual Elizabeth Stampede is a highlight, featuring rodeo events, food vendors, and enough cowboy hats to make you think you've wandered onto a film set. Just remember to bring your best western attire; you'll want to blend in with the locals who have a habit of looking like they just stepped off a horse—and some may actually have.

Empire

Empire, Colorado, is a tiny town nestled in the mountains, and it seems to have the same number of residents as it does opinions on whether it's a good idea to ski in shorts. With a population that hovers around 300, it feels like everyone knows each other—perhaps too well. Empire has a history as colorful as a winter coat on a summer day, having started as a mining hub during the Gold Rush. Picture prospectors with beards and dreams, scurrying around hoping to strike it rich, probably while yelling "Eureka!" at an alarming volume.

The town was founded in the 1860s and quickly became a hot spot for gold and silver mining, which is a fancy way of saying that some people got very rich, and many more ended up with dirt under their fingernails and zero gold to show for it. Fast forward to today, and you'll find that Empire is a blend of Old West charm and the modern-age mystery of how it has stayed off the radar while being so close to larger towns like Georgetown and Winter Park. One can only assume the townsfolk have perfected the art of camouflage, or maybe they just hide from the tourists in their incredibly cozy homes.

When it comes to attractions, Empire boasts the iconic *St. Mary's Glacier*, a delightful spot for both summer hikes and winter snowball fights. Just don't be surprised if you encounter more snow than you bargained for, because Mother Nature clearly has a sense of humor. The glacier is not so much a "glacier" as it is a patch of ice that stubbornly refuses to melt, and on a hot day, it can feel like a bizarre oasis of cold. The views are stunning, and you might even find yourself wondering if you're on a set for a reality show about hiking disasters.

For a historical twist, you might check out the *Empire Museum*, which feels like stepping into a time capsule that's somehow still relevant today. Filled with artifacts from the mining days and local lore, the museum's exhibits are a tribute to the tenacity of the folks who lived here. You'll find pictures of miners with their questionable fashion choices and stories that make you grateful for modern plumbing. It's the kind of place where you can learn about the struggles and triumphs of the past while feeling very much like you could win a local trivia night just by showing up.

Then there's the *Saddleback Golf Club*, which is less a place to work on your swing and more a backdrop for "what were they thinking?" photos. The golf course features views that are nothing short of breathtaking—assuming you can breathe after climbing the steep hills. For the casual golfer, it's a great way to play a round while simultaneously engaging in cardio. Just watch out for the wildlife; the deer here have an attitude and will likely judge your swing just as harshly as you do.

As for dining, Empire offers a few delightful spots where you can refuel after all that hiking and golfing. The local diners serve up comfort food with a twist, and the waitstaff knows how to keep you entertained with tales of ghost sightings and questionable life choices. The food is hearty, and you'll probably walk away feeling like you've eaten an entire bear. Just make sure you don't go during peak hours unless you enjoy waiting longer than it takes to build a log cabin.

On the flip side, let's address the "worst" things about Empire. First off, it's small. Like, "you could probably walk the length of the town in less than ten minutes" small. If you're looking for nightlife, you might be better off inventing a fun activity—like watching the grass grow or counting the number of stars in the sky. After dark, the town feels eerily quiet, like a movie set where they forgot to cast the extras. If you're afraid of the dark, just make sure you bring a good flashlight, because the only thing more terrifying than being alone in Empire at night is tripping over a rogue rock.

If museums and nature aren't your thing, you might try to find entertainment by engaging with the locals. Their stories are often laced with humor and a touch of mischief, but be prepared for some tall tales. You might hear about how someone once caught a fish so big that it had to be displayed in the local bar for two weeks before it could be stuffed and mounted—though you may also hear that the fish was actually a mere trout that was cleverly photo-shopped to look larger.

Lastly, no visit to Empire would be complete without a trip to the *Georgetown Loop Railroad*. While technically not in Empire, it's close enough that you could claim you went to the coolest train ride in the area. You'll hop on a vintage steam locomotive, which is a great excuse to wear your best "I'm a time traveler" outfit. The ride offers views of the beautiful Colorado mountains and a glimpse into the old mining history, all while making you feel like you're in an episode of a classic Western.

Englewood

Englewood, Colorado, is a charming little slice of suburbia that somehow manages to blend the essence of a bustling town with the laid-back vibes of your favorite aunt's living room. With a population that hovers around 35,000, it's big enough to avoid awkward small talk with everyone at the grocery store, but small enough that you might still bump into your ex at the local coffee shop. The town has an interesting history, originally founded in the late 1800s as a railroad stop. Back then, it was a simple farming community, where crops grew like weeds and life was as easygoing as a Sunday afternoon nap.

Fast forward to the 20th century, and Englewood morphed into a bustling suburb of Denver, bringing with it a mix of residential charm and the kind of traffic that can make you question your life choices. The name "Englewood" is said to have been inspired by a picturesque spot in New Jersey, but you won't find any swamps or marshlands here—unless you count the parking lots after a good rain.

One of the town's hidden gems is the Englewood Historical Society, which operates out of the Englewood Depot. This museum is a tiny time capsule that showcases the town's rich history through artifacts, photographs, and stories that will make you feel like a time traveler. There's something oddly comforting about learning that your favorite local diner has been serving pancakes since before the invention of sliced bread. The museum's exhibits can lead you on a journey through the past, complete with tales of the town's founding families and their dubious fashion choices. Pro tip: do not ask about the infamous "cowboy hat" incident of 1923 unless you're ready for an hour-long saga.

Now, if you're looking to experience the great outdoors without hiking a mountain or risking a bear encounter, Englewood offers a lovely array of parks. One standout is Belleview Park, which is basically a mini Disneyland for kids, complete with a petting zoo, train rides, and enough playground equipment to keep children busy while parents sip overpriced lattes and contemplate their life choices. Just be wary of the goats—they're cute but conniving, and they have a way of sneaking up on you when you least expect it, probably plotting some kind of goat rebellion.

For the culturally inclined, the Town Center at Englewood is home to the engaging Englewood Arts program, which hosts art exhibitions, live performances, and the occasional interpretive dance that leaves you questioning what you just saw. If you're lucky, you might catch a local band that makes you feel nostalgic for that garage band phase you swore you'd never revisit. The talent can range from impressive to "let's just say they're getting better" in a matter of minutes, and every performance is a reminder that Englewood has a vibrant arts scene just waiting to be discovered—if you're brave enough to venture out.

But every rose has its thorns, and Englewood is no exception. While the town has its fair share of attractions, let's not ignore the not-so-glamorous side of suburbia. Take, for instance, the traffic. The roads can be busier than a bee hive on a sugar high, especially during rush hour when everyone suddenly remembers they need to be somewhere ten minutes ago. If you have plans, leave an hour early, or just accept that you'll be fashionably late—forever.

Then there's the matter of the local cuisine. While Englewood boasts some great eateries, you might find yourself faced with an existential crisis while dining at a chain restaurant that claims to offer "authentic cuisine." You know the type: a menu that's thicker than a textbook and about as reliable as a fortune teller who just got out of a bad relationship. The food can be hit or miss; you might have a fantastic taco one day, only to bite into a flavorless brick of sadness the next. It's a culinary roulette, and sometimes you walk away with a full stomach, and other times, you just walk away.

Speaking of walking, Englewood is home to the famous "Englewood Civic Center," where you can engage in all sorts of civic-minded activities, from city meetings to recreational classes that promise to teach you everything from pottery to pickleball. The facilities are top-notch, and you might find yourself signing up for a class you have absolutely no business being in. Spoiler alert: if you can't tell the difference between a clay pot and a modern art installation, pottery class might not be your thing.

If you're up for some nightlife, Englewood isn't exactly known for its bustling party scene. You won't find clubs pulsating with beats, but there are a few bars where the locals gather to enjoy a drink or two. Just be prepared for a lot of conversation about the weather, the Broncos, and the occasional unsolicited opinion about politics that's more entertaining than a sitcom. The vibe is chill, and you might find yourself swapping stories with strangers who have a surprisingly extensive knowledge of Englewood trivia.

Finally, don't forget to check out the local shopping scene. The South Broadway area is lined with quirky shops, vintage stores, and all the thrift shops you could ever want. If you're looking for a one-of-a-kind outfit, this is the place to find that perfect vintage jacket that will have you saying, "I'm just quirky enough to pull this off." Or you might find a gem like an old vinyl record of an obscure band that was probably popular for five minutes in the '70s, and it's the perfect conversation starter—just not a great dance partner.

Englewood, Colorado, is a delightful mix of history, culture, and everyday quirks. It has its ups and downs, but if you're ready for some local charm, a hint of chaos, and the occasional goat encounter, you'll find yourself enjoying everything this suburb has to offer. Just remember, whether you're wandering through the historical society or dodging traffic, you're in for an adventure that's equal parts fascinating and hilariously unpredictable. And if all else fails, you can always join a pottery class, because who doesn't want to create a masterpiece that might just resemble a lumpy rock?

Erie

In the charming little town of Erie, Colorado, which is nestled snugly between Boulder and Denver, history and hilarity collide in a delightful mess of small-town quirks and suburban oddities. Originally established as a coal mining town in the late 1800s, Erie has transformed over the years from a gritty mining hub into a picturesque suburb with more new developments than you can shake a stick at. If the pioneers could see it now, they'd likely be confused—"Wait, where are the saloons and the gold rush? Is that a Starbucks?"

One of Erie's historical claims to fame is its namesake, the Erie Canal, which had nothing to do with this town but is a fantastic conversation starter at local coffee shops. You could almost hear the town's founders saying, "Hey, let's name our town after something famous. Who cares if it's in New York?" And thus, Erie was born, accompanied by an identity crisis that would echo through the ages.

As you stroll through downtown Erie, you might stumble upon the Erie Historical Society, which operates out of a quaint little building that looks like it was plucked straight from a Hallmark movie set. The museum is a treasure trove of artifacts from the town's coal mining days, and it's the kind of place where you can learn about the history of the town while secretly hoping they don't ask you to participate in a reenactment. Imagine donning a miner's helmet and being asked to shovel coal for the sake of "educational value." No thank you!

While you're at the historical society, take a moment to appreciate the plethora of photos showing the original Erie. They are charming, but if you squint hard enough, they almost look like they could be mistaken for black-and-white selfies from the Victorian era. The museum offers a delightful glimpse into the past, complete with stories of the town's founders who probably spent more time arguing about the best coal seam than they did planning for a future full of Starbucks.

Erie also has an impressive array of parks that would make any nature lover weep with joy—or at least sneeze a little from the pollen. One standout is the Erie Community Park, which boasts trails, sports fields, and a lake that is rumored to house more ducks than actual people. The ducks have formed a sort of union and occasionally hold meetings about their rights to bread crumbs, much to the dismay of local children trying to enjoy a day out. If you ever find yourself in a duck standoff, just remember: they're way more organized than you'd think.

If you're into art, Erie won't let you down. The town has a public art program that features installations scattered throughout, which is great if you enjoy strolling around with your coffee, pondering the meaning of abstract sculptures that look like they were made by a toddler on a sugar high. The local arts scene has a bit of everything—paintings, sculptures, and the occasional art piece that will have you scratching your head, thinking, "Is that a giant metal chicken or a tribute to the world's worst family reunion?"

When it comes to dining, Erie has plenty of options, but the culinary scene can be as unpredictable as a game of musical chairs. You might find yourself at a local diner where the special of the day is a mystery meat sandwich that promises to be "like nothing you've ever tasted!" which is both terrifying and strangely appealing. The town boasts a mix of chain restaurants and local spots that will make you feel like you've accidentally stepped into an alternate universe where food is either gourmet or takes "frozen" to a whole new level.

And let's talk about the events. Erie hosts an annual "Erie Town Fair," where you can enjoy carnival rides, food vendors, and the chance to participate in pie-eating contests. Just imagine: you, your friends, and an excessive amount of pie, all while trying not to get whipped cream in your hair. It's a classic small-town affair that draws in the crowds like moths to a flame, with everyone desperately hoping their kids won't end up in a giant inflatable bouncy house, leading to what could only be described as the "Bouncy House Apocalypse."

Now, every town has its secrets, and Erie is no exception. While on the surface it seems like a peaceful suburban paradise, there are whispers of the "Erie Ghosts." Local lore suggests that the ghosts of miners from the town's coal mining days roam the streets at night, possibly looking for their long-lost lunch pails. As someone strolls past the historical society, they might just hear a distant voice lamenting, "Why did I choose a career in coal mining? I could've been a barista!"

If you're searching for something a little more thrilling, Erie does have its share of local legends, including tales of strange lights appearing in the sky, prompting UFO enthusiasts to gather like moths to a porch light, hoping to catch a glimpse of intergalactic visitors. Nothing says "small town" like an evening spent looking up at the stars and wondering if that blinking light is a spaceship or just your neighbor's annoying porch light.

Shopping in Erie is a mixed bag. On one hand, you can find local boutiques that sell everything from handmade crafts to bizarre trinkets that you'll want to buy just for the story. On the other hand, you might accidentally walk into a store that seems like a front for something much more sinister, like an underground cat cult. Beware of the cat lady at the counter—her collection of feline figurines is impressive, but the intense gaze may haunt you for weeks.

As the sun sets, Erie takes on a different character, and you might find yourself contemplating whether to hit a local bar or simply head home to binge-watch your favorite show. The nightlife scene can be a bit subdued, but there are a few spots where you can grab a drink and experience the local gossip—usually revolving around who's got the best lawn or who accidentally mowed down the neighbor's prize-winning flower bed.

Estes Park

Estes Park, Colorado, is that picturesque mountain town that seems to have been plucked right out of a postcard, complete with stunning views, quaint shops, and enough tourists to make even the most patient person question their life choices. Nestled at the entrance of Rocky Mountain National Park, Estes Park is like that friend who always seems to have everything together, but you know deep down they're just one bad hair day away from chaos.

Let's kick things off with a bit of history. Estes Park was named after a certain William Estes, who probably thought, "Hey, this place is nice, let's slap my name on it!" The town has a long history of attracting adventurous spirits, from the Ute Native Americans who called it home to early settlers who thought living in the mountains sounded like a fantastic idea—until winter hit and they realized their biggest challenge was keeping warm without becoming dinner for bears.

One of the town's shining jewels is the Estes Park Museum, where you can dive deep into the town's history without drowning in boredom. You'll find artifacts ranging from old mining tools to the town's original zoning laws, which were probably just a list of "Don't build your house too close to the bears." The museum is charmingly quaint, featuring exhibits that remind you of your great-aunt's attic, minus the questionable taxidermy. The best part is the stories of the town's founders, who had dreams as big as the mountains but likely spent a lot of time trying to figure out how to keep their coffee warm in the unpredictable weather.

Speaking of weather, let's talk about the seasonal attractions. In winter, Estes Park transforms into a snowy wonderland, perfect for skiing, snowshoeing, or taking a picturesque sleigh ride. Just don't forget to bring your warmest gear, or you'll be the one in the group who looks like a popsicle with legs. If you're lucky, you might even witness the majestic elk rutting season in the fall, when the elk strut their stuff like they're auditioning for a reality show. Seriously, these guys are dramatic. Just make sure to keep a safe distance unless you want to be on the receiving end of a loud bugle call that sounds suspiciously like a foghorn.

When it comes to food, Estes Park doesn't disappoint, offering a mix of quaint cafés and more upscale dining options. One of the town's culinary claims to fame is its fudge shops, which are basically chocolate temples. But proceed with caution; the aroma alone might have you floating out of your diet plan. You could wander into a local bakery and leave with a slice of pie bigger than your head, thinking, "I can totally eat this for breakfast!" The downside? You might end up in a food coma on the nearest park bench, dreaming of a simpler time when your biggest worry was how to avoid chores.

Let's not forget about the annual events that make Estes Park a local favorite. There's the Estes Park Elk Festival, where the community celebrates its resident elk population with everything from educational talks to the questionable tradition of "Elk Calling." You haven't lived until you've witnessed someone trying to mimic an elk call, resulting in a sound that can only be described as a mating call gone horribly wrong. And yes, people will cheer as if it's the highlight of the day.

Another fun event is the Estes Park Music Festival, where you can enjoy live music while surrounded by the beauty of the Rockies. This is where you can sip craft beer while pretending to be cultured. Just remember, there's a fine line between appreciating the arts and wondering if you should have taken that music class in high school.

If you're feeling adventurous, take a drive up the Peak to Peak Highway. This scenic byway will have you questioning how many scenic overlooks you can actually handle. Spoiler: a lot. Each viewpoint is more breathtaking than the last, and by the time you reach the top, you'll feel like a mountain guru, complete with the wisdom of a thousand peaks. Just keep your eyes on the road, because nothing ruins a good mountain vibe like a squirrel darting across at the wrong moment.

For those seeking a more peaceful experience, the Stanley Hotel is a must-visit. It's not just a beautiful piece of architecture; it's also the inspiration for Stephen King's "The Shining." Yes, that means you can sip tea in the lobby while wondering if the ghost of a former guest is watching you make a fool of yourself. If you're brave enough, take a ghost tour at night. Just imagine wandering through a supposedly haunted hotel, trying to convince yourself that the icy chill down your spine is just a draft from the window and not a ghost with unfinished business.

Now, let's be real about the downsides of visiting Estes Park. First, there's the parking situation. It's a game of musical chairs, except the chairs are limited and the music never stops. You might find yourself circling the same block multiple times, mentally composing an ode to the parking gods who clearly favor only the lucky few. If you're not careful, you could end up parked several miles away and have to hike back in what feels like a mini-mountain expedition, complete with the right footwear and a map that might as well be written in hieroglyphics.

Also, be prepared for the tourist crowds. If you've ever dreamed of experiencing the joy of shoulder-to-shoulder walking while trying to find a good photo spot, Estes Park is your Mecca. Nothing says "serenity" like trying to capture the perfect mountain backdrop while dodging selfie sticks and groups of people in matching t-shirts. Just remember to smile and wave like you're in a bizarre reality show.

Estes Park is a delightful blend of history, stunning nature, and quirky attractions that make it one of Colorado's hidden gems—if you can call a town this popular a "hidden gem." Whether you're exploring the museums, hiking in the mountains, or simply indulging in some delicious fudge, there's something for everyone. Just remember to pack your patience, your best hiking boots, and a good sense of humor because in Estes Park, every day is an adventure, and you never know when a rogue elk might make a guest appearance. Oh, and if you happen to spot a ghost, just smile and say, "Hi, Stephen!"

Evans

Evans, Colorado, is one of those towns that many people pass through on their way to bigger destinations, but it's like that unassuming friend who surprises you with their knowledge of obscure trivia. You think you know them, and then they drop a fun fact about the history of sock knitting, and suddenly, you're intrigued. Located near Greeley, Evans has a history that could fill a small book—if that book were more of a pamphlet. It was established in the late 19th century, originally as a railroad town. Apparently, the railroad thought, "Let's plop a town down here," and thus Evans was born.

Now, let's dive into the charmingly mediocre attractions that Evans has to offer. First up, there's the Evans Community Complex. It sounds fancy, doesn't it? But it's really just a multipurpose facility where you can find everything from community meetings to the occasional roller derby. Imagine people zipping around in skates while you wonder if you should have brought a helmet and knee pads. The real highlight, though, is the giant inflatable slide that occasionally pops up at community events. Nothing screams "We take safety seriously" like watching adults hurl themselves down a bouncy slide with the enthusiasm of children on sugar highs.

If you're in the mood for a museum, you might want to adjust your expectations. Evans doesn't boast the Louvre or even a local art gallery that displays more than just finger paintings, but it does have the Evans Historical Society. It's a treasure trove of local artifacts that will make you think, "Wow, I never knew people collected this stuff!" You'll find everything from old photographs to historical documents that tell the tale of Evans as a once-thriving railroad town. The best part? You can leave feeling like you've just completed a PhD in local history without the student loans.

Food in Evans is where things get interesting—or should I say, "mysterious"? There's a local diner that's a bit of a culinary enigma. You might walk in expecting the usual greasy spoon fare, but end up with a dish that looks like it was created in a fever dream. One day, you'll find a plate of spaghetti smothered in a mysterious sauce that you can't quite place, while the next day you could be staring at a burger topped with jalapeños and something that may or may not be a slice of pizza. Dining in Evans is like playing a game of roulette—except if you lose, you just end up with an interesting story to tell your friends later.

And speaking of interesting stories, let's talk about the Evans River Park. It's a lovely spot for a stroll, but beware: you might get waylaid by some enthusiastic fishermen trying to convince you that the trout are biting like it's the last supper. "Just cast your line, and you'll catch something!" they'll say, as you nod politely, trying to remember if you've ever actually fished before. The park has trails for walking, biking, or just contemplating your life choices while surrounded by nature. Just make sure to keep an eye on your sandwich; local ducks are experts at swooping in when you least expect it.

When it comes to events, Evans has its fair share of community gatherings that can only be described as "small-town charming." The annual Evans Family Festival is a true spectacle of local culture. You can expect carnival rides, games, and more fried food than you can shake a stick at. There's even a pie-eating contest that will have you questioning your life choices. You think, "I can definitely eat four slices," but halfway through, you're left regretting every decision that led to this moment. If you make it to the finals, congratulations! You've officially entered the realm of local legend.

Of course, the festival wouldn't be complete without live music. You'll be treated to performances by local bands, some of which are surprisingly good, while others sound like they just learned to play their instruments yesterday. But hey, it's all in good fun! You'll sway along with your fellow festival-goers, who are probably just as confused about the lyrics as you are, while enjoying the festival's "artistic" interpretation of pop songs.

As for the worst things to do in Evans, you might want to avoid the old, abandoned schoolhouse. It's not officially on any tourist maps, but if you're feeling adventurous, take a stroll by. Rumor has it that it's haunted—by the ghosts of all the homework that was never completed. You could stand outside and try to hear the faint echoes of old math problems or even worse, the sound of gym class dodgeballs. It's best to admire from a distance, lest you start getting ideas about "urban exploration" and end up in a web of questionable choices. (I'm kidding, but only about the homework.)

One last note about Evans: it's a place where people know each other. If you're wandering around and accidentally get lost, don't worry. Someone will inevitably stop and offer you directions—or invite you to a barbecue. That's just how small towns roll. You could show up thinking it's a friendly invitation only to find yourself in a discussion about the local high school football team. Be prepared to nod along, feigning interest in the details of the last game and why "that one ref was the worst."

In the end, Evans, Colorado, is like a quirky aunt at a family reunion. You might not see her every day, but when you do, she's always got a story to tell and a snack to share. Whether you're hanging out at the community complex, diving into local history, or trying to navigate the local culinary scene, there's an undeniable charm to this small town. Just remember to keep your expectations in check and enjoy the ride—because in Evans, the journey is half the fun. And who knows? You might leave with a story about the time you accidentally joined a pie-eating contest or almost went fishing with a local who believed he was the trout whisperer.

Evergreen

Evergreen, Colorado, is that charming mountain town that looks like it was plucked straight out of a Hallmark movie, complete with picturesque scenery and a plot twist or two. Nestled in the foothills of the Rocky Mountains, Evergreen is a blend of natural beauty, quirky local legends, and just the right amount of touristy charm. Historically, this area was a hot spot for gold miners in the late 19th century, who probably thought, "Hey, let's dig through some rocks and see if we can find a shiny thing." Spoiler alert: they did, but that shiny thing led to a whole lot of trouble and a town that's still recovering from a serious case of "What do we do now?"

Fast forward to today, and Evergreen has transformed into a community that's half "outdoorsy nature enthusiasts" and half "let's sip lattes and pretend we're on a wellness retreat." Hiking trails abound, and if you wander around, you'll likely bump into folks dressed in gear that looks like it's more suited for a Vogue photoshoot than a trek through the woods. You can practically hear them thinking, "If my Instagram isn't stunning, did I even hike?"

One of the best things to do in Evergreen is to visit Evergreen Lake, which is not just a body of water but a magical realm where locals convene for paddleboarding, fishing, and maybe even a spontaneous duck conversation. The lake is surrounded by mountains, and you can find people jogging, walking their dogs, or attempting to look casual while trying not to trip over tree roots. If you're feeling particularly ambitious, rent a paddleboat and try to look graceful while you awkwardly navigate the water. Just be careful not to splash any unsuspecting ducks; they may not take kindly to your aquatic shenanigans.

Now, let's talk about the museums. Evergreen boasts the Evergreen Historical Society, which sounds sophisticated until you realize that it's essentially a collection of local artifacts that someone's grandma might have donated. Expect to see items like antique farm equipment, an old horse saddle, and photos of people who definitely looked like they were having a great time in black and white. The highlight, however, is the famed "Hall of Really Old Stuff," where you can ponder the question, "Did people really live without Wi-Fi?" as you look at the remnants of life from the days when you had to talk to your neighbors instead of scrolling through social media.

If you're in the mood for something more culturally enriching, check out the Center for the Arts Evergreen. Here, you can marvel at local artwork, watch performances that might range from the sublime to the bewilderingly avant-garde, and occasionally attend a workshop where you can learn to paint like a true Coloradoan. Just be ready to embrace your inner artist while trying not to spill paint on your clothes—because nothing says "I'm a serious painter" like a tie-dye look from an accidental encounter with a paintbrush.

As for dining, Evergreen has its fair share of culinary delights, or at least that's what the menus will have you believe. You can find everything from cozy coffee shops to restaurants serving up dishes that sound so gourmet you might need a dictionary to understand them. Ever had lavender-infused quinoa with a drizzle of artisanal olive oil? You might in Evergreen! But beware: you might also find yourself in a small café that serves a burger that's more bun than patty. That's right; you might just be paying for a very overpriced sandwich experience, so make sure to read the fine print. It's a gamble, much like your chances of running into a celebrity—because nothing says "I'm in Colorado" like spotting a star on a nature walk and wondering if they, too, are questioning their life choices while hiking.

And speaking of life choices, let's address the "worst" things to do in Evergreen, which could include hiking during a snowstorm. Sure, you might think you're the next great mountain adventurer, but soon you'll be contemplating your decisions while trying to stay upright on a slippery slope. There's also a local bar that, depending on the night, can either be a fun night out or a wild karaoke showdown where everyone suddenly believes they're a rock star. Spoiler alert: they're not. You'll be treated to renditions of 80s ballads that sound more like cats fighting than an actual musical number.

Evergreen is also famous for its events, like the annual Evergreen Rodeo. Yes, folks, it's a genuine rodeo, and nothing says "mountain town" quite like watching cowboys attempt to ride bulls while you sit in the stands, munching on cotton candy and wondering how you got roped into this. And let's not forget the parade, where you can enjoy floats that range from the heartwarming to the "Did they really just put that on a truck?" While you're there, don't miss the opportunity to catch a few candy bars tossed from the floats, but brace yourself: the competition is fierce, and you might need to elbow a toddler or two to secure your prize.

For outdoor enthusiasts, the Evergreen Open Space offers more trails than you can shake a walking stick at. You could spend hours wandering around, feeling one with nature, only to realize you've somehow ended up on a trail that's far less picturesque and much more "Why did I think this was a good idea?" It's not uncommon to hear someone mutter, "This doesn't look like the map," as they ponder their life choices.

Evergreen is a place that blends quirky charm with mountain majesty, offering a unique experience that's as delightful as it is bewildering. From paddleboarding on the lake to engaging in heated discussions about the best hiking trails, this little town is packed with surprises. You'll leave with stories that are better than any Instagram filter and maybe even a newfound appreciation for the simple joys of life—like a great cup of coffee or a perfectly questionable burger. And if you happen to bump into a local while you're there, just remember: they're probably just as confused about why they live in a town filled with ducks and old farming tools as you are.

Fairplay

Fairplay, Colorado, is the kind of town that makes you wonder if you've accidentally stepped onto a movie set from the Wild West—complete with tumbleweeds, cowboy hats, and more quirky characters than you can shake a stick at. Nestled at the foot of the majestic Mosquito Range, this charming little gem has a history as rich as the gold miners who flocked here during the 1859 gold rush. Yes, gold! The shiny stuff that led to more dreams, schemes, and poor life choices than any reality TV show could ever capture.

In its heyday, Fairplay was the bustling hub for prospectors looking to strike it rich. The town has seen its fair share of colorful characters, from miners who thought they could find gold in their morning coffee to merchants who realized selling shovels was a much more stable business plan. Fairplay even claims to be the inspiration for the fictional South Park, which means you can expect a healthy dose of absurdity alongside your scenic views.

One of the best things to do in Fairplay is to visit the South Park Historical Society Museum. Here, you can dive deep into the local lore, marvel at artifacts that look like they've been pulled straight from a time capsule, and contemplate why people thought it was a good idea to wear such uncomfortable clothing. Expect exhibits featuring everything from old mining tools to black-and-white photos of folks who looked suspiciously like they were in a perpetual state of confusion. You might even stumble upon a section dedicated to the infamous "Lost Treasure of Fairplay," which is less about actual treasure and more about the town's ability to lose any semblance of reality when it comes to local legends.

If you're feeling adventurous, head over to the nearby Mosquito Pass, one of the highest automobile passes in North America. Driving up there is like participating in a high-stakes game of "Will I make it, or will I end up stuck in a snowdrift?" The views are breathtaking, and you might find yourself wondering if you've accidentally stumbled into a postcard. Just be careful of the altitude; one too many selfies might leave you gasping for breath—both from the beauty and the sheer ridiculousness of your friends' poses.

Fairplay also has its fair share of outdoor activities, with hiking trails that range from "Oh, this is lovely" to "What in the world was I thinking?" Make sure to pack plenty of water because getting lost on a mountain trail can lead to some very philosophical conversations with yourself about life choices. And if you're lucky, you might even spot some wildlife. Just remember: if you see a moose, it's probably more interested in munching grass than in becoming your new best friend.

For those who fancy a more relaxed outing, the local eateries offer a variety of culinary experiences that are as varied as the town itself. You can find everything from down-home diners serving up burgers that could double as doorstops to cafes that act like they're in a cooking competition. Just be prepared for the occasional dish that might have you questioning the chef's sanity. "Is this a chili or a science experiment?" you may find yourself wondering as you take a brave bite.

Now, let's take a moment to talk about the best and worst things to do in Fairplay. On the "best" list, you have the annual Fairplay Colorado BBQ Challenge, where you can feast on smoked meats so good you'll forget your own name. It's an event that draws locals and tourists alike, all hoping to snag the title of BBQ champion while debating the finer points of sauce versus rub. Spoiler alert: no one really agrees, and the arguments often end in laughter and a collective decision to just eat more barbecue.

On the "worst" side, you might want to steer clear of the ghost tours. Yes, Fairplay is proud of its spooky history, and nothing says "fun" quite like wandering around a graveyard at night while someone tries to convince you that the spirit of a long-dead miner is following you. Sure, it sounds like a blast until you realize that the real horror is how much your friends are laughing at your nervous reactions.

One particularly memorable attraction is the iconic Fairplay Beach. Yes, beach. In the mountains. It's a small stretch of sand where you can spread out your towel and pretend you're at a tropical resort while the nearest lake is a brisk hike away. It's the kind of place that reminds you that sometimes, even in Colorado, you need a little imagination to enjoy the great outdoors. Just be prepared for the locals to look at you like you're a little unhinged for trying to tan in the high-altitude sun.

As you wander the town, you'll also come across the old Fairplay Town Hall. This historic building is a reminder of a time when town meetings didn't involve Zoom calls and endless debates about who forgot to bring snacks. Instead, it served as a community hub where residents gathered to discuss everything from road maintenance to the mysterious disappearance of the town's best pie recipe. One can only imagine the heated discussions that took place over such critical matters.

In Fairplay, you'll find a community that embraces its quirks, celebrates its history, and might just make you question your own sanity as you explore the eccentricities of life in a small mountain town. From the bizarre artifacts in the museum to the delightful oddities of local events, Fairplay is a place where laughter and adventure await at every turn. Whether you're hiking through stunning landscapes or contemplating the meaning of life over a plate of barbecue, this town offers a unique blend of experiences that are bound to leave you with stories to tell—and perhaps a newfound appreciation for the absurdity of it all. And who knows? You might just find yourself falling in love with a little slice of Colorado history that's as entertaining as it is picturesque.

Firestone

Firestone, Colorado, is one of those towns that seems to have more charm than residents, a place where the past and present collide in a delightful dance of contradictions. Nestled in the northern part of the state, it's a place where history lurks around every corner, mostly because the town itself has seen more changes than a soap opera character during a plot twist.

Firestone started as a sleepy little community in the late 1800s, born from the dreams of coal miners and railroad workers. The town was named after the Firestone family, who were all about innovation—much like the famous tire company, minus the rubber. You won't find tire factories here, but you will discover a town that has somehow transformed itself into a thriving suburb of Denver while still holding onto its quirky roots. It's a classic case of "I'm not lost, I'm exploring!" for those who think they've accidentally taken a wrong turn on the way to the mountains.

One of the first stops on any trip through Firestone should be the local museum, which might be less museum and more "let's cram a bunch of old stuff into one room and hope people enjoy it." It's the kind of place where you can gaze at artifacts that make you ponder how people ever survived without smartphones and Wi-Fi. Expect to see an array of intriguing items, from antique farming equipment to a collection of photos that look like they were taken with a potato. The curators, who likely have a deep passion for local history, are more than happy to share tales of the town's colorful past, often peppered with "Can you believe this?" and "What were they thinking?"

Speaking of history, let's dive into the best things to do in Firestone. One standout is the Firestone Regional Sports Complex, which boasts fields and facilities that are a magnet for youth sports enthusiasts. If you're into watching kids kick soccer balls around like they're on a caffeine high, this is the place to be. Just make sure to bring snacks because watching sports can be a serious endurance test—both for you and the athletes. If you're lucky, you might even catch a game where the winning team gets a trophy that looks suspiciously like it was purchased at a discount store. Nothing says "champion" quite like a plastic trophy that cost less than your lunch.

If you're a fan of the great outdoors, you might want to check out the parks. Firestone's parks are a mix of well-maintained green spaces and "creative interpretations" of what a park should be. You can enjoy a picnic, take a leisurely stroll, or have a deep philosophical discussion about why the ducks seem to have more social interactions than you do. Just be cautious of the local squirrels—they've been known to form small gangs that demand tribute in the form of snacks.

Now, onto the culinary scene. Firestone is home to a variety of dining options that range from delightful to "Well, I guess I'll eat this." One local favorite is a diner that proudly boasts a menu filled with comfort food. You know, the kind of meals that are delicious enough to make you forget about your diet and maybe even your sense of self-control. You can feast on greasy burgers and fries, all while feeling like you've stepped into a time capsule that hasn't been cleaned since the '80s. Just don't be surprised if you leave with a food coma that rivals that of a hibernating bear.

On the flip side, you might want to steer clear of that one restaurant that has more "Closed" signs than open hours. You know the place—where the menu looks like it hasn't changed since the dawn of time and the waitstaff appears to be either highly trained in the art of ignoring you or just plain confused about what day it is. It's the type of establishment where you might end up with a salad that is a little too creative for your taste, leaving you wondering if you've unwittingly wandered into a culinary experiment gone awry.

As you wander through Firestone, you can't help but notice the town's penchant for events that bring the community together—like the annual Firestone Arts and Crafts Festival. Picture a gathering of local artists, vendors, and the occasional overzealous face painter who has an alarming number of glittery unicorns in their repertoire. It's a celebration of all things artsy and crafty, where you can find everything from handmade jewelry to paintings that evoke deep existential questions about the meaning of life. Spoiler alert: they probably don't have the answers.

Then there's the infamous Firestone Fourth of July celebration. It's a day filled with more red, white, and blue than you thought possible, featuring parades that can only be described as "enthusiastic." Expect floats that look like they were thrown together at the last minute and enough patriotic fervor to make even the most jaded cynic crack a smile. Just remember to bring your earplugs because the fireworks show might have you questioning whether it's the Fourth of July or an impromptu battle for supremacy in the sky.

As you meander through the streets of Firestone, keep an eye out for the charming houses that look like they belong on a postcard, juxtaposed against the occasional "What on earth were they thinking?" architectural choices. It's a town that takes pride in its homes, even if some look like they were designed by someone who got lost in a Pinterest rabbit hole. You might even catch a glimpse of neighbors chatting over white picket fences, discussing everything from the weather to the latest gossip about that one guy who insists on mowing his lawn at 6 AM.

So, as you explore this delightful mix of history, quirkiness, and the occasional questionable dining decision, you'll find that Firestone, Colorado, is a town that embraces its past while offering a few surprises along the way. Whether you're pondering the mysteries of local legends at the museum or munching on comfort food while contemplating life's big questions, there's no shortage of laughter and adventure waiting for you in this small but vibrant community. Just remember to bring your sense of humor and an appetite for the unexpected because in Firestone, it's all part of the experience.

Flagler

Flagler, Colorado, is the kind of place that feels like it was plucked right out of a western film set, complete with dusty roads and an ambiance that whispers, "You can leave your high-speed internet behind—who needs it anyway?" Founded in the late 1800s, this small town sprang up thanks to the railroad, because what says "success" quite like the ability to transport goods across the plains while simultaneously raising the average age of your population to "slightly older than dirt"?

The town got its name from the railroad magnate Henry Flagler, who was so influential that he could have sold ice to penguins—if penguins were interested in purchasing anything at all. As you stroll through Flagler, you'll notice that its population hasn't changed dramatically since those early days. In fact, if you've ever wanted to experience what it was like to live in a town where the high school football game is the social event of the year, this is your chance.

One of the must-see attractions in Flagler is the Flagler Museum, which has all the charm of a small-town history exhibit combined with the thrill of wondering if the last person who visited left any crumbs behind. The museum is filled with artifacts that chronicle the town's colorful past, from farming implements that look like they were designed during the Stone Age to photographs that could double as evidence in a "What not to wear" fashion show. You can easily spend an afternoon marveling at items that make you question how humanity ever survived without Wi-Fi.

If museums aren't your thing, perhaps you'd prefer to explore the Flagler area's outdoor attractions. The Flatirons of Flagler might sound impressive, but they're really just some slight hills that give you an excellent view of, well, more plains. It's a great spot for nature lovers and those who think that spending an afternoon contemplating life while staring at flat land is a form of therapy. Be sure to bring a camera to capture the breathtaking scenery—or at least to prove to your friends that you were somewhere that wasn't just your couch.

Next, let's talk about food. Flagler has dining options that vary from "who thought this was a good idea?" to "I'd drive ten miles for this." There's the local diner that serves everything you could possibly want on a menu that resembles a novel. You can order a burger, a sandwich, or an enormous plate of fries that might give you a serious case of the munchies just looking at it. The diner is decorated with memorabilia that screams "nostalgia," making you feel like you've time-traveled to an era where people wore bell bottoms and paid with actual cash.

Then there's that other restaurant that everyone says to avoid, which serves food that looks suspiciously like it was made using a microwave and a questionable recipe found online. If you're feeling adventurous, you might consider stopping by to test your gastrointestinal fortitude. Just remember, there's a fine line between "gourmet experience" and "I hope I don't regret this in the morning."

If you happen to be in Flagler during a local festival, you're in for a treat. The annual Flagler Community Festival is a highlight of the year, featuring games, food stalls, and probably a pie-eating contest that will leave you wondering how anyone can consume that much pie in one sitting. The locals are always ready to showcase their talents, whether it's through an impromptu dance-off or a karaoke contest that features songs you forgot existed. It's the kind of event where you can indulge in some classic small-town charm while also questioning your life choices as you watch Aunt Edna belt out "I Will Survive" in a way that makes you believe she might actually mean it.

For those interested in a more serene experience, the town's parks offer a variety of outdoor activities, such as picnicking, hiking, or simply contemplating your life choices while staring into the vastness of the Colorado sky. Be prepared to dodge the occasional rogue soccer ball or frisbee that seems to have a personal vendetta against your head. The parks might not be large, but they provide a cozy space for relaxation, especially if you enjoy the sound of children's laughter punctuated by the occasional shriek of surprise when someone's dog makes a break for the nearest patch of grass.

If you're feeling particularly brave, you could also venture out into the surrounding area for some recreational opportunities. Flagler is known for its hunting and fishing spots, where you can channel your inner outdoorsman or woman while simultaneously battling the elements. It's a chance to embrace nature while you wrestle with the realization that you've brought more snacks than necessary, but hey, those snacks aren't going to eat themselves, right?

In terms of nightlife, let's just say that if you're looking for a booming social scene, you might want to turn back around. The closest thing you'll find to nightlife is the local watering hole, which may or may not have the ambiance of a set from a low-budget western. It's a place where you can enjoy a cold drink while swapping stories with locals who have lived in Flagler longer than most of us have been alive. Just be prepared for the inevitable "I remember when" stories that will leave you both entertained and mildly terrified at the idea of small-town life.

As you wrap up your visit to Flagler, it's impossible not to appreciate the quirky charm of this little slice of Colorado. It's a town that wears its history on its sleeve while embracing the present in a way that's both endearing and slightly bewildering. Whether you're exploring the museum, indulging in questionable culinary adventures, or basking in the tranquility of the outdoors, Flagler offers a unique experience that's worth every quirky moment. Just remember to pack your sense of humor and an open mind because in Flagler, the best moments often come from the unexpected.

Fleming

Fleming, Colorado, is the kind of place that makes you wonder if you've somehow stepped into an old postcard from the 1950s, complete with a charmingly dusty main street and a population that seems to have a collective age of approximately "let's just say older than the town itself." Founded in 1888, this little gem sprouted up in the midst of the vast Colorado plains, where the wind blows so fiercely you half expect to see a tumbleweed auditioning for a role in a spaghetti western.

Historically, Fleming was named after a railroad guy, which seems to be a recurring theme in Colorado—every town has a "guy" behind its name, usually one who liked trains. The railroad arrived, and like a giant caterpillar munching through the landscape, it helped the town grow, although you might argue that it didn't have much competition given that the area was basically a flat expanse of land and an occasional cow.

Let's talk about museums. Fleming has the unique privilege of being home to the Fleming Museum, which is a delightful collection of artifacts that can be best described as "vintage nostalgia meets 'why did anyone keep this?'" You'll find everything from old farm equipment to photographs of people who looked suspiciously like they'd never experienced air conditioning. It's the kind of museum where you can marvel at a collection of old tools and wonder how humans ever managed to survive without a smartphone in their pocket. The experience is like stepping into someone's attic, minus the creepy vibes and the risk of finding a taxidermy project gone wrong.

If you're feeling adventurous, you can stroll through town, which is about as action-packed as watching paint dry. Don't get me wrong—there's a charm in its simplicity, but it's a simplicity that might leave you questioning if you've accidentally taken a wrong turn and ended up in a parallel universe where time stands still. You might even spot the town sign that boldly announces, "Fleming: Population 206!" You have to admire their commitment to accuracy; it's a reminder that every resident counts—especially when you're in a place with a population that could fit comfortably in a high school classroom.

Dining in Fleming is an experience all its own. You have the local diner that serves up classic American fare, which could also be translated as "if it's fried, we've got it." The menu reads like a list of items designed to promote heartburn, with dishes that might leave you feeling like you've just consumed a brick. And the best part? You'll never be sure if the secret ingredient is love or a dash of good ol' Colorado dust. The waitstaff is friendly, possibly because they know that you'll be the talk of the town for the next month if you order the "super-sized heart attack on a plate."

Now, let's dive into the great outdoors—if you can call it that. Fleming is surrounded by fields that seem to stretch endlessly, which is perfect for anyone who enjoys staring into the horizon and contemplating their life choices. You might think, "Wow, look at that vast expanse of land!" only to realize that nothing has changed for miles and miles. It's the perfect spot for a picnic—if you're okay with eating while being serenaded by the rustling of grass and the occasional distant moo. Be sure to bring plenty of snacks, because the sheer vastness of the area can make you feel like you're on an expedition to find the last slice of pizza in the world.

For those interested in culture, Fleming doesn't disappoint. Each year, the town hosts a local festival that showcases everything from pie-eating contests to hay-bale rolling competitions. Yes, hay-bale rolling. You heard that right. If you've ever wanted to witness adults competing in an activity that could easily double as a scene from a sitcom, this is your moment. The festival is a veritable cornucopia of local talent, complete with handmade crafts and questionable culinary experiments that you can sample while holding your breath and hoping for the best.

Speaking of local talent, let's not forget about the charm of small-town entertainment. You might catch a local play that feels like it was written by someone who hasn't quite grasped the concept of dramatic tension. The performances are filled with heartfelt moments and lines that sound like they were borrowed from a 1950s sitcom. It's like watching your aunt perform a monologue at a family gathering—you're not quite sure if you should laugh or cry, but you're definitely entertained.

As the sun sets over Fleming, the nightlife is just beginning to stir—or perhaps it's just the wind rustling through the empty streets. If you're hoping for a vibrant bar scene, you might need to adjust your expectations. The local watering hole has all the ambience of a high school hangout, complete with a jukebox that plays songs from a time when gas was a quarter a gallon and the idea of texting was merely a fantasy. You can kick back with a cold drink, shoot some pool, and engage in the kind of deep conversations that make you question not just life, but the entire universe.

As you prepare to leave Fleming, you might find yourself reflecting on the unique charm of this little town. It's a place where the past mingles with the present in a way that feels both nostalgic and oddly comforting. Whether you've marveled at old tools in the museum, indulged in diner food that probably has a cult following, or just enjoyed the vast emptiness of the plains, Fleming has a way of making you appreciate the simple things in life—like knowing exactly where you stand in a population of 206. It's a town that may not be for everyone, but it definitely has a story to tell. And sometimes, that story is as simple as "I once visited a place where the most exciting thing to do was watch the grass grow."

Florence

Florence, Colorado, is the kind of place that makes you think, "Did I accidentally take a time machine to the Wild West?" With its charming small-town vibe, Florence seems to have a knack for preserving history in a way that feels almost like a quirky museum exhibit. Founded in the late 1800s, this town has more stories than it knows what to do with—most of which involve cowboys, miners, and an inordinate amount of dust.

The history of Florence is rich enough to rival that of any gold rush town, but instead of gold, it was the local coal mining that put Florence on the map. Picture it: a town full of hopeful miners who, after a long day of digging in the dark, had only a dust-covered sandwich to look forward to. But they persevered, and the mining boom brought an influx of people, dreams, and just the right amount of mischief. If you ever wanted to feel like a character in an old-timey novel, Florence is your stage.

Now, let's discuss the museums, because every good town needs at least one that's slightly odd and full of artifacts you never knew you needed in your life. The Florence Pioneer Museum is the crown jewel of local history. Here, you can find everything from old photographs of the town's founding fathers—who, let's be honest, looked like they were one bad haircut away from being sent to a ghost town—to antique tools that leave you wondering how humans ever managed to survive without modern conveniences. The museum's charm is that it feels like a treasure trove curated by your great aunt who refuses to throw anything away. If you're lucky, you might stumble upon the local lore about the town's infamous outlaws, who were less "bank robbers" and more "guys who might have borrowed a horse without asking."

When it comes to things to see and do in Florence, you might think the options are limited, but that's where you'd be wrong. First off, there's the iconic Florence Historical District, where the buildings seem to whisper tales of yesteryear while you stroll down the streets. Make sure to take a picture with the 1920s-era movie theater marquee—it's a relic that gives off serious retro vibes, just begging for a filter on social media. You can almost hear the echoes of jazz music and the sound of popcorn popping in a time when going to the movies didn't involve sitting in a recliner that can also make you a sandwich.

For those who appreciate a good laugh, the local diner serves food that could probably win awards for the most creative takes on classic American dishes. The "Florence Special" features a mystery meat that locals swear is delicious, though no one can quite agree on what it actually is. It's the kind of dish that makes you wonder if you should ask for the recipe or just prepare yourself for an adventurous meal. Don't forget to ask for the pie—rumor has it that the pie is so good, it might just convince you to stay in Florence for the rest of your life, or at least until the sugar high wears off.

And if you're looking for a little thrill, you might want to check out the Royal Gorge Bridge, just a short drive from Florence. It's a marvel of engineering that makes you question both your mortality and your sense of adventure. Standing on the bridge gives you a view that's breathtaking—if by breathtaking, you mean you might actually forget to breathe as you contemplate the long drop to the bottom. If you're feeling particularly bold, you can take a gondola ride that will swing you over the gorge like a squirrel on a wire, which is definitely not for those with a fear of heights or an aversion to spontaneous screaming.

Let's not overlook the local events, which are the lifeblood of Florence's social scene. Each year, the town hosts the Florence Heritage Festival, where you can indulge in a cornucopia of local crafts, live music, and food that would make even a gourmet chef question their life choices. The highlight? The parade, where you can see floats that look like they were designed by a committee of enthusiastic children who just discovered glitter. It's heartwarming and slightly chaotic, much like the town itself.

However, not everything in Florence is sunshine and roses. For every charming aspect, there are a few questionable decisions lurking in the shadows. Take, for example, the town's obsession with antique shops. While browsing through dusty relics can be entertaining, it can also be a test of endurance. You might find yourself sifting through enough porcelain cats to create a feline army, leaving you to wonder why anyone would need that many cat figurines in the first place. By the time you leave, you'll be asking, "Who collects this stuff? And why?"

Then there's the infamous local haunt, the "haunted" Old Jail Museum. Yes, you heard that right—this place claims to be haunted by the spirits of former inmates who didn't quite make it out. It's the kind of place where you walk through the creaky doors, and the chills creep up your spine as you wonder if the ghost of a long-gone outlaw is going to ask you for a sandwich. Tours are available, and you can expect your guide to embellish stories that make you question whether they've ever seen a ghost or if they're just really good at storytelling.

As the sun sets over Florence, you'll find that the nightlife is as lively as a gathering of retirement home bingo players. Local bars have all the flair of a neighborhood gathering spot, where you can enjoy a drink and swap tales of adventure—or, more likely, listen to the same three locals talk about their glory days. There's karaoke, of course, where you might witness performances that make you question whether you've stumbled into an audition for a bad reality show.

Florence, Colorado, is a town that embodies the phrase "small-town charm" in a way that feels both heartwarming and a bit bewildering. With its mix of history, museums, and the curious blend of the best and the worst, you're sure to leave with a few good stories to tell—or at the very least, a sense of wonder about how such a unique place could exist in a world of skyscrapers and high-speed internet. So, whether you're wandering through antique shops, indulging in questionable diner fare, or contemplating the meaning of life at the Royal Gorge, Florence invites you to embrace its quirky charm and laugh at its oddities, one dusty street at a time.

Fort Collins

Fort Collins, Colorado, is a place that feels like it's perpetually ready to be the star of a sitcom. With its perfect blend of college town energy, hipster vibes, and an abundance of craft beer, Fort Collins is a quirky gem nestled against the foothills of the Rockies. Founded in 1864 as a military outpost, the town was originally meant to protect settlers from the evils of Native American raids, wild animals, and probably the occasional grumpy neighbor. But thankfully, the military didn't stick around long enough to throw a boring welcome party, and instead, the settlers turned it into a hub of creativity, commerce, and craft brews.

You can't mention Fort Collins without mentioning its brewing scene, which is like a craft beer theme park for adults. With more than 20 breweries, including the famous New Belgium Brewing Company, the town has earned the nickname "Napa Valley of Beer." If you're not careful, a simple afternoon stroll could turn into a quest to taste every hoppy creation imaginable, leading to an impressive collection of pint glasses and a lack of coherent memories by sundown. One minute you're savoring a light lager, and the next, you're discussing the merits of barrel-aged stouts with a mustachioed stranger who swears he once brewed beer in his bathtub. Just remember, when in Fort Collins, pace yourself. There's no need to challenge your liver to a duel.

The historic Old Town area is another highlight of the city, where the buildings are so charming that even Instagram models get jealous. Stroll down the streets and take in the Victorian architecture that makes you feel like you've stepped into a postcard from the past. The town's founders clearly knew how to make a place look good, and they filled it with shops that sell everything from artisanal cheese to handcrafted leather goods. You might even find a store that sells exclusively tie-dye products, because why wouldn't you want a rainbow-colored onesie for that upcoming family reunion?

If museums are your jam, Fort Collins has you covered. The Fort Collins Museum of Discovery is a must-visit for anyone who has ever wanted to play with cool gadgets while pretending to be smart. With interactive exhibits that range from the region's history to science displays that make you feel like you're in a college lab, you can easily spend an afternoon getting lost in a whirlwind of knowledge and nostalgia. Just be careful not to get too carried away in the music exhibit—you might find yourself belting out classic rock tunes at a decibel level that could summon the ghost of Jimi Hendrix.

For those who appreciate a bit of weirdness, the city is home to the Cache la Poudre River, which offers not only stunning views but also an array of outdoor activities. You can hike, fish, or even white-water raft if you're feeling particularly adventurous. But be warned: the river is named after a cache of supplies buried by French trappers in the 1800s, which means it's also a prime spot for losing your dignity. Just picture it: one moment you're paddling with confidence, and the next, you're upside down in the water, desperately clinging to the remnants of your dignity while shouting at the universe, "Why did I think this was a good idea?"

When it comes to local events, Fort Collins knows how to throw a party. The annual Colorado Brewers' Festival is like a beer lover's fantasy come true. Picture thousands of people swaying to live music while clutching steins of frothy goodness, all while trying to balance a plate of food that could qualify as a small buffet. Just make sure you wear shoes that can handle the sticky ground; no one wants to go home with beer-flavored feet. If that's not your scene, the FoCo Food Truck Rally is a feast for both your stomach and your Instagram feed. You can sample everything from gourmet tacos to artisanal ice cream, all while trying not to be the person who trips over their own feet in front of a crowd.

As with any city, Fort Collins has its share of quirky oddities. For example, there's the infamous "Giant Blue Bear" sculpture peering into the Colorado Convention Center, which raises some serious questions about the aesthetic choices of the local art scene. It's like a giant blue plush toy decided it was time to make a statement, and now it looms over the city, reminding everyone that you can never be too fluffy. People come from far and wide to take selfies with the bear, which probably means that somewhere there's a bear-themed Instagram account with more followers than most celebrities.

Now, not everything is sunshine and craft beer in Fort Collins. For every charming coffee shop, there's a line so long you'd think they were giving away gold bricks instead of lattes. If you're not willing to wait twenty minutes for a cup of overpriced coffee, you might as well pack your bags and head back to your boring old hometown. And let's talk about the traffic—nothing quite prepares you for the experience of sitting in your car while wondering if you'll ever see the other side of the intersection. It's a thrilling adventure that might leave you questioning your life choices and contemplating the merits of walking everywhere.

Let's not forget about the infamous Poudre Canyon, where the views are breathtaking, but the roads are enough to give even the most seasoned driver a panic attack. The winding turns, steep drops, and occasional rockslide are a reminder that nature can be both beautiful and terrifying. Just remember to keep your hands at ten and two, and pray you don't accidentally drive off the side into a patch of trees that will undoubtedly laugh at your misfortune.

As the sun sets over Fort Collins, you might find yourself contemplating what to do for the evening. If you're looking for live music, there's a good chance you'll stumble upon a local band playing at a dive bar. These venues are like the land of misfit toys for aspiring musicians, where dreams go to either flourish or crash and burn spectacularly. Either way, you're in for an entertaining night filled with questionable dance moves and more than a few "unique" musical choices.

In summary, Fort Collins is a delightful mix of history, craft beer, outdoor adventures, and more oddities than you can shake a stick at. Whether you're sampling local brews, navigating the historic district, or discovering the quirks of the town, you'll find that Fort Collins is not just a place to visit but a wild ride of experiences that might leave you laughing or shaking your head in disbelief. So strap in and get ready for a journey through a town that knows how to embrace its quirks and celebrate the wonderfully strange tapestry of life.

Fort Garland

Fort Garland, Colorado, is a town that feels like it was plucked straight from the pages of a Western novel—complete with rugged mountains, dusty streets, and a historical narrative that's more colorful than a box of Crayola crayons. Founded in 1858 as a military outpost to protect settlers from Native American raids and the occasional angry bear, Fort Garland served as a crucial stronghold during the tumultuous days of the West. Picture soldiers, mustaches flapping in the wind, bravely patrolling the perimeter while dreaming of more peaceful pursuits, like knitting and baking bread.

The fort itself was named after the intrepid Colonel John Garland, who probably never imagined his name would be associated with a place where the most exciting thing to do is watch paint dry. Although the original fort is long gone, its legacy lives on in the tiny town that now boasts a population that could probably fit in a minivan. This is a place where everyone knows your name—and likely knows your business, too.

Speaking of knowing your business, let's dive into the museums. The Fort Garland Museum is the crown jewel of the area, offering a charming look at the history of the fort and the surrounding region. Exhibits range from military memorabilia to Native American artifacts, and you can even find a few items that probably came straight from a garage sale. It's a delightful mix of "wow, that's interesting" and "how did that end up here?" Visitors often marvel at the stories these artifacts tell, or they may just be bewildered by the randomness of it all. The museum staff, who could easily pass as historians straight out of central casting, are eager to share tales that blend fact with a dash of local legend. Who knew that a rusty horseshoe could spark such passionate debate about the town's most infamous horse thief?

Now, as for the best things to do in Fort Garland, let's start with the great outdoors. Surrounded by the stunning San Luis Valley, this place is an outdoor enthusiast's playground. Whether you're into hiking, fishing, or just pretending to be an outdoorsy type while sitting by a campfire roasting marshmallows, there's something for everyone. Take a hike up to the majestic Blanca Peak, where the view is so breathtaking you might forget to breathe altogether. Just remember to pack a water bottle, because nothing says "I love nature" quite like dehydrating in front of a picturesque vista.

If you're in the mood for a more relaxed outing, the local community park offers a range of recreational activities, including the age-old tradition of people-watching. You can sit on a bench, sip your coffee, and enjoy the spectacle of locals trying to figure out if that is indeed a dog or a very hairy cat. Just don't get too comfortable; before you know it, you might find yourself in a spirited discussion about the best local fishing spots or the merits of different types of barbecue sauce. Spoiler alert: there is no right answer, and everyone has an opinion.

Now for the "worst" things to do—let's just say Fort Garland is not exactly known for its nightlife. If you're looking for a vibrant club scene, you might want to recalibrate your expectations. The most excitement you'll find after sunset is probably a community potluck or a spirited game of bingo.

Imagine the thrill of yelling "Bingo!" as if you just won the lottery, only to realize your prize is a slightly used casserole dish. Still, there's a certain charm in the simplicity of small-town gatherings, where everyone shares stories and nobody needs a DJ to get the party started.

You might also want to steer clear of the local ghost tours. Yes, Fort Garland has its fair share of spooky tales, but you might find that the scariest thing about them is the realization that you're being haunted by your own boredom. If the thought of walking through the woods at night while listening to someone recount a ghost story that sounds suspiciously like a plot from a low-budget horror film doesn't excite you, perhaps a night in with Netflix and a pizza is the better option.

But fear not, if you're in the mood for some culture, the local art scene can be surprisingly vibrant. The town often hosts art fairs where local artisans showcase their crafts. You might encounter hand-painted pottery, homemade jams, and enough knitted goods to keep your grandma busy for a lifetime. Just be prepared to be approached by at least three people who will insist you buy something to support the local economy, because nothing says "I care" quite like being guilted into purchasing a knitted sweater in July.

For those who want to immerse themselves in the local culture, the Fort Garland Memorial Day Parade is a must-see event. It's the kind of parade where the floats are made from whatever happens to be lying around—think old tractors and hand-painted signs that might have been created during a particularly inspired bout of boredom. Everyone gathers to watch, and you might find yourself swept up in the excitement of it all, even if the highlight is the local marching band's enthusiastic rendition of "Yankee Doodle." Just make sure to bring a lawn chair, because standing for an hour in the Colorado sun is a rite of passage that can lead to some serious sunburn.

And let's not forget the occasional wildlife encounter. Deer are practically the unofficial mascots of Fort Garland, appearing in yards and parks with the nonchalance of someone who's just there to sip coffee and read the newspaper. Just don't be surprised if they give you the side-eye as if to say, "What are you doing here?" It's a humbling experience, especially when you realize they probably have a better social life than you do.

Fort Lupton

Fort Lupton, Colorado, sounds like a place where you'd expect to find cowboys, tumbleweeds, and maybe a saloon with a piano player in the corner. But don't let the name fool you; this town is more modern than you might imagine, and it has a history that's as colorful as a tie-dye shirt at a music festival.

The town's name comes from Fort Lupton, a military outpost established in 1859, named after a certain William Lupton, who apparently had a knack for getting his name attached to things. Originally a fur trading post, the fort was built to protect settlers and travelers moving westward. Picture a time when men wore hats taller than their ambitions and used phrases like "by thunder!" at the drop of a hat. As for the fort itself, it's long gone, but its spirit lives on in the town's charming, if slightly quirky, character.

Fast forward to the modern era, and Fort Lupton has transformed from a dusty military outpost into a bustling little town where the population is made up of friendly faces and the occasional cow that has wandered off its farm. The town sits snugly between the South Platte River and an array of delightful cornfields, and it's a place where you can easily experience the sweet aroma of hay mixed with the hint of something... suspiciously like adventure.

For those eager to soak up some local history, the Fort Lupton Museum is a must-visit. Housed in a charming building that seems to have been designed by someone with a fondness for both old bricks and new ideas, this museum showcases artifacts from the town's history and the surrounding area. You'll find everything from dusty old uniforms to photographs of people who probably have fascinating stories—if only they could tell them without fading into sepia tones. The highlight is undoubtedly the exhibit on the town's founding and the fort's role, complete with the kind of artifacts that make you wonder how people survived without smartphones.

As you stroll through the museum, you might notice that the docents possess a unique talent for making even the driest historical facts sound like the latest gossip from the schoolyard. "Did you know that back in the day, this place had more saloons than people? That's right! They had a 3:1 ratio of taverns to settlers! You could practically sip whiskey while riding a horse!" Who knew history could come with such a side of sass?

Now, on to the best things to do in Fort Lupton. If you're a fan of outdoor activities, the town is surrounded by parks, trails, and open spaces that beckon you to explore. The Fort Lupton Recreation Center is the heart of community activity, where you can partake in everything from swimming to yoga to the kind of fitness classes that make you question your life choices. You might find yourself surrounded by a mix of fitness enthusiasts and those just there for the free Wi-Fi.

If you're feeling particularly adventurous, hop on a bike and pedal along the scenic South Platte River Trail. Just remember, the only thing standing between you and that serene riverside view is your own level of fitness. No pressure. You might find yourself sweating like a sinner in church, but hey, it's all part of the experience. And if you happen to encounter a deer or two along the way, consider it a bonus—unless they give you the side-eye, in which case, just keep pedaling.

Let's talk food, shall we? Dining in Fort Lupton is a delightful journey through the town's culinary landscape. You'll find a mix of family-owned diners and chain restaurants that cater to every palate. Try the local diners for a hearty breakfast that's the equivalent of a warm hug. Just don't be surprised if the pancakes are larger than your head; the locals take breakfast seriously. On the flip side, if you're feeling a bit more adventurous, consider heading to one of the food trucks that pop up in town. You might discover a culinary treasure—or a questionable taco. The gamble is half the fun, right?

Now, let's get to the worst things to do in Fort Lupton. If you find yourself in town on a Sunday morning, you might want to avoid the local laundromat. Not because it's particularly terrible, but because it doubles as the unofficial gossip hub. You might find yourself entangled in conversations about the neighbor's cat, the latest town drama, or who was spotted at the grocery store wearing mismatched socks. If you're looking for peace and quiet, consider a different time to do laundry or bring headphones and pretend you're in your own little world.

And while we're at it, steer clear of trying to get a selfie with the town's welcome sign. You might think it's a quaint little photo op, but locals know that it's a rite of passage to have someone photobomb your shot. Whether it's a dog running by or a neighbor on a bike, the odds are high that you'll end up with a picture of someone's back rather than the sign itself.

For those seeking culture, Fort Lupton has its fair share of local events. Check out the annual "Farmers Day Festival," a celebration that features everything from a parade to pie-eating contests. Imagine competitive pie eating as a serious sport, where the winners wear their trophies—crumbs on their faces and slightly unhinged smiles—as badges of honor. The entire event is a mix of small-town charm and chaos, with children running amok while parents try to remember where they parked.

Fort Morgan

Fort Morgan, Colorado, a name that sounds like it could belong to either a military general or a character in a Western movie, has a rich history that makes it both intriguing and entertaining. Founded in 1865, Fort Morgan was named after Colonel Christopher Morgan, who was notably involved in the Civil War and possibly known for his impressive mustache—though historical records are a bit vague on that front. Originally established as a military outpost to protect settlers from Native American raids, the fort became a hub for trade and a strategic location on the overland stage route. You can imagine the scene: a bunch of grizzled pioneers, wide-brimmed hats, and maybe some dramatic piano music playing in the background.

Fast forward a bit, and you'll find that Fort Morgan transitioned from a military stronghold to a thriving agricultural community. Corn, sugar beets, and other crops started to dominate the landscape, transforming the town into a veritable buffet for the region. If you've ever wanted to know where your sugar comes from, look no further than Fort Morgan. The town has that lovely small-town feel, where everyone knows each other, and the latest gossip travels faster than a speeding horse.

One of the town's main attractions is the Fort Morgan Museum. This charming little establishment is like stepping into a time machine, except instead of being greeted by a futuristic robot, you'll meet friendly locals who have an uncanny ability to recount the town's history as if they were there for every significant moment. The museum features exhibits on the fort's history, the agricultural development of the area, and even the town's role in the World War II era. You can expect to see everything from dusty old uniforms to photographs that make you wonder how anyone managed to look so serious while wearing such questionable fashion choices.

While you're there, make sure to check out the museum's collection of artifacts from the fort itself. You might stumble upon a cannonball or two—though if they start rolling toward you, it's probably best to duck and cover. The museum's volunteers are often eager to share the quirkiest stories about the items on display, like the time someone tried to sell a cannonball as a decorative paperweight. Spoiler alert: it did not end well.

Now let's discuss some of the best things to do in Fort Morgan. Outdoor enthusiasts can take a stroll or bike ride along the South Platte River, where the views are stunning enough to make you contemplate becoming an amateur nature photographer. Just remember, if you're not careful, you might end up in the middle of a family of ducks that clearly have no interest in being part of your scenic shot.

For a true taste of local culture, swing by during the summer for the annual "Morgan County Fair." Picture this: livestock shows, pie-eating contests, and a rodeo that is as authentic as it gets. You'll find people of all ages sporting cowboy hats, boots, and a grin that suggests they might have just had a little too much funnel cake. This fair is the epitome of small-town fun, where you can experience the kind of community spirit that makes you feel warm and fuzzy inside—or maybe that's just the cotton candy.

But let's not forget the culinary scene. Fort Morgan is home to several delightful eateries that offer a mix of classic American fare and some surprisingly good Mexican food. Tacos that are so good, you might start planning your next visit before you even leave the table. And if you're in the mood for something truly unique, check out a local diner where the special might just be a burger that's bigger than your head. It's a culinary challenge you didn't know you needed in your life.

Now, onto the worst things to do in Fort Morgan. If you're ever tempted to go for a "relaxing" hike at the local park, be warned: you might find yourself lost in what locals affectionately refer to as "The Maze." This place is a patchwork of trails that look deceptively easy to navigate until you realize you've walked in circles and are now on speaking terms with a very judgmental squirrel. It's best to bring a compass or at least a friend who's good with directions.

Another pitfall? Attempting to visit the local laundromat during peak hours. It's like entering a social experiment where everyone shares their life stories while waiting for their delicates to finish drying. You might end up knowing more about your fellow laundromat patrons than you do about your own family. If you're looking for peace and quiet, consider doing laundry at 3 AM, when you can finally hear yourself think.

And for those adventurous souls looking to take a selfie with the town's welcome sign—good luck! The locals have a tradition of photobombing newcomers, and you might end up with a picture that captures a random dog leaping into the frame at the precise moment you press the button. "This is Fort Morgan!" you'll say, while the dog looks like it's about to claim its own Instagram fame.

Fountain

Fountain, Colorado, a name that brings to mind bubbling springs and perhaps a lot of overly enthusiastic fountain pens, has a history as colorful as a modern art exhibit gone wrong. Settled in the 1850s, the town was originally named after the Fountain River, which is more of a babbling stream than a grandiose fountain, leading to a slight identity crisis that the town has yet to fully resolve. Imagine the town hall meeting where someone suggested "Fountain" and the crowd collectively thought, "Sure, why not? It's better than 'Ruggedly Unremarkable.'"

The history of Fountain reads like a classic American tale: pioneers, gold rushes, and plenty of dust. It all began with a handful of settlers who rolled into the area, probably with an abundance of hope and not enough sunscreen. Originally part of the land that would become Colorado Springs, Fountain carved out its own niche, becoming a charming little hamlet that managed to hold on to its identity through the many changes surrounding it.

One of the best places to dive into Fountain's history is the Fountain Historical Society and Museum. This delightful little spot is like a treasure chest filled with artifacts from yesteryear, including the remnants of the local telephone exchange, which looks suspiciously like a wooden box with a crank on it. Volunteers are always eager to share their stories, and if you're lucky, you might hear the tale of the time someone mistook a very important historical document for a menu from a local diner. Spoiler alert: the document did not include "french fries."

If you're looking for more excitement, make your way to the Fountain Creek Regional Park. This isn't just any park; it's the kind of place where you can enjoy nature, contemplate your life choices, and dodge children on bikes who seem to have a vendetta against adults. With miles of trails, it's a great place for hiking, jogging, or simply contemplating why you decided to wear shoes that pinch your toes. Don't forget your camera, because the views can be breathtaking, even if the only thing you manage to capture is a blurry picture of a squirrel.

Speaking of squirrels, Fountain is home to the annual Fountain Fall Festival, a gathering that brings the community together for food, fun, and a questionable amount of pumpkin-themed activities. If you've ever wanted to see a pie-eating contest where everyone is fully committed to not getting any pie on their face—spoiler alert, it's messy—this is the place for you. Just don't get too close to the apple cider stand unless you want to end up with sticky fingers and a taste for fermented dreams.

When it comes to dining, Fountain offers a delightful mix of options. You can grab a bite at one of the local diners, where the portions are so generous that you might consider carrying a Tupperware just for leftovers. The local fare leans heavily on hearty American classics, so if you've ever wanted to enjoy a burger bigger than your head, you've found your mecca. Just be prepared for the inevitable food coma that will follow.

But let's not gloss over the worst things to do in Fountain, which can be just as entertaining as the best. For example, trying to navigate the local traffic during rush hour is a rite of passage that will test your patience and driving skills. It's like a game of Frogger, but with actual cars and a lot more honking. If you're feeling adventurous, you might even attempt to make a left turn during this time—good luck with that!

Another contender for the "worst" category is visiting the town's only laundromat. There's something about the fluorescent lights, the smell of fabric softener, and the quiet hum of the dryers that can make you feel like you've stepped into a parallel universe where small talk is an Olympic sport. Expect to hear tales of lost socks and laundry disasters as you wait for your clothes to dry, because nothing brings people together like the shared pain of doing laundry.

Fountain also has a quaint downtown area that is charming enough to make you feel like you've stepped into a Hallmark movie, but with slightly more potholes. As you stroll down the main street, you might encounter a variety of shops selling everything from local art to slightly questionable antiques that may or may not have come from a yard sale. It's a great place to pick up that unique souvenir, like a ceramic cow or a vintage "Welcome to Fountain" sign, because nothing says "I traveled" quite like a piece of slightly tacky decor.

For a taste of true local flair, check out the community events throughout the year. From holiday parades to craft fairs, there's always something going on that offers a glimpse into the heart of Fountain. Just be wary of the overly enthusiastic parade participants who might hand you candy while simultaneously waving a giant foam finger—trust me, it's a lot to process all at once.

Fountain, Colorado, is a place that offers a delightful mix of history, charm, and the kind of local flavor that makes you appreciate small-town life. Whether you're enjoying a day at the park, diving into the past at the museum, or navigating the local traffic like a seasoned pro, there's plenty to explore and experience. Just keep your sense of humor handy because, in Fountain, laughter is the best accessory you can bring along for the ride.

Fowler

Fowler, Colorado, sounds like the name of a character from a sitcom—maybe a well-meaning but bumbling neighbor who always borrows tools and never returns them. Located in Otero County, this tiny town has a history that feels like a mix of old Western charm and small-town quirks that you can't help but laugh at. Founded in the late 1800s, Fowler started as a railroad stop, a little dot on the map where weary travelers could get a drink, stretch their legs, and ponder their life choices—like how they ended up in Fowler.

The name itself is an homage to a local who probably thought they were doing a solid for the future generations. "Fowler" evokes images of flocks of birds or perhaps a family of ducks waddling across the street. It's hard to say what the original founders intended, but one can imagine a discussion that included a lot of "Well, what should we call it?" and someone yelling "How about Fowler?" as they pointed at a very confused bird.

Historically, Fowler was a hub for agriculture, and at one point, it boasted more cows than residents. Seriously, if you wandered around, you might have seen more Holsteins than people. The local economy was fueled by farming and ranching, making it a place where the phrase "That'll put hair on your chest" might have originated, usually in reference to the local chili cook-offs that had a reputation for being hotter than the sun.

If you're into history, the Fowler Museum is your best bet for a good dose of local lore. You'll find a delightful collection of artifacts that reflect the town's agricultural roots, quirky memorabilia, and maybe even a few items that make you question the sanity of past residents. Ever wanted to see a 1920s tractor that looks like it was designed for a Mad Max movie? Now's your chance! The museum volunteers are often enthusiastic and can regale you with tales that sound suspiciously exaggerated—like that time someone claimed to have caught a fish so big it needed its own zip code.

For outdoor enthusiasts, Fowler offers the picturesque charm of the Arkansas River nearby, perfect for fishing or just standing around trying to look contemplative. You can fish for trout, but if you don't know what you're doing, you might end up with a healthy respect for the local ducks instead. Just remember, if you see someone in waders who looks suspiciously like they've fallen in three times that day, they're probably local.

Now, let's talk about the annual events that can either make or break your love for Fowler. The Fowler Harvest Festival is a highlight, bringing the community together for a good old-fashioned celebration of all things farm-related. You can expect pie-eating contests, which are less about technique and more about seeing who can emerge victorious without requiring immediate medical attention. If you're thinking of joining, maybe wear a poncho—you know, just in case.

On the downside, Fowler does have its share of small-town quirks that can be a little, well, underwhelming. The local diner serves a meatloaf that could probably double as a doorstop, and while the service is friendly, the wait can feel like you're auditioning for a reality show titled "Survivor: Small

Town Edition." If you plan on eating there, be sure to bring a good book or a friend who can entertain you with stories of their more exciting life.

Speaking of excitement, the town has its moments of questionable charm, particularly when it comes to local attractions. There's the infamous "World's Largest Prairie Dog" statue, which is a must-see if you enjoy life-sized rodents made out of concrete. It's a local landmark that can make for a great photo opportunity—just make sure to keep an eye on the prairie dog; some say it has a mischievous streak and may steal your snacks if you're not careful.

As for the best thing to do in Fowler? It might just be enjoying the sheer quietness of the town. With more stars in the sky than people on the streets, you can easily find yourself in a state of blissful solitude. Just remember to bring a good sense of humor along with you, as the locals have a tendency to laugh heartily at the oddities of small-town life.

The worst part of Fowler, you ask? Well, it's hard to pinpoint just one thing. The lack of a Starbucks could be a deal-breaker for some, especially if you're addicted to overpriced coffee drinks with names longer than the ingredients list. The town does boast a few local coffee shops, but they may leave you feeling more like you've just consumed a cup of lukewarm disappointment than an invigorating espresso.

If you're looking for nightlife, prepare yourself for a long search. Fowler's idea of a hot night out might include gathering at the local park for some corn hole and lemonade, while sharing stories of "that one time at the Harvest Festival." Forget about wild parties; your biggest adventure will be debating the merits of different types of lawn mowers.

Fowler, Colorado, is a charming little slice of Americana, packed with quirky history, a museum that doubles as a trip down memory lane, and enough small-town charm to fill a coffee cup. Whether you're fishing, visiting the local diner, or snapping a photo with the world's largest prairie dog, you'll find that laughter and good humor are the true highlights of this hidden gem. Just make sure you're prepared for the adventures—and misadventures—that await in this delightful town.

Fraser

Fraser, Colorado, has a name that sounds like it belongs to a character in a sitcom or perhaps a fancy cocktail. You can just imagine someone ordering a "Fraser Fizz" at a trendy bar, and the bartender giving you a quizzical look as if you've just asked for a unicorn smoothie. This charming little mountain town sits snugly in the Rockies, not too far from Winter Park, and boasts a history that's equal parts rugged and quirky.

Founded in the late 1800s during the gold rush, Fraser began as a railroad stop for the trains hauling precious metals and hopeful dreamers. The town was named after a local pioneer, which is a classic tale. But it also feels like one of those names that could have been conjured up by a group of tired settlers sitting around a campfire after too many beans, debating what to call their new town. "Fraser! Let's go with that! It sounds strong, like a lumberjack but also kind of posh!"

The early days were not without their challenges. Fraser faced the typical struggles of a frontier town—harsh winters, wild animals, and the ever-present risk of running out of coffee. If you were brave enough to be a part of Fraser's history, you probably spent many a day building cabins, dodging grizzly bears, and trying to figure out how to grow vegetables in rocky soil. The town eventually transitioned from a mining hub to a tourism hotspot, which seems to happen in every small town that realizes it can profit from people who don't know how to dress for winter sports.

For those with a penchant for history, Fraser's very own Fraser Valley Historical Society offers a delightful peek into the past. This museum is the kind of place where you might find an ancient mining cart that looks like it survived a battle against a giant hamster. The exhibits tell the story of the town's evolution from mining town to ski resort, with a few detours into quirky anecdotes that make you question how anyone survived back then without a smartphone.

As for things to do, Fraser is the ultimate playground for outdoor enthusiasts. If you love skiing or snowboarding, Winter Park Resort is just a hop, skip, and a jump away—assuming that hop, skip, and jump are made while wearing snow boots and trying not to slip on ice. Fraser itself is also home to some stunning trails for hiking, biking, and even snowshoeing, if that's your idea of a fun time. Nothing quite like strapping giant tennis rackets to your feet and wandering through the woods while wondering who thought that was a good idea.

But let's not sugarcoat everything. Fraser does have its challenges, particularly when it comes to amenities. The local dining scene can be a bit, let's say, rustic. If you're hoping for gourmet cuisine, you might end up in a diner where the biggest seller is a burger that may or may not be from a cow that lived in the nearby fields. And while the charm of small-town dining is endearing, nothing quite prepares you for the experience of ordering "the daily special" only to discover it's last week's leftover casserole that has transformed into a new life form.

Now, if you're into events, Fraser hosts the annual Fraser River Valley Music Festival, which is a delightful mix of music, community spirit, and maybe a bit too much local craft beer. Imagine a crowd of friendly folks bobbing their heads to tunes while dodging the occasional stray frisbee and trying to figure out how to balance a plate of food in one hand while holding a drink in the other. It's a glorious sight, and if you're lucky, you might even catch a few local bands that are just one YouTube video away from stardom.

On the flip side, Fraser's winter can be a double-edged sword. The snow brings joy and adventure, but it can also lead to situations where you find yourself knee-deep in powder and questioning all your life choices. Skiing is a blast until you realize that you're more likely to tumble down the mountain like a rolling snowball than to gracefully glide like a pro. And don't get me started on the ski lifts. There's something both exhilarating and terrifying about being hoisted high above the ground while trying to hold on for dear life and pretending you know what you're doing.

When it comes to nightlife, Fraser might not be the first place that pops into your mind. You won't find any clubs that rival the big city; instead, you'll get a cozy bar scene where locals gather to share stories, sip on craft beer, and relive the glory days of their high school sports. If you're lucky, someone might even break out the karaoke machine, leading to a night of questionable musical talent that can only be described as "unique." Just remember, there's no such thing as too many renditions of "Sweet Caroline" in a small town.

As for the best and worst things about Fraser, it's all about perspective. The best? It's a haven for outdoor lovers and offers stunning scenery that will make you want to pull out your camera at every turn. The worst? If you find yourself stuck in a snowstorm, the charm of small-town life might begin to wear thin as you wonder when the next hot meal will appear. The key to surviving Fraser is to embrace the quirks, enjoy the community, and always be ready for whatever the weather—or a giant snowball fight—might throw your way.

Frederick

Frederick, Colorado, sounds like a character from a classic novel, perhaps a dapper gentleman with a monocle who solves mysteries on horseback. But this Frederick isn't galloping through the pages of Victorian literature; it's a quaint town nestled just north of Denver, sporting a history that's as colorful as a box of crayons left out in the sun.

The name Frederick comes from a local landowner, Frederick H. Smith, who must have felt that "Smithville" was just a tad too ordinary. His ambition paid off, and the town grew around the railroad in the late 1800s, attracting a mix of miners, farmers, and those who simply wanted to escape the hustle and bustle of bigger cities. The residents probably thought, "Why not settle in a place where the most excitement comes from watching cows cross the road?" And so Frederick was born, a place where life was simple, and the biggest event was the annual pie-eating contest, complete with a trophy made from recycled hubcaps.

As for the history, Frederick has had its fair share of ups and downs. Once a thriving coal mining town, it experienced the usual boom and bust that accompanies any mining endeavor. The mines, of course, eventually played out, leaving behind a few relics and a lot of "What do we do now?" The transformation into a suburban haven began in the late 20th century when folks from Denver discovered that living in Frederick was much more affordable than living in the city. And with that, the town saw a wave of new residents who were probably lured in by the promise of wide open spaces and the occasional sighting of a cow in the front yard.

Now, let's get into the museums, because what's a small town without a place to showcase its history? Frederick's Museum of Natural History may not have the grandeur of the Smithsonian, but it offers a charming collection of local artifacts, including an impressive array of dinosaur bones. You can practically hear the echoes of ancient roars as you walk through, imagining what it was like when those gigantic lizards roamed the land. The museum is a delightful place to bring the family, unless, of course, you have that one kid who insists on asking a thousand questions about why dinosaurs aren't still around, which may or may not lead to an existential crisis for everyone involved.

But what are the best things to do in Frederick? Well, if you enjoy outdoor activities, you're in luck. The town is crisscrossed with trails that are perfect for walking, biking, or even trying to outrun a particularly energetic dog. The Coal Ridge Trail is a local favorite, where you can stroll and soak in the stunning views while wondering how on earth you managed to forget sunscreen yet again. You'll also find parks that cater to every family's need for space to run, play, or have a picnic that inevitably ends up with ants as uninvited guests.

Frederick is also home to various annual events that add a dash of excitement to the calendar. The Frederick in Flight Balloon Festival is a highlight, featuring hot air balloons floating gracefully above the landscape. It's a picturesque sight until you realize that you forgot to bring a camera and will now have to rely on your memory, which, let's be honest, is probably not that reliable after last weekend's barbecue.

Now, let's talk about the worst things about Frederick. While it has charm and character, it's not without its quirks. The dining scene can be a bit limited, and you might find yourself frequenting the same few establishments. If you're lucky, they'll have a rotating menu that will keep your palate guessing—"Will it be the 'House Special' again or something adventurous like the 'Chef's Surprise,' which might just be last week's chili?" There's a certain thrill in dining where you can count the number of menu items on one hand, but don't expect Michelin-starred cuisine unless you're prepared to redefine what "gourmet" means.

Frederick does have its fair share of local breweries, which are perfect for unwinding after a long day of work or trying to convince your friends that the local craft beer is way better than that mass-produced stuff. Just be cautious; you might end up joining a heated debate about the merits of IPAs versus lagers. And heaven forbid you mention the word "stout" in front of the self-proclaimed beer connoisseurs—you might get a three-hour lecture on how it's "too heavy" for a sunny day.

When it comes to the nightlife, Frederick doesn't exactly rock the party scene. You won't find trendy nightclubs or fancy cocktail lounges. Instead, the locals gather at neighborhood bars where the most exciting activity is pool. If you're lucky, someone might organize trivia night, where you can test your knowledge of obscure facts while desperately hoping no one asks about pop culture after 2005. But the beauty of it all lies in the laid-back atmosphere where everyone knows everyone, and strangers are welcomed with a friendly nod, assuming they can keep up with the local gossip.

Frisco

Frisco, Colorado, sounds like a charming little town that's about as far from the San Francisco Bay Area as you can get without hitting a tumbleweed. You might think it got its name from some romantic vision of the Golden Gate Bridge, but no, the name actually comes from the railroad. The Denver and Rio Grande Western Railroad decided to drop a "Frisco" into the mix, likely because "Boring Town" was already taken. So, there you have it: a name that has nothing to do with fog, sourdough bread, or tech startups.

Historically, Frisco was established during the gold rush of the 1800s, when every other town was sprouting up like mushrooms after a rain. It was a classic case of "there's gold in them there hills," and people flocked to the area, hoping to strike it rich. Unfortunately, many of them realized they were better suited for other pursuits, like selling shovels or becoming expert nugget polishers. Fast forward a couple of centuries, and Frisco has transformed from a dusty mining town into a trendy little hub for outdoor enthusiasts, tourists, and people who think "après-ski" is a lifestyle choice.

The town's history is well-preserved, and one of the best places to soak it all in is the Frisco Historic Park and Museum. Imagine a charming collection of buildings that looks like it was pulled straight from a Christmas card. There's a schoolhouse, a log cabin, and a church, each more picturesque than the last. You half-expect to see Santa peeking out from behind the wooden fence, just waiting for the perfect moment to jump in for a photo op. The museum offers a glimpse into the town's past, showcasing artifacts that make you wonder how people survived without smartphones. How did they communicate? Smoke signals? Carrier pigeons? It's all a bit of a mystery, but it definitely makes you appreciate the wonders of texting.

Now, let's dive into the best things to do in Frisco. If you're an outdoor enthusiast, this place is like a candy store for adults. You can hike, bike, ski, and snowboard until your legs feel like jelly. The Frisco Peninsula Recreation Area is a local favorite. In the summer, it's perfect for hiking and mountain biking, but in winter, it transforms into a snowy wonderland where cross-country skiing and snowshoeing reign supreme. Just be warned: if you're not careful, you might accidentally end up in a snowball fight with a group of kids who take their snow sports way too seriously.

Speaking of sports, let's talk about the Frisco Adventure Park. This place is like Disneyland for adults who've traded in their Mickey ears for ski helmets. It offers everything from tubing hills to Nordic skiing. You'll find yourself laughing uncontrollably as you race down the tubing hill, hoping you don't end up in a face-first snowdrift. Nothing says "adulting" like screaming your head off while trying to maintain some semblance of dignity.

And if you're into water sports, the Dillon Reservoir is just a stone's throw away. Boating, fishing, paddleboarding—you name it, you can do it. Just be sure to watch out for the rogue paddleboarders who seem to think they're auditioning for a water ballet. You might get splashed, and then your daydreams of serene relaxation will be replaced with thoughts of revenge through an unexpected wave of your own.

But let's not gloss over the worst things about Frisco. The dining scene can sometimes feel like a high-stakes game of "Guess What's on the Menu." You could find a fantastic little bistro one day and the next day it's transformed into yet another pizza place. Pizza? Sure, it's a classic. But when you're trying to enjoy some local cuisine, being served pizza at every turn can feel a bit monotonous. You might find yourself longing for something adventurous, like, I don't know, a salad? The horror.

And let's talk about parking. It's a sport unto itself. If you're not prepared to channel your inner contortionist to squeeze into a space that's about the size of a postage stamp, you may end up walking from a remote location that's farther than the hike you just completed. The battle for parking spots is fierce, especially during peak seasons when everyone and their dog decide to come to Frisco at the same time. You might as well bring a tent and some snacks because you could be waiting a while.

Let's not forget the weather. While it's lovely most of the time, Colorado's mountains have a way of changing moods faster than a toddler who's missed nap time. One minute you're basking in the sun, and the next you're dodging hail the size of golf balls. If you don't pack layers, you might find yourself buying a $50 sweatshirt from the gift shop just to avoid hypothermia. It's all part of the Frisco experience, or at least that's what they tell you as they hand you a brochure on "How to Dress for All Four Seasons in One Day."

Now, on to the events. Frisco hosts a variety of festivals, but be prepared for the fact that they can sometimes feel like they're going for quantity over quality. You'll find events celebrating everything from art to beer to the grand opening of a new taco truck. Sure, you might discover a hidden gem or two, but you'll also encounter a few quirky offerings that leave you scratching your head. "Do we really need a festival dedicated to the appreciation of pinecones?" you might ask. The answer, surprisingly, is yes. In Frisco, anything is possible.

Fruita

Fruita, Colorado, a name that sounds like it was plucked straight from a fruit basket, actually has its roots in the early settlers' fondness for the local produce. When you think of Fruita, you might picture a quaint little town where apples and peaches reign supreme, but hold onto your hats because this place has a history that's as juicy as a ripe peach.

Originally, Fruita was home to the Ute people, who were probably rolling their eyes at the settlers who arrived later, thinking they could just plop down in the valley and call it home. Fast forward to the late 1800s, when the town was founded around 1880, thanks to a combination of irrigation systems and a desire for agriculture. Farmers flocked to the area, undoubtedly hoping to create the next great fruit empire. Little did they know that Fruita would eventually morph into a mountain biking mecca. Talk about a plot twist.

Fruita's history is preserved at the Museum of Western Colorado's Fruita Branch, which is a delightful way to dive into the past. You'll find everything from old farming equipment to quirky artifacts that tell the story of the town's evolution. Imagine walking through a small museum filled with dusty relics and stories that could put even the most energetic toddler to sleep. It's a treasure trove for history buffs, though you might occasionally question why a town needs an exhibit dedicated to vintage fruit crates. They really went all out.

Now, let's talk about the best things to see and do in Fruita. If you've ever wanted to experience mountain biking while simultaneously being smacked in the face by the gorgeous Colorado scenery, look no further than the Kokopelli Trail. This trail system is practically a rite of passage for anyone who enjoys two wheels and gravity-defying downhill thrills. Just make sure to wear a helmet, because you'll want to protect that precious noggin when you take the inevitable tumble down a steep slope. The adrenaline rush of flying downhill is only slightly diminished by the impending bruises that come with it.

For those who prefer their adventures a little less adrenaline-pumping, Fruita offers the Colorado River. Kayaking and paddleboarding on the river is a lovely way to cool off and pretend you're a water sports pro, even if your only experience involves splashing around in the kiddie pool. The riverbanks are lined with trees, and you might even spot a heron or two, judging you from afar as you struggle to balance on your board. Remember, it's not about the destination; it's about how spectacularly you can fall into the water.

If you're not one for getting muddy or wet, don't worry; Fruita has you covered with its array of local wineries. Yes, you heard that right. The town is home to some charming vineyards where you can sip on local wines and pretend to be a connoisseur, swirling your glass and nodding thoughtfully as you try to discern the "notes of berry." It's all fun and games until someone spills their wine or mistakenly declares that they taste hints of shoe leather. Don't worry; it happens to the best of us.

Now let's get to the worst things about Fruita, because every town has its quirks. For starters, the dining scene can sometimes feel like a roll of the dice. You could find a fantastic little eatery that serves the most divine tacos one day, only to return the next week to find it has mysteriously transformed into yet another sandwich shop. You may very well end up sampling a dozen mediocre burgers before you stumble upon the hidden gem that serves up the most delicious chili you've ever tasted. Or, you might just end up with a plate of something that looks suspiciously like a science experiment gone wrong.

Then there's the weather. While the sun shines brilliantly most of the time, don't let that fool you into thinking you're safe from sudden temperature drops or unexpected storms. One minute you're basking in the sun, and the next you're huddled under an awning, praying that the dark clouds will pass without ruining your day. Make sure to pack layers; otherwise, you'll be forced to buy that overpriced hoodie from the local gift shop, which may or may not have a "Fruita: It's a Peach of a Place" slogan plastered on it.

Fruita also has a population of about 13,000 people, which means you might run into the same friendly faces several times during your visit. This can be charming or slightly unnerving, depending on your social skills. If you're someone who enjoys small talk, you'll fit right in. But if you're more of the "please don't ask me about my day" type, you might find yourself dodging conversations like they're an aggressive dog in the park.

Let's not forget about the local events. Fruita loves to celebrate, and that means festivals galore. The Fruita Fall Festival, for instance, is a delightful time when the town transforms into a carnival of sorts. You'll find parades, arts and crafts, and more food than you can shake a stick at. Just be prepared for the fact that some of those food vendors might still be perfecting their recipes, leading to a few questionable culinary choices. And don't even get me started on the annual bike festival. If you're not into biking, you might feel a bit left out while everyone else is gearing up for an epic ride through the mountains.

Genoa

Genoa, Colorado, a name that might sound like an Italian city but is actually a small town in the eastern plains of Colorado, is one of those places that seems to have escaped the notice of time and the 21st century altogether. Founded in 1887, this tiny spot in Lincoln County has a history that is equal parts fascinating and bewildering. It's as if the town was frozen in a vintage postcard—complete with sepia tones and a healthy dose of quirkiness.

The name "Genoa" is said to have been inspired by Genoa, Italy, but locals might tell you it's more about the abundance of weeds and wildflowers than Mediterranean charm. Picture early settlers looking at their scraggly homesteads and thinking, "You know what this needs? A fancy name!" And thus, Genoa was born. It thrived for a time as a bustling railroad town, but like many places in the West, it saw its glory days fade as the trains moved on and so did the townsfolk, leaving behind a town that is now a shell of its former self.

If you're ever inclined to visit, the first stop on your Genoa tour should undoubtedly be the Genoa Historical Society Museum. Don't let the unassuming exterior fool you; inside, you'll find an array of artifacts that could make any history buff's heart flutter with joy—or at least raise an eyebrow. This museum is a delightful jumble of local history, from dusty old photographs that look like they were taken when the camera was still a new invention, to tools that could be mistaken for medieval torture devices. It's a snapshot of life in the late 1800s, minus the Instagram filters.

As you wander through the museum, you might come across a collection of quirky items that reflect the oddball spirit of the town. There are old farming tools, vintage clothing, and even the original high school mascot costume that looks like it was crafted by someone who took the phrase "make it cute" a little too literally. It's both charming and mildly terrifying, and you'll probably find yourself trying to decipher how a town could end up with a mascot that looks like a mutant potato.

Once you've soaked up enough history to impress your friends back home, it's time to explore the great outdoors—or at least the not-so-great outdoors of Genoa. One of the best things to do is to take a stroll through the lovely parks, where you can experience the sheer joy of being outdoors while simultaneously wondering what to do next. The parks are an ideal place for a picnic, assuming you don't mind sharing your sandwich with a curious squirrel or two. Just make sure to pack extra snacks because those little guys can be persistent, and they have a knack for judging your snack choices.

For the adventurous type, nearby options abound for outdoor activities, like hiking and biking. Just be prepared to explain to your friends that yes, you did indeed hike up that hill, even if it was more of a gentle slope. The scenery is picturesque, with vast fields of grass stretching to the horizon, occasionally interrupted by the odd cow or tumbleweed. It's the kind of place that makes you feel like you're on the set of a low-budget Western film.

Now let's talk about the culinary scene, or lack thereof. The dining options in Genoa can be a bit sparse. You might find yourself perusing the local diner menu, which could feature anything from hearty breakfasts to cheeseburgers that seem to have seen better days. The food might not win any awards, but there's something endearing about sitting in a diner where the décor hasn't changed since the '70s. Just don't ask about the "daily special." It might be better left to the imagination.

The worst part about visiting Genoa, however, is the lack of nightlife. If you're looking for vibrant bars and clubs, you might as well pack your bags and head to Denver. The nightlife here consists of cozy chats with the locals, which might turn into a spirited debate about the best way to cook a steak or the merits of different tractor brands. It's all very friendly and wholesome, but if you're hoping to dance the night away, you're better off twirling in your living room.

Despite its small size, Genoa does host an annual event that brings the community together—The Genoa Community Festival. Imagine a small-town fair with local vendors, games for the kids, and maybe a parade featuring floats that look like they were crafted from whatever materials happened to be lying around. It's the kind of festival where you can get your fill of cotton candy while contemplating how the cotton was grown in the first place.

As charming as it is, Genoa does have its peculiarities. For one, the population hovers around 200 people, which means if you're not careful, you might end up at the same event as everyone else in town. This can lead to some awkward encounters, especially if you accidentally comment on someone's choice of hat. You'll quickly find out that in a small town, everyone knows everyone else's business, and gossip travels faster than the wind.

Genoa is a town where time stands still, and the quirks of small-town life thrive. With its rich history, oddball museum, and delightful outdoor activities, it offers a unique experience that blends nostalgia with a pinch of the absurd. Sure, you might not find a bustling nightlife or gourmet dining options, but who needs those when you can revel in the charm of a town that feels like it's living in a sepia-toned postcard? Whether you're a history buff, an outdoor enthusiast, or just someone looking to experience the quirks of small-town life, Genoa has something for you, even if it's just a bizarre conversation with a local about the virtues of homemade pie.

Georgetown

Georgetown, Colorado, a name that rolls off the tongue as easily as a ski slope rolls downhill, is a town that looks like it was plucked straight from a storybook and dropped into the Rocky Mountains. Founded in the mid-1800s during the Gold Rush, this picturesque little enclave was once a booming mining town. Picture miners running around with pickaxes, dreams of gold in their eyes, and an unyielding thirst for adventure—and probably a bit too much whiskey.

The name "Georgetown" supposedly comes from George "Pegleg" Williams, who stumbled upon gold in the area and decided to celebrate his fortune by naming the town after himself. If only he knew how it would become a historic site instead of just a barroom tale. The town's mining heyday didn't last long, and soon Georgetown transitioned from a bustling center of commerce to a charming ghost of its former self, like the last few pieces of fruit in a sad, neglected fruit basket.

One of the first stops in Georgetown should undoubtedly be the Georgetown Loop Railroad. This isn't just any old train ride; it's a majestic, scenic journey through the mountains that makes you feel like you've been transported back to a time when trains were the height of luxury and speed. The ride weaves through some breathtaking landscapes, and let's be honest, it's also an excellent opportunity to take a million pictures for your social media, even if you end up looking like a tourist in a giant hat. Just remember, if you hear a whistle, it's probably the train and not your Instagram account reminding you that you haven't posted in a week.

Then there's the Georgetown Heritage Center, a museum dedicated to preserving the town's rich history. Imagine walking through a collection of artifacts that could have come from a scavenger hunt gone wrong. You'll find everything from old mining equipment that looks like it could double as medieval torture devices to sepia-toned photographs of people who were probably way too excited about their mining hats. You'll marvel at the juxtaposition of the past and wonder how anyone ever thought that a miner's mustache was a good idea.

Once you've had your fill of history and nostalgia, take a stroll through the town. The charming architecture will have you feeling like you've stepped onto a film set, and it's easy to see why Georgetown has been featured in movies and TV shows. Just be careful where you step; you might trip over a historical landmark. If you're lucky, you might even stumble upon one of the town's many ghost stories, because who doesn't love a good tale about a long-lost miner wandering the streets looking for his gold?

Now, let's get real about the food scene in Georgetown. It's a bit of a mixed bag, much like a box of chocolates that you forgot was there and only discover when you're trying to clean out the pantry. You can find some local diners serving hearty fare that might remind you of grandma's cooking, assuming your grandma wasn't too into healthy eating. Think comfort food with a side of nostalgia, served with a dash of "Is that what I think it is?" But if you're looking for gourmet dining, you might want to recalibrate your expectations.

And while we're on the subject of dining, the town does host a couple of charming eateries. Some of them have outdoor seating, perfect for soaking in the mountain air—unless you're there during one of the infamous summer rain showers, which can sweep in faster than you can say "I should have checked the weather." Nothing says fine dining like huddling under an awning, trying to enjoy your meal while the heavens decide to unleash their fury.

For those seeking a bit of adventure, there are hiking trails galore. The hiking in the area is spectacular, with paths winding through lush forests and stunning views that make your Instagram followers weep with envy. Just be sure to pack plenty of water because nothing ruins a hike faster than turning back halfway due to dehydration and shame. You'll also want to keep an eye out for the local wildlife, which might include anything from a curious deer to a bear that looks like it just stepped out of a reality show about foodies.

Now, let's not sugarcoat everything. Georgetown does have its fair share of quirky downsides. The weather can be as unpredictable as a toddler with a sugar rush. One minute you're basking in the sun, and the next, it's snowing. You might even witness the phenomenon known as the "Georgetown Wind," which has been known to pick up unsuspecting tourists and send them tumbling down the street like tumbleweeds in a Western film.

The nightlife, if you can call it that, is on the quieter side. Don't expect a bustling party scene; you're more likely to find locals gathered around a fire pit, sharing ghost stories and hot cocoa. This may sound idyllic, but if you're looking for late-night dancing, you might want to bring your own disco ball and some glow sticks. The town might be small, but that doesn't mean you can't have a good time—just remember to keep the music low so as not to disturb the ghosts.

And let's not forget about the annual events, which range from quaint to quirky. The Georgetown Christmas Market is a delightful affair, featuring local crafts, local authors, hot cider, and enough holiday cheer to make even the Scroogiest among us crack a smile. If you time your visit right, you might even catch the famous Georgetown Ghost Tour, which will take you around the town and tell you tales of its haunted past. It's like a history lesson but with more spookiness and fewer textbooks.

Gilcrest

Gilcrest, Colorado, a name that sounds like it could be a character in a whimsical children's book, is a small town with a big personality and a history as quirky as its name. Founded in the early 20th century, Gilcrest emerged as a charming little community primarily thanks to the railroad and the agricultural boom. Imagine farmers in overalls and wide-brimmed hats chasing their dreams of crops and cattle, while the trains puffed along, serving as a lifeline to the wider world. The name "Gilcrest" itself supposedly comes from a combination of the family names of the town's founders, and you can almost picture them nodding at each other, saying, "Let's slap our names together and call it a day!"

One of the first things to note about Gilcrest is that it's the kind of place where everyone knows everyone—if you're looking for anonymity, you might want to rethink your life choices. The town is small enough that you might even bump into the same person twice while searching for a parking spot. But this tight-knit community atmosphere is what makes Gilcrest feel cozy, like a warm blanket on a cold day, even if that blanket is a little dusty and in need of a wash.

In terms of museums, don't expect a grand Smithsonian-style experience. The Gilcrest Historical Society operates a small museum dedicated to preserving the town's heritage. Here, you'll find artifacts that could be described as "fascinating" only if you've got an insatiable curiosity for rusty farming tools and photos of people whose hairstyles belong firmly in the last century. It's a place that invites visitors to marvel at how far we've come, especially in the realm of fashion. After all, there's nothing like a good old-fashioned sepia-toned photo of a mustachioed man in suspenders to make you appreciate modern grooming standards.

If you're lucky, you might visit during one of Gilcrest's town events, which range from charmingly quaint to bewilderingly odd. The annual Gilcrest Community BBQ is a highlight, where locals gather to feast on grilled meats and enjoy a side of small-town gossip. It's a culinary experience that could make even the most indifferent meat-lover swoon, as long as you don't mind the possibility of inadvertently discovering someone's secret recipe for coleslaw that they probably swore they'd never share. Just remember to pace yourself; too much BBQ can leave you feeling like you're about to roll home.

For outdoor enthusiasts, Gilcrest is near some decent spots for hiking and nature walks, though it's essential to understand that "nature" in Colorado often includes a healthy dose of unpredictable weather. The views are stunning, the air is crisp, and there's always the chance you might run into a deer who looks slightly annoyed to have its photo taken. Pro tip: if you do see a deer, don't be that person who tries to feed it. It's not a petting zoo; it's a wild animal with standards, after all.

Now, let's not sugarcoat everything. The "best" things about Gilcrest can sometimes double as the "worst." For instance, if you're expecting vibrant nightlife, you're in for a shock. The nightlife in Gilcrest can best be described as "hushed," resembling more of a cozy gathering around a fire pit than a club scene. Don't expect dance floors and DJ booths; instead, you'll find locals swapping stories over cups of coffee or perhaps a glass of home-brewed lemonade that may or may not have an extra kick.

The food scene is equally endearing and perplexing. While there are a few dining establishments, your culinary options will likely consist of diner classics and the occasional "what is that?" on the menu. You might find a dish called "mystery casserole" that gives you pause. While your adventurous spirit might urge you to try it, remember that some mysteries are better left unsolved. However, if you're fortunate, you'll stumble across a hidden gem of a diner where the pancakes could easily become the highlight of your trip—just ignore the off-kilter pictures on the wall and the weirdly enthusiastic waitress who seems to know your life story after a single conversation.

As for the local culture, Gilcrest can feel like a time capsule. The residents take pride in their history, which means you might encounter the occasional reenactment of historical events—because who doesn't want to see a bunch of locals donning old-fashioned clothing and trying to figure out how to use a rotary phone? These events, while charming, sometimes lead to awkward situations, like when someone accidentally brings their smartphone to a historical reenactment and sparks an existential crisis among the participants.

Don't forget the surrounding scenery, which is as diverse as the personalities of its inhabitants. With the majestic Rocky Mountains as a backdrop, the town provides an Instagram-worthy panorama that'll leave you wondering why your phone camera isn't quite capturing the beauty of it all. It's almost poetic—if you squint hard enough and tilt your head to the side.

In conclusion, Gilcrest, Colorado, is a delightful blend of history, small-town charm, and just a sprinkle of the absurd. Whether you're exploring the historical society's modest museum or sampling the local BBQ, the town offers a unique experience that captures the essence of rural Colorado. You might not find the latest trends or the hottest nightlife, but you will find a place where everyone knows your name—whether you like it or not—and where the stories of the past are as rich as the food you'll consume. Just be prepared for anything, because in Gilcrest, the unexpected is part of the charm, much like the town itself.

Glenwood Springs

Glenwood Springs, Colorado, a name that rolls off the tongue as smoothly as the waters that bubble up from its famous hot springs, is a town that offers more than just a chance to soak your stress away. It's nestled in the Rocky Mountains, giving it an enviable position as a picturesque vacation destination. The town is named after the very springs that have drawn visitors since the 1800s. Imagine early settlers gazing in wonder at the bubbling waters and thinking, "Hey, let's build a town right here! What could possibly go wrong?" Spoiler alert: they were right.

The history of Glenwood Springs reads like a textbook of wild tales, from the days of Native American tribes who used the springs for their healing properties to the arrival of white settlers in search of fortune and a hot bath. In the late 1800s, the town became a playground for the rich and famous, including Ulysses S. Grant, who took a dip in the hot springs and proclaimed them "better than a day at the spa." Okay, that may be a slight exaggeration, but you get the picture.

Fast forward to today, and Glenwood Springs is a bustling hub of activity. The town boasts a range of museums, though if you're expecting a Louvre-like experience, you might want to recalibrate your expectations. The Glenwood Springs Historical Society & Museum offers a charming glimpse into the past with exhibits that include artifacts from the railroad era and some truly riveting tales about the infamous "Glenwood Canyon Gang," a group that seems to have engaged in the kind of mischief that would make a good episode of a Wild West show.

If you're looking for the crème de la crème of museum experiences, you can also visit the Frontier Historical Museum. Here, you'll find displays that could easily inspire a game of "Guess What This Tool Was Used For." The artifacts are a testament to human ingenuity, or perhaps a testament to how much stuff people accumulate over the years. Spoiler alert: some of the items may leave you scratching your head.

Now, let's talk about the hot springs that made Glenwood Springs famous. The Glenwood Hot Springs Resort features the world's largest mineral hot springs pool. Picture yourself lounging in the warm waters while gazing up at the stunning mountain backdrop. It's as if nature conspired to create the perfect relaxation spot, and you're the lucky recipient of that cosmic favor. Just be prepared for the occasional awkward moment when someone accidentally splashes you while doing an enthusiastic cannonball—nothing says relaxation quite like being drenched by an overzealous swimmer.

For the adventurous souls out there, Glenwood Springs is home to some of Colorado's best outdoor activities. Hiking, biking, and river rafting opportunities abound. You could hike up to Hanging Lake, a stunning gem that looks like it was plucked straight from a fairy tale. Just be warned: it's popular, so you might find yourself in a conga line of fellow hikers, all silently judging each other's fitness levels. Remember, it's not about how fast you go, it's about how many picturesque selfies you can snap along the way.

If you're feeling especially brave (or foolish), you might want to tackle the Glenwood Canyon Bike Path. This scenic ride runs alongside the Colorado River, providing stunning views and occasional heart-pounding moments as you navigate the twists and turns. Just remember to bring your sense of adventure—and perhaps a little insurance.

Now, let's not sugarcoat everything. While Glenwood Springs has its charms, it also has its quirks. The town can get crowded, especially during peak tourist season, and the quest for a parking spot may turn into a game of musical chairs that no one wants to play. If you're not careful, you could end up driving in circles while listening to the same catchy pop song on the radio for the fifth time.

Then there are the dining options. While there are some gems, you may also stumble upon places that could generously be described as "quirky." Ever tried a restaurant where the menu looks like it was designed by someone with a penchant for chaos? You might find items like "Mysterious Meat Surprise" or "I Hope This Is What You Ordered." The thrill of dining in Glenwood Springs lies in the unexpected—just remember to ask a lot of questions before committing to anything.

And of course, there's the infamous Glenwood Caverns Adventure Park, where you can explore the depths of the Earth and experience thrilling rides at the same time. It's like a theme park for geology enthusiasts, where you can feel both exhilarated and educated. Just try not to think too hard about how many layers of rock are above you while riding the roller coaster—your stomach might appreciate it.

All in all, Glenwood Springs is a town of contrasts, blending natural beauty, a rich history, and the occasional bizarre experience. From soaking in the soothing hot springs to hiking breathtaking trails, every corner of this town offers something to enjoy—or at least to chuckle about. It's a place where you can embrace the peculiarities of small-town life while soaking in the grandeur of the Rockies, reminding you that sometimes the best adventures are the ones you didn't quite expect. So pack your bags, leave your inhibitions behind, and prepare for a delightful escapade filled with history, hot springs, and a healthy dose of the unexpected.

Golden

Golden, Colorado, a name that conjures images of gleaming mountains and, strangely enough, a fair amount of beer. Yes, this charming little town, nestled at the foot of the Rockies, has a rich history that includes everything from gold mining to being the home of Coors Brewery. It's the kind of place where the locals might proudly proclaim, "We've got gold in our name and a brewery on our block!"

Let's take a stroll through Golden's history, shall we? Founded during the Colorado Gold Rush in 1859, Golden quickly became a hotspot for those looking to strike it rich. As fortune-seekers flocked to the area, they probably looked at the surrounding mountains and thought, "If we can't find gold, we might as well have a scenic view." Fast forward a few decades, and Golden evolved from a dusty mining town to a vibrant community that has somehow managed to retain its charm while embracing modernity. It's like that friend who, despite getting older, still shows up to parties in the coolest clothes.

When it comes to museums, Golden has its fair share of options. First on the list is the Golden History Museum & Park. Imagine stepping into a time capsule that's been meticulously curated by someone with a love for old-timey artifacts. You'll find everything from pioneer exhibits to a replica of a historic 1800s cabin that could have easily been home to the "Little House on the Prairie" cast. You might even learn about the town's fascinating role as a center for the railroad—yes, that means trains and maybe even a few overly excited children running around.

Not to be outdone, the Colorado School of Mines Geology Museum is a gem (pun fully intended) for anyone with a penchant for rocks. This museum is packed with more minerals than a health food store and features exhibits that could make even the most rock-averse person reconsider their stance on geology. You can gawk at everything from giant crystals to fossils, all while trying to convince your friends that you, too, could have been a geology major if only you had better study habits.

Now, if you're a fan of beer—let's be honest, who isn't—then a trip to the Coors Brewery is practically a rite of passage. Tours are available, and you can witness the magic of beer-making while trying not to think about the number of college parties that ended with Coors in hand. The highlight? A sampling of the golden brew itself, served in a glass that may or may not have been washed by the same interns who accidentally spilled it on their shoes.

For those who prefer outdoor activities, Golden is a playground for the adventurous. Hiking in the nearby foothills offers spectacular views, and if you're lucky, you might catch sight of a deer that looks slightly more majestic than you feel in your old hiking boots. Don't miss out on a stroll down the Clear Creek Path, where you can contemplate life's mysteries while watching people attempt to navigate the river in their kayaks—mostly unsuccessfully, if we're being honest.

On the flip side, Golden isn't without its quirks. The town can get a tad crowded, especially during the summer when tourists flock to experience the outdoor life. Finding a parking spot may require more strategic planning than an advanced chess match. And let's not forget the weather—one minute you're basking in sunshine, and the next, a rogue hailstorm could appear, turning your leisurely hike into a frantic dash for cover. If you're not careful, you might find yourself seeking shelter under a less-than-reliable tree that's more likely to drop a branch on your head than provide actual protection.

Now, let's address the food scene. Golden boasts an array of eateries that cater to every palate, from foodies to picky eaters. However, be wary of the "quirky" restaurants where the menu might include items that sound more like a dare than a meal. You might encounter dishes like "Mystery Meat Tacos" or "Surprise Ingredients Pizza," which could leave you questioning your life choices—or at least your dining partner's judgment.

For a truly unique experience, there's the Buffalo Bill Museum and Grave. Yes, you read that right. This is the final resting place of the legendary William F. Cody, a.k.a. Buffalo Bill. You can pay your respects while contemplating how someone could have made a living showcasing cowboy life in a world where most of us just sit at desks. The museum features artifacts that make you feel like you've stepped into a Wild West show, complete with photos, memorabilia, and more hats than you knew existed. And if you're feeling particularly adventurous, take a hike to the grave—it's a workout and a history lesson all rolled into one.

Granada

Granada, Colorado, a name that rolls off the tongue like an overly ambitious Spanish dancer. Tucked away in the southeastern part of the state, Granada has a history that's as colorful as its name. Founded in the 1870s, the town was initially a bustling hub for the railroad and agriculture, primarily known for its thriving beet sugar industry. Yes, you heard that right—beet sugar. When you think of the sweet stuff, you probably picture cane sugar, but Granada said, "Why not beets?" This bold choice meant a whole lot of sugar and a whole lot of farming, with farmers likely high-fiving each other over their crop yields while pondering what to do with all that excess beet pulp.

As you explore Granada, you'll stumble across the Prowers County Historical Museum, which is an absolute treasure trove for those who enjoy dusty artifacts and stories about days gone by. Here, you can learn about the town's rich history, including its role as a stop for people traveling west. Imagine folks back in the day disembarking from a train and asking, "Is this where we're supposed to find our dreams or just a decent cup of coffee?" The museum features everything from vintage clothing to a replica of a one-room schoolhouse, which might make you feel nostalgic for a time when education involved more memorization and less scrolling through TikTok.

Now, if you're a fan of the outdoors, the surrounding area offers opportunities for hiking, fishing, and pretending you're a pioneer while avoiding modern conveniences like Wi-Fi and coffee shops. Granada's proximity to the Arkansas River means you can go fishing, or as I like to call it, "sitting quietly while contemplating life choices." But be careful; the river can get a little rambunctious, much like a toddler on a sugar high.

Then there's the charm of Granada's downtown, which is more quaint than bustling. Picture a scene from a Western movie, but with fewer cowboys and more people trying to remember where they parked their cars. The streets are lined with small businesses that are just waiting for you to stop by, provided you don't mind the occasional tumbleweed rolling by. You might encounter a diner that boasts the best green chili this side of the Rockies. Or you might find a quirky antique shop filled with items that make you wonder about their past lives—like that one porcelain cat figurine that looks like it's seen some things.

Speaking of food, let's talk about the culinary scene, which ranges from downright delightful to "did I really just eat that?" You'll find classic diner fare that's as comforting as a warm hug, and then there are the adventurous spots that might make you reconsider your life choices. A local favorite is the famed Granada Taco Shop, where the tacos are delicious, and the hot sauce could set your mouth on fire faster than you can say, "Why did I order extra hot?"

Now, if you're a history buff, you'll appreciate Granada's connection to the infamous Amache Internment Camp, located just a few miles outside of town. During World War II, this camp housed Japanese American internees, and today, the site serves as a poignant reminder of that chapter in history. There's a small memorial and interpretive site that tells the story of the camp and its residents, complete with the kind of historical depth that leaves you both thoughtful and slightly somber. It's a place where you can reflect on how history isn't always a straightforward tale of heroism and glory—sometimes it's about learning from past mistakes, which is a heavy load for a little town like Granada to carry.

In terms of what to avoid, Granada is as close to a sleepy town as you can get. If you're looking for nightlife, you might want to bring your own disco ball and a playlist, because the after-dark options are limited. The most excitement you'll find might be a local bingo night or the occasional town hall meeting where someone discusses the benefits of beets. Thrilling, I know!

As for seasonal events, Granada has its share of small-town charm, including an annual festival that could be described as "cute" at best. Picture vendors selling homemade crafts, a pie-eating contest, and the kind of community spirit that makes you wish you had baked something to contribute. You'll definitely feel a sense of camaraderie, even if you're just a curious traveler passing through.

Granby

Granby, Colorado, a name that sounds like it could be a mispronunciation of a fancy cheese but is, in fact, a charming mountain town nestled between the Rockies. The name "Granby" is derived from the Granby River, which itself sounds like a name you'd give a rather enthusiastic dog. Established in the late 19th century, Granby initially flourished thanks to the railroad and a healthy dose of good ol' fashioned mining. It was like the Gold Rush but with more pine trees and fewer mustaches.

Fast forward to today, and Granby still embodies that classic Colorado spirit, where the locals are as friendly as a Labrador puppy, and the air is so crisp it feels like nature's way of giving you a refreshing slap in the face. If you're looking for history, the Granby area is rich with tales of rugged pioneers, ambitious railroad tycoons, and a smattering of colorful characters that would make a great sitcom if you added a laugh track and some strategically placed commercial breaks.

One of the gems in Granby's crown is the Granby Museum. This delightful establishment isn't exactly the Louvre, but it certainly has its own charm. It's filled with artifacts that tell the story of the town and its surroundings, featuring everything from old photographs that could make you question fashion choices of yesteryear to tools that likely belonged to people who were way tougher than you. Visitors can marvel at the stories of settlers and see just how far civilization has come from those early days of hand-carved furniture and no indoor plumbing.

The town's outdoor attractions are where Granby truly shines—provided you're not allergic to nature or fresh air. Just nearby is Granby Ranch, a ski area that boasts winter sports opportunities for everyone, from the daredevils attempting to become the next Olympic champion to the folks who can barely manage to stay upright on a flat surface. During the summer months, the place transforms into a mecca for mountain biking and hiking. You might even feel inspired to take a selfie with a majestic mountain backdrop, capturing a moment of faux bravery that will make your friends on social media wildly jealous.

Now, if you fancy a leisurely day, head to Lake Granby, where you can engage in activities that range from fishing (a sport that involves a lot of waiting and very little actual catching) to boating (because nothing says relaxation like trying to avoid a sunburn while steering a boat). Don't forget your sunscreen, because nothing ruins a trip to a beautiful lake like the unmistakable scent of regret and fried skin.

For those who appreciate the finer things in life, Granby does offer some local dining options. You might find a cozy diner serving up comfort food that'll make you feel like you've been wrapped in a warm blanket. The granola bars here probably taste better than anything you'd find in a fancy city café, and if you're lucky, you might even stumble upon a place serving a slice of pie that could rival grandma's secret recipe. Just be careful not to ask for the recipe; it's a dangerous path filled with betrayal and unexpected family feuds.

Now, let's talk about the downside. Granby is definitely not the life of the party. If you're looking for nightlife, your options are about as sparse as a hairline on a bad comb-over. Most nights, you'll find yourself gazing at the stars, which is nice until you realize that you could be watching Netflix in your pajamas. The most excitement you might encounter could be a local trivia night or a town meeting discussing the merits of paving another road. Riveting stuff, I assure you.

Seasonal events in Granby provide a bit of flavor to the otherwise calm calendar. The Granby Rodeo is a highlight, where you can witness the thrill of cowboys attempting to tame bucking broncos while you munch on cotton candy, blissfully unaware that you're about to become the butt of a million jokes. Picture families gathered around, cheering on the brave souls who willingly climb onto animals that are far more powerful than any of us will ever be. It's like a live-action version of "America's Funniest Home Videos," and you can't help but root for the cowboys, even as they eat dirt.

One quirky site that could easily be a double feature in a horror film is the infamous "Granby's Haunted Hotel," which is rumored to have more ghosts than guests. While you might find it hard to decide if the shivers you feel are due to paranormal activity or simply the cold Colorado air, it's a fun stop for those who enjoy a good ghost story or just want to feel a little spooked. Be prepared for a few overly enthusiastic local legends that might make you question your decision to spend the night.

Granby is like that favorite old sweater you can't part with—it's cozy, familiar, and has its own unique charm, even if it's not the trendiest piece in your closet. With its rich history, friendly locals, and ample outdoor activities, Granby offers a slice of life that feels both refreshing and nostalgic. Sure, the nightlife might be lacking, but you'll have more than enough nature, history, and small-town warmth to fill your days with memorable moments. Just remember, when in Granby, it's not about the wild nights out; it's about the beautiful sunsets, the quiet moments, and perhaps the best slice of pie you'll ever taste.

Grand Junction

Grand Junction, Colorado, is a name that evokes images of sprawling mesas, rugged canyons, and the distinct possibility that you're lost somewhere between Denver and Utah. Located at the confluence of the Colorado River and the Gunnison River, Grand Junction is a place where nature and civilization awkwardly coexist, and it wears that title like a badge of honor. The name itself is a straightforward homage to its geographical features, hinting at the junction of two rivers and a few questionable life choices made by travelers seeking a shortcut.

The history of Grand Junction is a colorful tapestry woven with the threads of Native American heritage, pioneering settlers, and a dash of cowboy flair. Initially inhabited by the Ute tribe, this area saw its first influx of white settlers in the late 19th century, thanks in part to the arrival of the railroad. Yes, nothing screams "progress" quite like laying down some tracks and hoping for the best! The town was founded in 1881, and it quickly became a hub for agriculture and trade, as the fertile land surrounding the rivers lured in farmers eager to make their mark. It's safe to say that if you had a green thumb, you were in business.

Fast forward to today, and Grand Junction is a blend of small-town charm and the distinct flavor of an aging college town. The locals proudly proclaim themselves as the "wine country" of Colorado, and they have the vineyards to prove it. You can tour the wineries, sip on some surprisingly decent vino, and pretend you're a connoisseur while secretly Googling what "terroir" means. This area is a surprising powerhouse in the Colorado wine scene, with vineyards that range from quaint to absolutely Instagrammable.

Speaking of things that are picturesque, let's talk about the outdoors. Grand Junction is a stone's throw from some seriously stunning landscapes. The Colorado National Monument, a short drive from downtown, boasts breathtaking views and enough hiking trails to make even the most apathetic couch potato consider lacing up their sneakers. You can marvel at the sheer cliffs and rock formations that seem to challenge gravity, all while hoping that your phone has enough battery to capture the moment for your social media followers. Just be sure to watch your step—there's a difference between "cliffhanger" and "plummeting to your doom."

If you're more of an indoor enthusiast or someone who believes that "fresh air" is just a conspiracy, fear not. Grand Junction has its museums, like the Museum of the West, which showcases the rich history of the area, from Native American artifacts to the kind of Old West memorabilia that makes you want to don a cowboy hat and talk like you just stepped off the set of a John Wayne film. Here, you can learn about the local history while trying to suppress your desire to yell, "Yeehaw!" at inappropriate moments.

For those looking to immerse themselves in culture, the city hosts a vibrant arts scene. The downtown area is dotted with galleries, murals, and art installations that give off a "we tried really hard" vibe. One particularly amusing sight is the "Sculpture in the Park" program, where you can stroll through parks and pretend to appreciate modern art while pondering why anyone would think a giant metal chicken deserves a spot next to a serene pond.

Now, let's address the elephant in the room—or perhaps the tumbleweed in the landscape. Grand Junction's nightlife is, how should we put this, as lively as a retirement home at 3 PM. Sure, there are a few bars and restaurants where you can grab a drink, but don't expect wild parties or anything resembling a "rager." You might find yourself at a local pub, sipping on a craft beer while discussing the merits of local gardening practices. That's not to say there isn't fun to be had; it's just a different kind of fun. Think more "artistic jam sessions" and less "wild bachelorette parties."

As for the local dining scene, prepare your taste buds for a rollercoaster ride. On one hand, you have charming cafes that serve up hearty breakfasts that could put a diner to shame. On the other hand, you might stumble upon a bizarre fusion restaurant that combines sushi with tacos—because who doesn't love a little culinary chaos? You might want to tread carefully here; sometimes, creativity leads to fantastic flavor explosions, and other times, it results in dishes that leave you questioning your life choices.

And if you're looking for the "best" things to do in Grand Junction, they can be summed up in a few delightful activities. Visit the Grand Junction Botanical Gardens, where you can pretend to be a plant expert while admiring flowers you can't name. Go for a hike in the aforementioned Colorado National Monument, where you can capture that perfect selfie of you looking all adventurous—because nothing says "I'm a well-rounded individual" like a photo of you with a rock formation. And, of course, partake in the local wineries, where you can get tipsy on fermented grapes while discussing the finer points of the grape harvest with fellow enthusiasts.

Now, on the "worst" side of things, you might encounter a few quirks that can test your patience. The weather can be as unpredictable as a cat on a caffeine high, swinging between scorching heat and surprising cold snaps. The local wildlife can also be a little too friendly—don't be surprised if a deer decides to stroll right into town like it owns the place. And if you're not prepared for the occasional dust storm, you might find yourself wondering why you suddenly feel like you're part of a Western movie set in a sandstorm.

Grand Lake

Grand Lake, Colorado, sounds like a dreamy postcard destination, doesn't it? You can almost hear the gentle lapping of water against the shore, see the majestic peaks framing the scene, and picture tourists wrestling with inflatable swans while their children scream with glee. But let's not get too lost in the idyllic visuals; there's plenty of humor to mine from this small mountain town.

The name "Grand Lake" might suggest something vast and regal, like a royal banquet hall for the elite, but in reality, it's more of a charmingly modest spot. The lake itself is indeed grand—at least by Colorado standards. It's the largest natural lake in the state, which means if you ever find yourself at a trivia night in a bar somewhere, you can confidently shout that fact and impress no one but your equally bored companions.

The history of Grand Lake is a delightful romp through the past. Originally inhabited by the Ute tribe, this area has a rich Native American heritage that predates the arrival of white settlers by, oh, about a thousand years. The town was founded in the late 19th century, around the time when settlers realized that Colorado wasn't just a barren wasteland but rather a beautiful and bountiful place, perfect for, you guessed it, mining! Because when you think "beautiful nature," what better way to celebrate than digging it up for gold?

Fast forward a bit, and you have a quaint town thriving on tourism and fishing, a town that thought, "Why not lure in a few city folks looking for a weekend escape?" Grand Lake became a summer destination for weary travelers and an ideal spot for those wanting to escape the sweltering heat of the lowlands. The town's charm lies in its picturesque views and cozy cabins, but also in its blatant ability to attract people who want to pretend they're outdoorsy without actually having to do anything too strenuous.

Now let's dive into the museums, shall we? Grand Lake is not exactly bursting at the seams with cultural institutions. The town does boast the Kauffman House Museum, a historic hotel turned museum that offers a peek into the past. Imagine stepping into a place where the air is thick with the scent of old wood and nostalgia, and where you can marvel at the fact that people once traveled across the country just to sleep on a creaky bed while hoping for a good breakfast. You'll find plenty of artifacts from the early days, including furniture, photographs, and stories of tourists who didn't have Instagram to document their every move. Ah, the good old days when memories were just that—memories and not over-filtered snapshots of every mediocre latte.

On the outdoor front, Grand Lake is a paradise for those who claim to love nature but also enjoy the comfort of a hot shower and a plush bed. The lake itself is perfect for fishing, kayaking, and paddleboarding, as long as you don't mind the occasional goose honking at you like it's trying to take your lunch money. The views are stunning, and if you get tired of the scenery, you can always look at your fellow tourists and judge their choice of swimwear instead.

If hiking is your thing, you'll find trails that range from "I thought this was a nature stroll" to "I need a paramedic, stat!" The surrounding Rocky Mountain National Park is just a hop, skip, and jump away, offering ample opportunities for those who like to pretend they're rugged explorers. Just be sure to pack a sufficient supply of snacks, because nothing says "I'm ready for an adventure" like a granola bar and some high hopes.

Now, let's address the "best" things to do in Grand Lake. First and foremost, there's the annual Grand Lake Arts and Crafts Festival, where local artisans showcase their wares, including jewelry, pottery, and paintings. It's a delightful way to feel cultured while also secretly judging how much you'd pay for a handmade wooden spoon. If you're not careful, you might end up with more trinkets than you bargained for—perfect for cluttering up your house or giving as awkward gifts.

The Grand Lake Beach is another must-see, where you can lounge on the shore, dip your toes in the water, and contemplate the existential dread of life while avoiding splashes from the enthusiastic kids around you. You might even see a few locals trying to catch fish or convince their dogs to fetch sticks. It's a charming scene, if not a little chaotic.

And if you're in the mood for some culinary delights, you'll find a few restaurants serving up everything from hearty breakfasts to slightly questionable dinner options. You can enjoy a meal with a view, all while pondering why it's so hard to find a decent taco in a mountain town. As you dine, keep an eye out for the local wildlife—nothing like a chipmunk darting by to remind you that nature is still very much in charge.

Now, let's flip the coin and explore the "worst" things to do in Grand Lake, shall we? Prepare yourself for the winter months when the weather can be as unforgiving as your high school gym teacher. If you're not a fan of freezing temperatures and snowstorms that make you feel like you're in a snow globe, you might want to stay away during those months.

The town can also feel a bit sleepy, especially during the off-peak seasons. If you're someone who thrives on hustle and bustle, you may find yourself staring into the abyss of the quiet streets, wondering if this is how people end up in cults. When the summer crowds thin out, the silence can be deafening, and the only sounds you'll hear are your own thoughts or the distant call of a lonely bird.

Additionally, the occasional tourist trap is a must-mention. You'll find shops selling every conceivable type of souvenir, from overpriced t-shirts to random knickknacks that will gather dust on your shelf for years to come. There's nothing quite like spending money on a foam moose hat that you'll regret wearing in public. The more you try to fit in with the rustic vibe, the more likely you are to end up with an armful of unnecessary trinkets that serve no purpose other than to remind you of that one time you went to Grand Lake and questioned all your life choices.

Greeley

Greeley, Colorado, a name that evokes images of sprawling fields, lively cattle, and perhaps an alarming number of students on bicycles, is not just a place; it's an experience, one filled with its own brand of charm and chaos. The name itself might sound like a mix between a jovial gremlin and a slightly confused garden gnome, but it has roots that stretch back to the mid-19th century, named after the famous newspaper editor Horace Greeley, who once proclaimed, "Go west, young man!" It's as if he was putting out a cosmic ad for adventure, not knowing that his name would forever be associated with a town that enjoys a good rodeo and an awkward family reunion.

The history of Greeley is a wild ride. Founded in 1869, the town sprang up as part of a utopian experiment led by a group of Easterners who believed they could create the perfect agricultural community. Spoiler alert: they quickly realized that growing crops in the Colorado plains isn't as easy as it looks on Pinterest. The town developed around farming, which means that today, if you wander around Greeley, you might catch a whiff of something—part cow, part hay, and part the realization that you're not in the city anymore.

Greeley prides itself on its rich agricultural heritage, which can be both its charm and its curse. The town is home to the annual Greeley Stampede, a rodeo that's basically the Super Bowl of cowboy hats. Here, you can watch people in denim and boots grapple with bulls, all while trying to maintain a level of dignity that just isn't possible when a 1,500-pound animal is involved. It's a spectacle of laughter, cheers, and the occasional cringe as someone inevitably gets tossed into the dirt, perhaps serving as a reminder that life is all about taking risks—even if they result in a face full of mud.

As for museums, Greeley isn't a metropolis brimming with cultural institutions, but it does have a few gems that are well worth a visit. The Greeley History Museum is a delightful spot where you can discover the town's past through exhibits that range from the mundane to the bizarre. Imagine standing in front of a dusty old wagon while contemplating the lives of those who trekked across the plains, wondering how they managed to survive without Wi-Fi or even a good cup of coffee. The museum's collection of artifacts is like a time capsule filled with the curiosities of days gone by—everything from vintage farming tools to the odd stuffed animal that seems to have lost its way.

Then there's the Union Colony Civic Center, a place that aims to bring a bit of the arts into the heart of Greeley. The venue hosts everything from concerts to theatrical performances, which means you might find yourself seated next to someone who is way too enthusiastic about community theater. On a good night, you could witness a masterpiece, but on a bad night, you might find yourself questioning your life choices while watching an interpretive dance piece that feels like a collective cry for help.

When it comes to things to do in Greeley, the best option is arguably the Poudre River Trail, where you can enjoy a leisurely stroll while pondering the existential dread that comes with living in a small town. The trail winds alongside the river and offers picturesque views, as long as you don't mind the occasional biker whizzing past you, leaving you to question whether they're training for the Tour de France or simply trying to escape their own thoughts.

Then there's the Greeley Farmers Market, where locals gather to sell everything from fresh produce to homemade jams. It's a delightful way to support the community, though it often leads to an overwhelming number of impulse buys that leave you wondering how you ended up with 12 jars of artisanal pickles and a pair of hand-knitted socks. The vendors here are enthusiastic, and you might just end up chatting with a potato farmer who shares stories of the best fertilizer, turning what should be a simple errand into a fascinating lecture on soil quality.

Now, for the "worst" things to do in Greeley. One might think that a stroll through downtown would be a charming endeavor, but it's a bit of a mixed bag. You'll find a collection of quirky shops and eateries, which sounds delightful until you wander into a place that sells "vintage" items that are really just old junk marketed to hipsters. The thrill of finding a perfect treasure can quickly dissipate when you realize you've just purchased a chipped coffee mug that used to belong to someone's grandma from a guy with a rap sheet as long as my hair.

Another downside is the weather, which can be as unpredictable as a toddler on a sugar rush. One minute you're enjoying a sunny afternoon, and the next, you're dodging hail like it's an Olympic sport. Greeley has a way of keeping you on your toes, and if you're not careful, you might find yourself underdressed for a sudden snowstorm in July.

Speaking of weather, let's not forget about the wind. Greeley is famous for its blustery gusts, which can turn a casual stroll into an epic battle against nature. You might find yourself clinging to your hat, praying that it doesn't get whisked away to Kansas, while also contemplating the irony of living in a place known for its agricultural roots yet having to wrestle with Mother Nature on a daily basis.

Green Mountain Falls

Green Mountain Falls, Colorado, is a town that sounds like it should be the backdrop for a cheesy rom-com or the next great adventure of an eccentric family. Picture it: a name that conjures images of nature, tranquility, and the occasional bear trying to sneak off with a picnic basket. This charming little hamlet is nestled at the foot of Pikes Peak, where the elevation is high enough to make you feel like you can conquer the world, or at least find a good spot to sip overpriced coffee while contemplating your life choices.

The history of Green Mountain Falls is as eclectic as its name suggests. Established in the late 19th century, it was initially envisioned as a resort community. Picture wealthy Easterners trading in their top hats for hiking boots, ready to frolic in the wilderness while wondering if they packed enough plaid shirts. In the early days, the town attracted folks who wanted to escape the sweltering summers and urban chaos, seeking the sweet embrace of fresh mountain air. Little did they know that the local wildlife might also be seeking them out for dinner.

The town quickly grew into a popular retreat, boasting charming cottages, hotels, and a variety of amenities that would make even the most discerning city slicker feel at home. But the real draw? The stunning waterfalls that cascade down the surrounding mountains, providing a perfect backdrop for family photos—or a romantic getaway that inevitably turns into a battle against the elements when the rain comes pouring down.

Now, if you're in the mood for museums, prepare yourself for the Green Mountain Falls Historical Society. It's a small gem that offers a delightful glimpse into the town's past. Walking into the museum is like stepping into your quirky great-aunt's attic: you never know what you'll find. You might see vintage postcards, old photographs, and enough memorabilia to fill a garage sale. The volunteers, often local historians who have lived through the town's many phases, can regale you with tales of the past, including ghost stories that are likely more entertaining than true. Just don't expect a fully modern, flashy museum experience; this is a small-town affair, where the charm often outweighs the polish.

When it comes to things to do in Green Mountain Falls, the best activities often involve embracing the outdoors. Hiking trails abound, with paths that lead you through breathtaking scenery and up to those majestic waterfalls that lured so many in the first place. There's nothing like the thrill of trying to keep your balance on rocky paths while contemplating the existential question of whether this hike was a good idea after last night's pizza binge. If you make it to the top, though, the views are more than worth it—a perfect chance to take that Instagram shot that says, "Look at me, I'm adventurous!" while trying not to tumble down the mountain in the process.

For a slice of local life, the Green Mountain Falls Arts and Crafts Festival is a must-see, unless you're allergic to creativity and charm. Picture local artisans displaying their wares: hand-knitted scarves, pottery, and maybe even a few paintings that look suspiciously like they were made by someone's toddler. The festival is a colorful explosion of creativity, complete with live music, laughter, and a variety of food stalls. Just be careful where you step, as you might find yourself in a discussion about the merits of organic cotton versus conventional fabric. It's a real thrill.

Now, let's address the worst things to see and do in Green Mountain Falls, which, honestly, is a bit of a challenge because the town is so charming. However, one downside might be the unpredictable weather. You know that saying, "If you don't like the weather, wait five minutes?" In Green Mountain Falls, you could find yourself sweating under the sun only to be blasted by a sudden hailstorm minutes later. It's the kind of climate that makes you question whether you should carry an umbrella, sunscreen, and a snow shovel all at once.

And then there are the wildlife encounters, which can range from the delightful to the downright terrifying. Sure, spotting a deer munching on a bush might seem picturesque, but wait until you stumble upon a family of raccoons trying to break into your car. Suddenly, your peaceful getaway turns into a slapstick comedy as you flail around trying to shoo them away. Wildlife is one thing; the town's occasional bear sightings are another story altogether. Nothing screams "vacation" like a bear wandering through the local park, prompting everyone to consider the practicality of bear spray versus a solid picnic plan.

In terms of dining options, you might find that the selection is limited, which can lead to a rather interesting culinary adventure. The local diners have their charm, but ordering a burger could lead to a surprise of "today's special," which might just be whatever the chef found in the back of the fridge. Sometimes, that's an adventure in itself, especially if you're in the mood to try something adventurous like the "mystery meat surprise." It's the gamble of a lifetime—will you get a culinary masterpiece or a lesson in what not to order again?

As you explore Green Mountain Falls, don't forget to take a stroll through the town's parks. The lush greenery provides a great backdrop for a leisurely walk or an intense game of "how many squirrels can I spot before they notice me." Just be cautious if you find yourself near the lake; it's a great place for a picnic, but also a prime spot for the local ducks who may see you as a walking snack bar. Nothing says "relaxation" like being aggressively pursued by a gaggle of quacking birds.

Gunnison

Gunnison, Colorado, sounds like a high-altitude breeze—refreshing and slightly bewildering. The name itself has a storied past, named after John W. Gunnison, an army officer and explorer who ventured into this wild territory in the mid-1800s. One can only imagine the moment he laid eyes on the breathtaking scenery and thought, "Yes, I shall be immortalized as a town name, and my likeness will probably end up on a coffee mug." Spoiler alert: it did.

The history of Gunnison is a delightful tapestry woven with tales of mining booms, cattle ranching, and enough rugged pioneer spirit to fuel a hundred Westerns. It all began in the 1860s when gold was discovered in the area. The rush was on, with hopeful prospectors flocking to the mountains like moths to a campfire. Unfortunately, the gold was more elusive than a shy mountain goat, leading many to turn their sights to ranching instead. Apparently, ranching is a lot like dating; you have to find the right pasture and hope the cows are feeling cooperative.

One of the highlights of Gunnison is the Gunnison Valley Historical Museum. This little treasure trove is a bit like your eccentric uncle's attic—packed with artifacts that tell the stories of the town's colorful past. From Native American artifacts to relics from the mining days, you'll find everything except the actual ghosts of miners wandering around. The museum offers a slice of life that is charmingly reminiscent of a time when people wrote letters instead of texting, and a "good time" meant gathering around a potbelly stove and telling tales of misadventure.

If you're itching to stretch your legs, the Gunnison River is your ticket to outdoor adventures. The river flows like a meandering ribbon through the valley, providing ample opportunities for fishing, rafting, and general frolicking. Whether you fancy yourself a seasoned angler or just want an excuse to wear your fancy new waders, the river is a picturesque spot. Just be prepared for the occasional splash from an overzealous fish or the sudden realization that your fishing skills are on par with a potato. But hey, at least you'll have a great story to tell.

For those seeking more organized fun, the annual Gunnison River Festival is a highlight of the social calendar. Imagine a gathering where kayakers and floaters of all kinds come together to celebrate the river's beauty while competing in zany events like a "slalom race" or a "cardboard boat challenge." The sight of people paddling around in makeshift vessels is enough to make anyone chuckle, especially when it inevitably ends in a glorious splash. It's the kind of event where you can genuinely feel the spirit of community, even if that spirit is mostly fueled by laughter and the occasional adult beverage.

Now, let's discuss the best and worst things to do in Gunnison. Best: exploring the stunning landscapes of the surrounding Gunnison National Forest. Hiking trails wind through mountains, providing views so beautiful that they make you question if you've accidentally stepped into a postcard. Just remember, the higher you go, the thinner the air gets, and suddenly that extra slice of pie at dinner seems like a regrettable decision.

The worst thing? Well, let's just say that while the scenery is breathtaking, the weather can be as fickle as a cat on a hot tin roof. One minute it's sunny, and the next it's snowing. If you're not prepared, you could find yourself in a snowstorm while wearing flip-flops and wondering why you didn't check the forecast. It's a wild ride in the mountains, and you better pack layers—or you might just end up as a local legend for all the wrong reasons.

In terms of dining, you'll find a mix of delightful eateries and... let's call them "quirky" culinary experiences. The local diners serve up hearty breakfasts that could fuel a small army. If you ever wanted to experience a pancake that could double as a frisbee, look no further. But tread carefully with the local specialties; ordering the "wild game" can lead to an adventurous meal. You might discover that "wild game" means anything from venison to the less appealing roadkill surprise. Always read the fine print on that menu; your stomach will thank you.

And let's not forget the nightlife! Gunnison isn't exactly known for its pulsing club scene, but there are a few local bars where the drinks flow freely, and the live music might just blow your socks off—or at least make you tap your foot in appreciation. Just don't expect to find a VIP section; the closest thing you'll get is a corner booth with a view of the dartboard.

As for museums, in addition to the historical society, there's also the Western State Colorado University Museum, which offers a slightly more academic take on local history. They dive into topics like geology and natural history with displays that are both informative and slightly baffling. You might find yourself staring at a rock that you're told is over a billion years old, contemplating your own life choices while a helpful guide enthusiastically explains why it's important. Spoiler alert: it's not because it's pretty.

Gypsum

Gypsum, Colorado, might sound like the name of a rare rock band or the latest hipster smoothie blend, but it's actually a quaint little town nestled in the Rockies that's got some stories to tell. The name "Gypsum" originates from the mineral found in abundance here, which is quite fitting since the town is about as subtle as a rock concert in a library. When the town was founded in the late 1800s, folks were probably thinking, "We need a name that reflects our mineral wealth." And just like that, Gypsum was born, probably with a fanfare of miners and a few skeptical goats wondering what the fuss was about.

The history of Gypsum is a tale of ambition and geological discovery, filled with dreams of striking it rich and, ironically, more than a few hard knocks. Early settlers flocked to the area, lured by the promise of gypsum mining, which they thought would make them wealthy beyond their wildest dreams. Spoiler alert: not all of them were living large after the gold rush craze died down. They soon realized that mining gypsum was less about discovering shiny rocks and more about digging holes in the ground, which, let's be honest, is a much less glamorous endeavor.

As for museums, if you're expecting the Louvre, you might want to recalibrate your expectations. Gypsum is more about the charm of small-town history than high art. The Gypsum Historical Society Museum is a delightful little stop. Here, you'll find artifacts and exhibits that will make you feel like you've traveled back in time to when life was simpler, and people spent more time worrying about how to farm than how to farm Instagram followers. The museum's collection is like a time capsule, preserving everything from early settlers' tools to the stories of those who toiled under the sun and occasionally fought off the odd bear looking for an easy meal.

Now, let's dive into the best things to do in Gypsum. For the outdoor enthusiast, the Eagle River is a playground. You can fish, kayak, or just stare at the water, contemplating the deep questions of life like, "Why didn't I bring a snack?" Or if you're feeling adventurous, there's the Gypsum Creek Trail, which offers views that are so beautiful they'll make you reconsider every landscape photo you've ever posted. Just be prepared for the elevation—nothing says "I'm out of shape" quite like gasping for breath while trying to take in the scenery.

Another highlight is the annual Gypsum Daze celebration, a town festival that could easily double as a scene from a feel-good movie. The locals come together for food, music, and a parade that's charmingly local, featuring floats that might include everything from high school marching bands to, let's be real, the world's most enthusiastic bake sale. It's the kind of event where everyone knows your name, and you can eat your body weight in funnel cakes while reminiscing about the good old days of gypsum mining.

On the flip side, the worst thing to do in Gypsum? Attempting to navigate the local roads after a snowstorm without a decent map or a prayer. Trust me, you might think you're just going for a scenic drive, but you could easily end up in a snowdrift, contemplating your life choices while waiting for a snowplow that may or may not show up.

Dining in Gypsum is an experience unto itself. Local eateries range from cozy diners where you can get a plate of comfort food that feels like a warm hug to spots serving up gourmet fare that will make you feel like a culinary explorer. Just remember to ask what "daily special" means; you might find yourself trying a dish that includes ingredients you've never heard of, combined in a way that makes you question the laws of food science. Always read the reviews—or at least ask the locals for their opinions. They're the ones who have likely sampled everything on the menu and survived.

For nightlife, you won't find any extravagant clubs or sprawling bars, but the local scene has its charm. The occasional open mic night or trivia contest brings the community together, creating an atmosphere that's both entertaining and surprisingly competitive. Expect to witness passionate debates over who knows more about obscure 80s movies or who can recite the most ridiculous trivia. It's like living in a sitcom, where everyone knows everyone, and the stakes are never too high, except maybe for the karaoke champion who's convinced they can out-sing the rest.

Haxtun

Until I sat down to write this book, I'd never heard of this place. Haxtun, Colorado, sounds like a character straight out of a dusty old Western film. With a name that rolls off the tongue like a forgotten cowboy ballad, you might think it's a place where outlaws sip sarsaparilla while plotting their next heist. In reality, it's a small town with a charm that's less about gunslingers and more about friendly faces and local legends—mostly involving the best places to get a slice of pie.

The town's history is as colorful as a sunset over the plains. Founded in the early 1900s, Haxtun was born out of the relentless push for agricultural expansion. The name itself is a tribute to a local railroad official, which is fitting, since this town could easily be the poster child for "Let's Build a Railroad and See What Happens." The original settlers had dreams bigger than their pockets, leading to a delightful mix of determination, a few blunders, and a lot of "let's hope this works" moments. And you better believe that's where the real stories come from.

Museums? Oh, Haxtun has one! The Haxtun Historical Society Museum might not rival the Smithsonian, but it's packed with enough artifacts to make you feel like an accidental time traveler. From vintage farming equipment to photographs that show just how much the town has changed (spoiler: a lot less mud and a few more cars), the museum is a delightful little pit stop. You might even find yourself fascinated by the stories of early pioneers and their struggles, all while chuckling at the fact that their biggest concern was probably not having Wi-Fi.

Now, when it comes to things to see and do in Haxtun, the options are as varied as a buffet at a family reunion. For the outdoor enthusiasts, the nearby Logan County is an absolute playground. Whether you fancy yourself a fishing aficionado or just someone who enjoys staring at water while contemplating life choices, the area has plenty of fishing holes. Just be prepared for the occasional surprise, like a rogue duck deciding it's your new best friend while you're trying to enjoy a quiet day by the water.

If you're feeling particularly adventurous, take a stroll through the town's charming streets. You might be treated to sights of historical buildings, a few well-placed benches, and the occasional tumbleweed that's taken its time rolling through. If you're lucky, you might even stumble upon a local event, perhaps a bake sale or a small festival. Nothing brings a community together quite like the smell of freshly baked goods and the unyielding competition for the best pie in town. Just remember: if someone challenges you to a pie-eating contest, it's less about the food and more about the pride.

On the flip side, what are the worst things to do in Haxtun? Well, for starters, trying to find a late-night dining option might prove to be a challenge. The town is charmingly small, which means that once the sun sets, the options dwindle faster than your energy during a long meeting. If you find yourself starving at 10 PM, you might be reduced to eating whatever snacks you packed or, heaven forbid, calling it a night. There's only so much "ranch-style" living one can take.

Let's not forget about the weather. Haxtun can be a tad unpredictable. One minute, you're basking in the sun, and the next, you're dodging hail like you're in a scene from an action movie. Planning outdoor activities requires a weather app and a good luck charm. The lesson here? Bring layers. Lots of layers. You never know when you'll need to switch from shorts to a parka in less than five minutes.

When it comes to dining, Haxtun has a few local spots that promise to feed you, but don't go in expecting Michelin-star cuisine. Instead, you'll find hearty meals served with a side of "let's not talk about calories." The local diners are filled with friendly faces who'll greet you with a smile and possibly a few anecdotes about the town's history. Just be sure to check the daily specials, which can range from delicious home-cooked meals to the occasional mystery meat that's best left unexamined.

In terms of nightlife, don't expect neon lights and pulsing music. Haxtun's idea of a wild night involves a few locals gathered around a table at the local pub, reminiscing about the good old days while possibly engaging in a spirited game of cards. The atmosphere is more "cheerful chatter" and less "nightclub chaos." If you're in the mood for excitement, you might have to create your own, like challenging someone to a dance-off to a song that definitely should not be danced to.

Hayden

Apparently this is more than just the name of my favorite local pharmacist. Hayden, Colorado is located in Routt County. This delightful spot has a history that might just surprise you—if you can stay awake long enough to read about it. Founded in the late 1800s by a railroad mogul named Hayden, it became a hub for agriculture and ranching. You see, the man had a knack for naming places after himself, which is either the height of confidence or a serious case of ego.

As for museums, Hayden is a tad shy. While it doesn't boast a sprawling metropolis of exhibits, it does have its fair share of historical markers and local lore that can easily fill an afternoon of "what are we doing with our lives?" The Yampa Valley Historical Society might be your best bet for digging into the past, as they host events that let you mingle with history buffs who can regale you with tales of early settlers, their struggles, and their penchant for mud.

Now, when you're looking for things to do in Hayden, it's essential to know that options can be limited, but that's part of the charm, right? The best activities revolve around the stunning natural surroundings. If you're the outdoorsy type, the nearby Routt National Forest offers hiking trails that are likely to leave you breathless—not just from the altitude but also from the sheer beauty. Just be cautious not to wander off the beaten path unless you're looking to discover new ways to question your life choices or have a chat with a bear.

Hayden might not be bustling with nightlife, but it does have the kind of atmosphere that could make a night of stargazing feel like a major event. The lack of city lights makes it a prime location for spotting constellations, although you might be tempted to play a game of "Name That Star" until you realize you've been making up names for the last 20 minutes. Is that one a "Fluffy McFlufferson"? Absolutely.

The town also boasts a community vibe that can be quite delightful. Local events, like the Hayden Daze celebration, provide a chance to rub elbows with the friendly residents while indulging in classic fair food. Don't be surprised if you find yourself neck-deep in cotton candy while attempting to win an inflatable dinosaur at the local games booth. Spoiler: the inflatable dinosaur will become your new best friend.

However, let's not gloss over the less-than-stellar aspects of Hayden. If you're looking for a vibrant nightlife scene, you might want to recalibrate your expectations. Unless you consider a few locals gathering for karaoke night at the one bar in town to be the height of entertainment, you might find yourself yearning for a dance floor that doesn't consist of a linoleum square in the corner. The music selection may also leave much to be desired—imagine a mix of 80s hits and country ballads that will make you question your sanity.

Dining options in Hayden are like a box of chocolates—if the box only had three kinds and they were all slightly outdated. You've got your local diner serving up hearty meals that would make your grandma proud, but don't go in expecting gourmet fare. The burgers are solid, but if you're in the mood for a fancy salad or sushi, you might be out of luck. Best to stick to comfort food, or you might find yourself staring longingly at your neighbor's plate of fries while contemplating the choices that led you to this moment.

Let's also touch on the weather, because if you're in Hayden, you're going to need to be prepared for anything. One moment it can be sunny and inviting, and the next, you're getting pelted with hail that feels like Mother Nature is playing dodgeball with your face. Layering is essential, and it's wise to have a backup plan for any outdoor adventures. If you're planning a picnic, keep an umbrella and a raincoat handy—just in case.

Hayden's charm lies in its simplicity, which can either be a wonderful escape from the chaos of modern life or a slow crawl toward existential dread, depending on your perspective. It's a place where you can slow down, breathe in the mountain air, and enjoy a slice of pie that's probably made by someone's grandmother. Just be sure to check your expectations at the door, because in Hayden, it's all about embracing the quirks of small-town life. So grab your favorite book, settle into a cozy chair, and prepare for an adventure filled with a little bit of history, a lot of fresh air, and a healthy dose of humor.

Hillrose

Hillrose, Colorado, a name that sounds like it belongs to a quaint garden party hosted by a retired librarian, is actually a small town in Morgan County with a history that's surprisingly rich for its size. Founded in the late 1800s, Hillrose was originally a railroad town, and as all good railroads go, it was more about getting people to places than any sort of destination itself. The town was named for the charming hills and the wild roses that once graced the area, though one could argue that calling it "Hillrose" was simply an attempt to make it sound more picturesque than it actually is.

Fast forward to today, and Hillrose is a community that's well-versed in the art of keeping things low-key. The population hovers around a few hundred, making it a perfect spot for anyone who thinks cities are just too darn noisy. The vibe here is laid-back, so if you're in the mood for a high-energy atmosphere, you might want to double-check your GPS and head back toward the nearest urban sprawl.

Museums in Hillrose? Well, let's just say they take a more creative approach to the term. Instead of a sprawling museum filled with artifacts, you're more likely to stumble upon a few old buildings that may or may not house a collection of fascinatingly dusty items that might make you question how civilization ever advanced. There's an old schoolhouse and some remnants of the railroad, and while you won't find the Louvre here, you may find a genuine sense of local history. Just be prepared for the possibility that "interactive exhibits" might involve chatting with an elderly resident who remembers when the biggest excitement was a new tractor arriving in town.

One of the best things to do in Hillrose is simply to soak in the peaceful surroundings. This is the kind of place where you can take a stroll and contemplate life's greatest mysteries, like why there are so many different types of corn. The landscape features the kind of rolling hills that will make you feel like you've stepped into a postcard, minus the airbrushed models and impossibly blue skies. Nature lovers can bask in the vastness of the plains and gaze at the sky while trying to decide whether that cloud looks more like a dinosaur or a weirdly shaped potato.

If you're looking for a thrill, though, you might want to temper your expectations. The most exhilarating thing you'll find in Hillrose is probably a local barbecue or potluck, where the excitement revolves around which neighbor brought the best dessert. Competition can be fierce, with everyone secretly judging each other's potato salad recipes and assessing the number of marshmallows in the ambrosia salad. Don't underestimate the tension that can arise over baked goods. It's practically a sport in these parts.

As for dining, Hillrose embraces a strong sense of simplicity. The local diner is a go-to spot, serving food that could make a heartier meal out of a single potato. Think classic American fare—burgers, fries, and pie that can only be described as "grandma-approved." Expect a menu that could be easily replicated by anyone with a can opener and a basic understanding of how to fry things. The food is comforting in its familiarity, like a warm hug from your aunt who never stops asking about your love life.

Now, let's address the worst things to do in Hillrose. First off, avoid trying to convince anyone that the town is the next big vacation hotspot. The locals will look at you with a mix of confusion and pity, wondering if you've accidentally wandered in from another dimension. If you're hoping for a vibrant nightlife, you'll be disappointed. The most action you'll see after sundown is the occasional coyote howling at the moon, which is not quite the party scene you might have envisioned.

In terms of weather, Hillrose gets its fair share of surprises. One minute, you're basking in sunshine, and the next, it's like Mother Nature decided to play a prank and send down a thunderstorm. Make sure you've got layers, because the temperature can fluctuate faster than you can say "I thought we were in summer." You might even find yourself googling "how to dress for all four seasons in one day" while you sip your coffee and stare out the window.

Ultimately, Hillrose, Colorado, embodies the spirit of small-town life where simplicity reigns supreme. It's a place where everyone knows everyone, and the biggest news usually revolves around who's gotten a new tractor or whether the local high school team won last Friday's game. Embrace the charm, laugh at the quirks, and you might just find a slice of life that feels refreshingly unfiltered. Just don't expect any red carpets or paparazzi—unless you count the goats, which can be surprisingly judgmental.

Holly

Holly, Colorado, a name that sounds like it could belong to a particularly jolly Christmas elf, is actually a small town nestled in the southeastern part of the state. Founded in the late 19th century, Holly has the kind of history that could inspire a documentary, but only if that documentary was produced on a shoestring budget and featured a lot of grainy footage. Originally established as a railroad town, Holly quickly became a hub for agriculture and trade. The first settlers probably thought, "Hey, let's build a town in the middle of nowhere," and, miraculously, that town came to life, mostly due to the sheer determination of the locals and a couple of enterprising merchants who probably had really bad poker faces.

The town itself is a pocket of Americana, where life is simpler, and the biggest excitement is probably deciding which diner to visit for breakfast. The locals will tell you that Holly is known for its friendly folks, and if you can survive a few waves from the residents, you might just become a part of the fabric of this charming little community. On the surface, it's the kind of place where "how's the weather?" is the most riveting conversation starter, yet it's surprisingly rich in quirks that make it uniquely lovable.

Now, museums in Holly are as rare as a snowstorm in July, but there are some hidden gems. One notable spot is the Holly Historical Museum, which is a small collection of artifacts that tell the story of the town's founding. It has that quintessential small-town museum vibe: walls adorned with black-and-white photos that look like they haven't been dusted since the town's inception. You'll find relics from the days when the town was bustling with trains and dreams, alongside the usual assortment of outdated farming equipment that looks like it could star in its own horror movie if it were ever brought back to life.

Visiting the museum is like stepping into a time capsule where every hour feels like it could be an episode of "Antiques Roadshow" featuring items that no one knows the value of. You might even come across an exhibit dedicated to the world's most fascinating agricultural achievements—like the giant zucchini that a local once claimed would have won a county fair if he hadn't eaten it first.

The best things to do in Holly include embracing the small-town charm. You can wander the streets, where the pace of life is so slow you might think you've entered a time warp. It's the kind of place where a leisurely stroll could turn into an impromptu chat with a stranger who will tell you about the great pumpkin shortage of '89 or the time the town's annual rodeo almost ended in a cow stampede. Expect nothing short of pure entertainment.

One of the town's most notable events is the annual Holly Days celebration, a joyous gathering that combines a bizarre mixture of food, games, and a lot of questionable decisions made after too much funnel cake. Locals come together to showcase their best potluck dishes, and competition is fierce. You'll find everything from grandma's secret recipe casserole to suspiciously gelatinous desserts that seem to have a life of their own.

For outdoor enthusiasts, the surrounding landscape provides opportunities for activities like hiking and fishing, but let's be real—if you're planning a nature adventure in Holly, you might want to bring along a guidebook and an adequate supply of snacks. The locals can only point you to the nearest field and tell you which way is north, but that's about it.

Now let's address the worst things to do in Holly, which includes attempting to navigate the local social scene. If you're not a fan of small talk about the weather or the local high school football team, you may want to prepare for some awkward silences that will leave you questioning your life choices. Trying to be the new cool kid in town is about as effective as bringing a surfboard to a desert.

Another hazard is attempting to visit during the winter months without proper attire. The weather can turn colder than a polar bear's toenails, and you'll want to dress like you're preparing for an Arctic expedition. The locals might have laughed at your stylish but impractical shoes as you slipped and slid your way down the icy sidewalks, while they confidently navigate the terrain in what looks like dad sneakers.

Holly is also home to the highly competitive sport of "who has the biggest backyard garden." If you thought your prize-winning tomatoes would impress, you clearly haven't seen what the locals can grow. Be prepared for some serious horticultural envy, and if you dare mention your gardening skills, you might as well resign yourself to a lifetime of losing bets.

Ultimately, Holly, Colorado, is a town where life moves at a pace that could make a snail feel speedy. It's a place where the charm is palpable, the conversations are simple, and the stories shared are rich with character. Just remember to bring your sense of humor, a sturdy pair of shoes, and a hearty appetite for whatever culinary surprises the local potlucks throw your way.

Holyoke

Holyoke, Colorado, is a town whose name sounds like it should be the title of a children's book about a very enthusiastic choir of angels. Spoiler alert: it isn't. Instead, Holyoke is a small community nestled in the northeastern part of the state, where the landscape is as flat as a pancake and the biggest excitement is figuring out how to pronounce "Holyoke" correctly. Is it "Holy-yoke," like a divine egg? Or "Holy-kay," as in a casual acknowledgment of your presence? Either way, you'll probably find yourself just nodding along when the locals say it with a nonchalant drawl.

The town was founded in the late 19th century, primarily as a railroad stop. Think of it as the unassuming sibling in the family of Colorado towns that's often overlooked in favor of its flashier counterparts like Aspen or Denver. Holyoke began with dreams of grandeur, but those dreams were slightly tempered when they realized that the most exciting thing to happen was the arrival of the first train, which everyone treated like it was the second coming of rock 'n' roll. The settlers, armed with hope and a hearty appetite for adventure, established agriculture as their lifeline, and soon enough, Holyoke was producing crops that could probably outgrow your house.

The Holyoke Historical Museum is the town's pride and joy, housing artifacts that scream, "We were here!" It's filled with relics that give visitors a glimpse into the past, and by "glimpse," I mean you can look at old photos and imagine what life was like when people dressed like they were going to a fancy church event for every outing. You'll find everything from farming tools that look like they belong in a museum of medieval torture to a collection of dusty old yearbooks that could provide ample material for a town roast. The museum's charm is enhanced by the fact that it feels like it could be run by a couple of well-meaning but slightly eccentric volunteers who likely have stories about every single item on display—whether those stories are accurate is entirely up for debate.

In terms of things to do in Holyoke, you can enjoy the annual Holyoke Prairie Days, a festival that feels like a high school reunion but with more corn and fewer awkward silences. The locals come together to celebrate their agricultural roots, and it's a fantastic opportunity to marvel at livestock that are clearly living their best lives. You'll find contests for the largest pumpkin, which is basically an Olympic event for local farmers, and it's here that you can witness the fierce competition and whispered strategies about how to coax a squash into greatness.

For those who enjoy outdoor pursuits, the surrounding area offers opportunities for fishing, hiking, and—if you're feeling particularly adventurous—trying to find the nearest hill, because let's face it, flatland can be a bit monotonous. You can wander along the South Platte River and try to convince yourself that you're in a real-life postcard. If you're lucky, you might spot some wildlife, though the local critters probably know better than to get too close to humans.

But let's not sugarcoat everything; there are a few things best avoided in Holyoke. If you think you're going to get lost in a cultural hub of fine dining, you might be in for a surprise. The culinary scene is less Michelin star and more "How many ways can you fry a potato?" You'll have a plethora of diners and burger joints, but if you're looking for fancy cuisine, you might want to bring a picnic basket and prepare for disappointment. The locals have a deep love for comfort food, and any attempt to introduce quinoa might get you kicked out of the nearest diner.

Another thing to avoid is trying to make small talk about anything other than the weather, farming, or the local high school football team. You might think you're being clever by discussing the latest trends in urban fashion, but you'll likely find yourself met with blank stares that scream, "We wear flannel because it's practical, not because it's trendy." Small talk here is an art form, and if you get it wrong, you'll feel like you just tried to perform a Shakespearean monologue at a talent show for toddlers.

One of the more comical aspects of visiting Holyoke is the phenomenon of "the town meeting." If you've ever wondered what it's like to witness a public forum that's somehow both riveting and excruciating, look no further. The community gathers to discuss everything from local taxes to the fate of the town's most beloved historical sign. You might find yourself caught up in a passionate debate about whether or not the park should invest in new benches, complete with heartfelt anecdotes about the old benches that have been there since the dawn of time.

Hot Sulphur Springs

Hot Sulphur Springs, Colorado, is a name that sounds like a spa day gone slightly off the rails. If you've ever found yourself imagining a magical place where the waters are hot, the sulphur is abundant, and the townsfolk can tell you all about the benefits of minerals that you didn't even know existed, then congratulations! You've already arrived at the essence of Hot Sulphur Springs.

The name itself is a mouthful, evoking imagery of bubbling springs that not only promise relaxation but also the faint scent of hard-boiled eggs. The town's history dates back to the mid-1800s when settlers stumbled upon these naturally heated pools and realized that they were onto something special—namely, a natural hot tub that didn't require a Pinterest board to assemble. Initially frequented by Indigenous tribes, these waters quickly caught the attention of pioneers who figured, "Why not bathe where the steam comes out of the ground?"

In the late 1800s, the town became a hotspot, quite literally, for visitors seeking to soak their troubles away. Picture a lively scene where ladies in long dresses and gentlemen in top hats gathered around the springs, perhaps clutching their hats to avoid steam-induced mishaps. They came seeking health benefits that ranged from the medicinal to the absurd, and let's just say that the springs probably had their fair share of converts. It was a time when the phrase "taking the waters" meant something entirely different than it does in a modern spa.

Fast forward a bit, and you'll find the Hot Sulphur Springs Resort and Spa, where visitors can experience the joys of soaking in natural mineral pools while simultaneously contemplating life choices. The resort boasts a range of baths, and if you've ever dreamed of lounging in a pool that smells like a hard-boiled egg factory, this is your paradise. Some may find it a therapeutic experience; others may just feel like they've walked into a culinary nightmare.

The museum scene in Hot Sulphur Springs isn't as bustling as you might find in larger cities, but there's the history museum where you can marvel at artifacts that once belonged to the early settlers, including tools that look like they were crafted in an era when "user-friendly" was a concept still in the brainstorming phase. It's a tiny place, but it has a certain charm, and the volunteers are likely to have more stories than the items on display. Prepare for some lively anecdotes about the town's founding, complete with exaggerated tales of pioneers facing down bears and brewing their own beverages, possibly involving the hot springs as a secret ingredient.

For those who are keen on outdoor adventures, you'll find ample opportunities to hike, bike, and marvel at the scenic beauty surrounding the town. Just remember, though, that "hiking" can sometimes feel like a polite way of saying, "Let's walk uphill until we can't feel our legs." But if you persist, you might just be rewarded with views that make you feel like you've conquered something monumental, even if it's just a very small mountain.

As for events, the annual Hot Sulphur Springs Rodeo is a must-see. It's a lively gathering where cowboys and cowgirls come together to showcase their skills while the audience eats popcorn and debates the finer points of rodeo etiquette. Don't forget to try the local cuisine while you're at it—think burgers, BBQ, and an assortment of foods that can only be described as "down-home." Just remember, anything you order might be served with a side of ranch dressing, regardless of whether it makes sense.

Now, let's not gloss over the less-than-stellar aspects of Hot Sulphur Springs. For one, if you're expecting a lively nightlife scene, you might be in for a rude awakening. The biggest "night out" is likely a trip to the local diner, where you can enjoy the unique ambiance of watching the local cats compete for your fries while you try to have a conversation. If you're searching for wild nights and neon lights, you'd be better off looking for the nearest disco ball and some questionable dance moves.

Also, if you happen to visit during the off-season, you might find that the town resembles a ghost town, minus the actual ghosts, although some locals might argue that a few of the older buildings are haunted by the spirits of pioneers who got lost on their way to the next hot spring. The eerie quietness can be a little unsettling, but on the bright side, you'll have plenty of space in the mineral pools without having to share with the summer crowd.

Hotchkiss

Hotchkiss, Colorado, is a name that might conjure images of a quaint little town nestled in the mountains, perhaps with a quirky sense of humor to match its unusual name. One might wonder if the town was named after a particularly memorable breakfast item or a delightful character from a Victorian novel, but no, it's actually named after a certain early settler, a Mr. Jacob Hotchkiss. This Jacob was so charmingly unremarkable that he ended up lending his name to an entire town instead of becoming famous for something much more glamorous, like inventing the pancake or revolutionizing the way we brew coffee.

Established in the late 1800s, Hotchkiss started off as a hub for agricultural innovation, a place where farmers and ranchers realized that their dreams of cultivating the land could become a reality. Imagine a bunch of rugged pioneers wielding pitchforks, contemplating how to grow crops in a region that could, at times, be more arid than a desert. It was a struggle, but they persevered, proving that the human spirit can indeed endure even the toughest of droughts.

Now, let's not forget about the museums. The Hotchkiss-Crawford Historical Museum is a must-visit, though "must" may be a strong word, depending on your enthusiasm for local history. Housed in an old schoolhouse, the museum offers a veritable treasure trove of artifacts from the town's past. Here, you can marvel at items that appear to have been pulled directly from your great-grandmother's attic, like vintage farm equipment and old photographs of people who may or may not have been smiling due to their lack of knowledge about cameras.

As you meander through the exhibits, prepare for an onslaught of historical stories, from the farming techniques of yesteryear to tales of how the town managed to survive the Great Depression with little more than grit and a lot of potatoes. There's also a collection of Native American artifacts, a reminder that this land had a rich history long before the settlers showed up, likely with dreams of farming and a slightly naive confidence.

When it comes to the best things to see and do, outdoor enthusiasts will find Hotchkiss a gem, as it's surrounded by stunning landscapes perfect for hiking, biking, and even pondering life's biggest questions—like how did we get here, and why didn't we bring snacks? The nearby Black Canyon of the Gunnison National Park offers views so breathtaking that you might wonder if you've accidentally wandered onto a movie set designed for nature documentaries. Just be careful not to fall in; there are no safety nets in nature, just gravity and your poor life choices.

If you're in the mood for some local flavor, look no further than the annual Hotchkiss Cherry Days Festival, which is an event where cherries reign supreme. Imagine a small town transformed into a cherry-themed wonderland, complete with pie-eating contests, parades, and perhaps an impromptu competition to see who can eat the most cherry-flavored anything without exploding. It's a true celebration of community spirit, and you might even find that the cherries are so good that they can temporarily erase the memory of everything else in life—at least until the inevitable sugar crash kicks in.

Now, let's not gloss over the potential downsides of a visit to Hotchkiss. For starters, if you're expecting the glitz and glamour of a big city, you may be in for a shock. The nightlife here revolves around cozy dinners and perhaps a game of cards with the neighbors. If you're craving neon lights and dance clubs, you might need to take a road trip. The biggest social event of the week might just be the bingo night at the local community center, where the stakes are high—pride, glory, and maybe a pie if you're lucky.

And speaking of luck, there's also the weather to consider. Hotchkiss experiences its fair share of seasonal changes, meaning you could go from a sunny day perfect for hiking to a surprise snowstorm in the blink of an eye. This unpredictability can lead to some unforgettable moments, like deciding to wear flip-flops in a snowstorm because, really, who needs proper footwear?

If you're not careful, you might also discover the local critters—deer, rabbits, and the occasional wandering cow. While they might seem harmless, these creatures can provide unexpected excitement, especially if one decides to cross your path at the exact moment you're trying to navigate a bend in the road. Suddenly, the serene countryside becomes a high-stakes game of "Will I get hit by a deer?"

In terms of local cuisine, Hotchkiss offers a mix of classic diner fare and surprisingly good Mexican food, where the salsa is spicy enough to make you question your life choices but delicious enough that you'll keep coming back for more. Just be prepared for the inevitable debate over whether the chili or the enchiladas are the true stars of the menu. It's a conversation that may never be resolved, but at least you'll have a full stomach while discussing it.

Hudson

Hudson, Colorado, a name that sounds like a forgotten character from a mid-century sitcom—perhaps the neighbor who always borrowed a cup of sugar but never returned the favor. Founded in the early 1900s, Hudson was originally a stop along the railroad, which was great for the delivery of goods and people, but not so much for the gossip. You could say the town is the quintessential "blink and you'll miss it" place, where the pace of life is slower than a snail on a leisurely stroll.

Historically, Hudson began as a farming community, where settlers decided that the plains of Colorado were the perfect spot to grow things like sugar beets and, let's be honest, a lot of boredom. The original settlers likely gathered around the dinner table, dreaming of turning this vast, flat land into a thriving agricultural wonderland. Little did they know, their ambitions would culminate in a town that's basically known for having a population that's more excited about a good sale at the local hardware store than any wild nightlife.

Now, if you're in the mood for museums, Hudson might not be the first town that comes to mind—unless, of course, you're an enthusiast for small-town history, in which case you might be overjoyed to discover the Hudson Historical Society. While the collection of artifacts might not rival the Louvre, you'll find a charming assortment of photographs, documents, and relics that paint a picture of a community that has persevered through decades of existential quiet. The historical society's motto could easily be "We've got stories, just not enough visitors to tell them to!"

One of the best things to do in Hudson is to simply embrace the local vibe. The Hudson Recreation Center provides opportunities for some community bonding over various activities, from swimming to working out. Just imagine, a whole afternoon spent sweating it out while making small talk with someone who may or may not be a distant relative. The best part? No one expects you to take it seriously. Exercise in Hudson seems less about fitness and more about finding the most creative ways to chat about local weather patterns.

Now, let's not overlook the annual Hudson Days celebration. This delightful event is essentially a town-wide excuse for everyone to come together and pretend they have something in common—like an unyielding love for corn on the cob and the thrill of a pie-eating contest. Picture locals gathered around, eagerly participating in activities that range from a parade to games for children, all while secretly hoping for a celebrity sighting, which will never happen. You're more likely to see someone's grandma win the three-legged race, and let's be real, that's the kind of drama people live for in Hudson.

If you find yourself in need of a good meal, Hudson has you covered—provided you like diners. You'll find plenty of cozy establishments that serve up hearty breakfasts and comfort food that can only be described as "we promise it's homemade, and yes, we still have that weird Jell-O salad." One local favorite might even feature a sign proclaiming "Best Coffee in Town!" which, in Hudson, is essentially like declaring yourself the tallest person in a room filled with toddlers.

But not everything is sunshine and sugar beets. The worst thing about Hudson? It might just be the lack of activities if you're seeking a whirlwind adventure. If you're looking for nightlife, you might as well be looking for Bigfoot. The closest thing to excitement after sunset is the sound of crickets harmonizing with the occasional train whistle, which might lull you into a deep sleep before you can even say "What happened to my Friday night?"

For those with a sense of humor and a taste for the absurd, there's a peculiar charm to Hudson's quietude. It's a place where you can unwind, sip some coffee, and contemplate your life choices—like why you chose to visit a town that appears on few travel itineraries. And if you're feeling particularly adventurous, you might find a local willing to share ghost stories about the old railroad days, which may or may not include exaggerated tales of runaway trains or spectral farmers.

On the flip side, the landscape surrounding Hudson offers ample opportunities for outdoor activities. With rolling plains and nearby parks, you can engage in hiking, fishing, or simply basking in the knowledge that you've escaped the hustle and bustle of the city for a while. Just be prepared to dodge the occasional tumbleweed; they have a knack for appearing out of nowhere, much like the random thought that maybe you should have just stayed home to binge-watch your favorite show.

So, what's the verdict on Hudson, Colorado? It's a quirky little town where the historical society is your best shot at a riveting afternoon, the community is tight-knit to the point of feeling like one big family reunion, and the only real danger is the overwhelming desire to take a nap because, let's face it, there's not a whole lot of adrenaline pumping here. Whether you find yourself sipping coffee in a diner, visiting the local museum, or simply taking a stroll to contemplate the mysteries of life, Hudson offers a slice of small-town America that's refreshingly unpretentious and completely comfortable in its own skin.

Hugo

Hugo, Colorado, a name that sounds like a character straight out of a 19th-century novel, possibly the one who always seemed to end up in trouble for reasons that no one quite understood. Nestled in Lincoln County, this charming little town was founded in the late 1800s and originally served as a stop on the railroad. You know, the kind of place where the trains would stop, the conductor would glance around to see if anyone wanted to hop on or off, and the townsfolk would wave cheerfully, hoping to catch a glimpse of someone interesting, perhaps a cowboy or a traveling salesman.

The history of Hugo is a delightful tapestry of the American frontier experience. Originally, the area was inhabited by Native American tribes, but then, in the name of progress (and railroads), settlers arrived to stake their claim, bring their dreams, and likely some really questionable fashion choices. The town quickly developed a reputation for its agricultural prospects, as farmers decided that growing crops in the middle of a vast, dry plains was a good idea. Spoiler alert: it was a mixed bag. Some crops thrived, while others served as the local wildlife's personal buffet.

Hugo is perhaps best known for its role as the "Gateway to the East." The locals might even have a t-shirt that proudly declares this, though whether anyone ever thought that was a selling point is up for debate. What is certain, however, is that the town features a few attractions that would make even the most seasoned traveler raise an eyebrow, or at least crack a smile.

Now, if you're looking for museums, Hugo has you covered—or at least partially covered. The most notable site is the Hugo Historical Museum, which is a quaint little place that could be mistaken for someone's living room if you squint just right. Here, you can find a delightful collection of artifacts, photographs, and relics that chronicle the town's journey from dusty outpost to… well, slightly less dusty outpost. It's the kind of museum where the excitement is palpable; you might even encounter a local volunteer who's genuinely enthusiastic about showing you a 1950s rotary phone. Thrilling, right?

Speaking of excitement, you can't talk about Hugo without mentioning the famed "Hugo Co-Op," a grocery store that has somehow become a beloved gathering place for the townsfolk. Picture this: locals mingling while picking up essentials like milk, bread, and the latest gossip. Rumor has it that if you hang around long enough, you might even hear the infamous "Hugo Whisper," a secret language spoken only by the most seasoned locals, consisting of half-formed sentences and knowing nods.

When it comes to things to see and do, there's a healthy mix of both fantastic and, let's just say, "interesting" options. For the outdoor enthusiast, Hugo is close to several parks and recreational areas. You can spend your afternoons fishing, hiking, or simply pondering the mysteries of life while staring at the endless horizon. Just be prepared to defend your choice of a hike when the most exciting thing you've encountered so far is a particularly feisty tumbleweed.

One of the best things about Hugo is its annual events, which can be quite the spectacle. The Hugo Rodeo is an experience to behold—complete with cowboy hats, boot-scootin' music, and more denim than you thought possible. Attending this rodeo is like stepping into a time capsule where the past and present collide in a spectacular display of rodeo clowns, bull riding, and barbecue that makes your taste buds do a little dance. And let's not forget the inevitable parade of locals attempting to show off their latest belt buckles, which they assure you were "won" rather than simply bought online.

On the flip side, if you're on the hunt for nightlife, you might want to temper your expectations. Hugo offers a quieter vibe than your average bustling city. Your choices for evening entertainment might include playing cards at the local diner or trying your hand at trivia night, where the hardest question could easily be about the best way to cook a potato. The fact that the biggest scandal in town involves someone showing up at the grocery store in last year's summer flip-flops is both amusing and a little sad.

If you're craving some culinary adventure, Hugo's dining scene is an eclectic mix. You have your classic diners that serve hearty plates of food so large they could double as coffee tables. The local cuisine is an ode to simplicity: burgers, fries, and the occasional salad—if you're feeling fancy. Just be prepared for the waitress to ask if you want extra gravy on your fries because, in Hugo, that's not just an option; it's practically a way of life.

But let's not ignore the worst parts about visiting Hugo. The isolation can be stifling; it's the kind of place where the nearest "big" city is at least an hour away, and even then, "big" is a relative term. If you're used to a bustling nightlife, the sound of crickets might start to feel like a personal soundtrack. And good luck finding a coffee shop that's open past 5 PM—local coffee drinkers are usually in bed by 8, dreaming of sugar beets and rodeos.

Idaho Springs

Idaho Springs, Colorado, a name that conjures images of adventurous pioneers, gold rush dreams, and an overwhelming number of people trying to figure out how to pronounce "Idaho." Nestled in the Rocky Mountains, this town has a history that reads like a rollercoaster ride—complete with sharp drops, unexpected turns, and the occasional loop-de-loop.

Founded in the 1850s during the gold rush, Idaho Springs became the place to be for anyone who thought they could strike it rich. Legend has it that the first gold discovery was made by a man who was likely just trying to find a good place to camp and accidentally tripped over a nugget while looking for his wayward dog. And thus, Idaho Springs was born—a town that quickly became a hub for miners, gamblers, and those who simply enjoyed living dangerously on the edge of a mountain.

The town was named after the hot springs that were discovered in the area. These springs became a vital source of both relaxation and questionable decisions for the miners who thought that soaking in natural hot water would cleanse them of their gold-seeking misadventures. Spoiler alert: it did not. People still flock to these springs today, which are just as likely to soothe your sore muscles as they are to give you a few moments to ponder life choices while the scent of sulfur wafts through the air.

Idaho Springs is not just a gold rush relic; it also boasts a surprisingly vibrant culture, which is a euphemism for a smorgasbord of eccentricities. The history is peppered with tales of the railroad, which rolled into town with the same kind of enthusiasm you'd expect from a toddler on Christmas morning. The Denver & Rio Grande Railroad linked Idaho Springs to the outside world, allowing visitors to marvel at its natural beauty and miners to find more places to trip over shiny rocks.

One of the town's highlights is the Idaho Springs Historical Museum, a gem that somehow manages to look like someone's attic but with fewer dust bunnies and more ancient artifacts. Here, you'll find an assortment of exhibits that tell the story of the town's colorful past—like how people used to make their own soap and why that was probably a bad idea. The museum also has artifacts from the gold rush days, including tools, photographs, and the world's largest collection of "what were they thinking?" memorabilia. Also make sure to stop by the Argo Mill Tour. You won't forget the 100 vertical feet over a series of five staircases. Not to worry, there are strategically placed benches if you need to take a break.

As you stroll through Idaho Springs, your eyes will inevitably be drawn to the numerous buildings that seem to have been plucked from a storybook. The quaint storefronts and charming architecture are a visual feast, as long as you don't look too closely. Behind the charm lies a series of questionable renovation decisions, as evidenced by the odd paint choices and signs that appear to be straight out of a yard sale. It's as if the entire town collectively decided that anything remotely tasteful was far too mainstream for their rugged, mountain vibe.

Let's not overlook the natural beauty surrounding Idaho Springs. The town is a gateway to the great outdoors, with trails that beg you to explore while simultaneously whispering, "Remember to wear sturdy shoes, or else you'll end up in a bush." Hiking, biking, and white-water rafting are all on the agenda, though be prepared for some locals to casually remind you that "white-water" means you might want to bring an extra pair of shorts—just in case you tumble in.

Speaking of water, the hot springs still attract a good number of visitors, even if they do smell like a thousand boiled eggs. Relaxing in these mineral-laden waters is said to rejuvenate the body and spirit, or at the very least, give you an excuse to wear a swimsuit in freezing temperatures. Many visitors find themselves in the hot springs wondering how they ended up in a glorified bathhouse while simultaneously feeling at one with nature.

As for dining options, Idaho Springs offers a curious mix of eateries. The local diners serve up hearty breakfasts that could fuel a small army, and you'll find burgers that are basically a rite of passage. But then there's the notorious pizza joint that has the audacity to serve toppings you never knew existed. Ever had pickles on a pizza? You can do that here. Just make sure to bring a good attitude and maybe a backup meal plan.

And then there are the town's events, which range from charming to downright baffling. The annual Idaho Springs Film Festival celebrates indie films with the same fervor one might reserve for a local bake sale, though it's hard to tell if it's more about the films or the free popcorn. The town also hosts the "Georgetown Loop Railroad Festival," where you can ride a train that's older than your grandparents and question your life choices as you traverse the mountainside. If you're lucky, you might even get a front-row seat to someone's rendition of "I think I'm gonna be sick" as the train sways around sharp turns.

Now, let's talk about the worst things about Idaho Springs, which could fill a book of its own. First, there's the infamous traffic, especially during peak tourist season. You'll experience the joy of creeping along the main road, contemplating the meaning of life while watching cars ahead of you turn into food trucks and gift shops. It's as if the entire town collectively decided to have a "Let's Make Everyone Late for Everything" party, and you're on the guest list.

The altitude can be a double-edged sword. Sure, you're breathing in the crisp mountain air, but that same air can turn you into a wheezing mess if you dare to exert yourself too much and you're not used to the Colorado altitude already. Hiking, biking, or even just walking to the nearest ice cream shop may leave you gasping like a fish out of water.

Ignacio

Ignacio, Colorado, a name that rolls off the tongue like a mouthful of marbles, is nestled in the breathtaking San Juan Mountains. You might think it sounds like a character from a spaghetti Western, and in many ways, it is—a small town with a big history and even bigger personality. Founded in the late 1800s, Ignacio started as a trading post for the Ute people and quickly evolved into a mining town that attracted fortune seekers faster than you can say "fool's gold."

The town's name comes from the nearby Ignacio Ute Indian Reservation, named after a local Ute leader. If you ever wondered whether local leaders were ever good at naming things, the answer is a resounding yes. It's a name that has survived the test of time, much like the town's habit of perplexing newcomers with its array of quirky charms.

Now, let's dive into the rich tapestry of history that has woven itself into the very fabric of Ignacio. Initially, the town was all about mining and trading, with prospectors scouring the mountains for shiny rocks, convinced that each little nugget would solve their financial woes. The 1890s saw a boom that made Ignacio the talk of the region, though not always for the right reasons. You could say it was a real gold rush situation—lots of excitement, some disappointment, and a few too many individuals with outlandish claims.

Today, the town is a delightful blend of old-school charm and modern quirks. One of the notable spots is the Southern Ute Cultural Center and Museum, which is a treasure trove of history, art, and culture that would make even the most hardened history buff shed a tear of joy. Here, you can learn about the Ute people, their traditions, and perhaps the correct way to pronounce "Ignacio" (hint: it's not like you're trying to order a fancy coffee). The museum is like a time capsule, except this one doesn't require a DeLorean to explore.

But let's be honest, while museums can be riveting, sometimes the real fun is found in the town's more eccentric offerings. Take the annual Ignacio Pine River Festival, where you'll witness an impressive array of local talent, food, and possibly some questionable dance moves. This festival could be described as the town's way of showcasing how to have a good time without losing your dignity—though opinions on that last part vary greatly. Here, the locals come together to celebrate all things Ignacio, which includes competitive canoe races and a fair amount of homemade pie. It's a good time until someone takes the pie-eating contest a bit too seriously.

Speaking of pies, let's take a moment to address the culinary scene in Ignacio. It ranges from the truly spectacular to the hilariously questionable. You'll find quaint diners serving hearty breakfasts that could fuel a rocket launch, and restaurants where you can order traditional Native American dishes. But venture a bit too far into the culinary scene, and you may stumble upon some peculiar food fusions. Ever had green chili ice cream? Neither have most people, but Ignacio believes in living life on the edge of flavor exploration.

And if you find yourself craving some outdoor adventure, Ignacio doesn't disappoint. The town is surrounded by stunning landscapes, perfect for hiking, biking, and more importantly, getting lost while trying to take the scenic route. The area boasts trails that range from "This is a nice stroll" to "You might want to call someone if you can't find your way back." Nature lovers will feel right at home, as long as they don't mind the occasional encounter with wildlife that seems to have mistaken hikers for long-lost friends.

Now, let's talk about the not-so-great things to see and do in Ignacio, because every town has its quirks. First on the list is the traffic situation, or rather the distinct lack of it. You might think that a small town wouldn't have traffic problems, but let me assure you that nothing tests a visitor's patience quite like waiting behind a local who suddenly decides that now is the perfect time to admire the view. If you find yourself stuck behind someone pondering the magnificence of a cow, just remember that you're in the heart of Colorado—patience is key.

If you're expecting a bustling nightlife, you might want to adjust those expectations. Ignacio is not exactly known for its club scene. The local watering holes have their own charm, offering a mix of karaoke nights and dart tournaments that could make you question your life choices. Just imagine belting out 80s power ballads while your friends cheer you on from the corner, wondering how they ended up in a small town with more stars in the sky than people in the bar.

Let's not forget about the weather, which can change faster than a toddler's mood. If you're in Ignacio, be prepared for everything from sunny skies to sudden snow flurries, often within the same hour. It's the kind of unpredictability that keeps you on your toes, or at least makes you question whether you need to bring a snow shovel or a beach towel for your day out.

Iliff

Iliff, Colorado, is one of those charming little towns that feels like a cozy, well-worn blanket—familiar, slightly askew, and just a bit dusty. Nestled in the eastern plains of Colorado, Iliff boasts a name that sounds like it could belong to a wizard or perhaps a long-forgotten superhero. Imagine a character donning a cape made of corn stalks, soaring over the flatlands in search of lost cattle and a good cup of coffee. But alas, this is not a comic book; it's a place with a rich history and a few amusing quirks of its own.

Founded in the late 19th century, Iliff sprang to life in 1887, likely after someone yelled, "Let's build a town!" over a poker game. The town was named after a local landowner, John Iliff, who was a cattle baron with a flair for self-promotion. Apparently, if you wanted a town to be named after you in the Wild West, owning a lot of cows was a surefire way to do it. John Iliff's empire was built on raising cattle, and his name became synonymous with the area, almost as much as cow manure and tumbleweeds.

Fast forward to today, and Iliff has transformed from a bustling cattle hub into a sleepy little community with a population that barely cracks 500. This transformation could be likened to a slow but steady descent into a peaceful existence—like a turtle taking its time to cross the road but in a very nice pair of boots.

Now, let's dive into the history, because Iliff has some stories that are more colorful than a patchwork quilt. During its early days, the town was a stopover for travelers and ranchers, with businesses sprouting like daisies after a spring rain. There were saloons where cowboys would drown their sorrows after a tough day on the range, alongside general stores that sold everything from canned beans to the latest gossip. Those who frequented these establishments were not shy about sharing their opinions on life, politics, and the best way to roast a marshmallow—debates that were often more heated than the campfire.

As for museums, Iliff is somewhat light on the full-blown exhibits but doesn't lack charm. The Iliff Historical Society may not be a sprawling museum with dinosaur bones and interactive displays, but it boasts a collection of artifacts that paint a vivid picture of the town's past. You might find items like old photographs, dusty farming tools, and a handful of quirky items that make you wonder who on Earth would collect such things. Want to see a collection of vintage potato peelers? Iliff could have you covered.

But you won't want to miss the grand display of community spirit at the local events. Iliff hosts the annual Potato Festival, a celebration that's equal parts homage to the humble spud and a testament to the town's agricultural roots. Imagine a gathering of enthusiastic potato lovers, parading around in potato costumes and showcasing creative culinary masterpieces. Potatoes prepared in every conceivable way—from fries to casseroles—are presented with a pride that would make any food critic weep with joy. The festival includes games, live music, and, of course, the Great Potato Toss, where the locals compete to see who can throw a spud the farthest. It's like the Olympics, but with less training and more starch.

Now, let's explore the less glamorous aspects of Iliff, because every town has its peculiarities. First, the weather. If you're visiting, pack a wardrobe that could rival a character from "The Adventures of Tintin." The winds can be so fierce that you might think Mother Nature is auditioning for a tornado movie. The locals have been known to joke that if you don't like the weather in Iliff, just wait five minutes—because you're probably going to get a snowstorm, a rain shower, or a sandstorm all in the same afternoon.

And speaking of local quirks, let's talk about the town's dining scene. While Iliff may not be known for five-star restaurants, it offers a few dining options that can only be described as "homey." You might stumble upon a diner that specializes in good ol' American comfort food, where the wait staff knows your name, your life story, and how you like your coffee. The special of the day is usually something hearty—perfect for folks who've spent the day working the fields or perhaps just binge-watching Netflix.

However, not every dish is a winner. Some culinary experiments can lead to "unique" flavor combinations that leave you questioning if someone accidentally spilled a bottle of mustard into the mashed potatoes. Still, it's all part of the experience, much like accidentally walking into the local barber shop thinking it's a coffee shop—surprise!

For outdoor enthusiasts, the plains surrounding Iliff offer scenic views that are as vast as the ocean, minus the water. Here, you can enjoy leisurely walks and hikes, allowing the gentle breeze to remind you that nature can be relaxing...until a sudden gust sends your hat sailing into the nearby cornfield. Just remember to look out for the occasional rattlesnake, which adds an element of adventure that can spice up any stroll.

And let's not forget the town's lack of nightlife, which can be charming in its own right. If you're looking for vibrant nightlife, Iliff might leave you a bit disappointed. The most excitement you'll find after dark is the glow of a porch light or the flickering of a TV in a nearby home. The local "nightlife" consists mainly of gathering at someone's house to play board games or share stories about that one time they almost saw a bear. So, if you're after wild nights, you might want to adjust your expectations to wild nights of conversation about the weather.

Indian Hills

Nestled snugly in the foothills of the Rocky Mountains, Indian Hills, Colorado, is the kind of place that feels like it was plucked from the pages of a novel titled "How to Live the Dream in a Tiny Mountain Town." Picture this: a collection of cozy homes, quirky locals, and the occasional deer that seems to think it's a neighborhood dog, strutting down the road like it owns the place. With a name like Indian Hills, you might expect to stumble upon some mystical vibe or at least a few ethereal beings floating around. Instead, you're more likely to find someone wearing socks with sandals while discussing the best way to compost kitchen scraps.

The name "Indian Hills" is a nod to the region's rich Native American heritage. It's a reminder that this land was once home to tribes who undoubtedly had a much better grasp of the outdoors than most modern-day residents, who might still struggle with a simple map app. The hills themselves are dotted with aspen trees and pines, providing a picturesque backdrop that has drawn in nature enthusiasts and people simply looking to escape the hustle and bustle of life. It's not exactly a bustling metropolis; more like a sleepy little hamlet where time moves slower than molasses in January.

History buffs might find the tale of Indian Hills amusingly tangled. The area started gaining traction in the late 1800s as a resort destination, attracting folks who wanted to escape the sweltering heat of Denver. They came for the fresh mountain air and to pretend they were rugged pioneers, even if their idea of roughing it was staying in a cabin with indoor plumbing. As the years rolled on, the town embraced its quirky charm, with a strong sense of community and a penchant for unique traditions that are sometimes hard to explain to outsiders.

One of the main attractions in Indian Hills is the community vibe, which is as palpable as the aroma of fresh pine trees. Local events often feel like family reunions—if your family consisted of friendly but slightly eccentric folks who might just challenge you to a friendly debate about the best way to make homemade granola. The Indian Hills Community Center serves as the town's beating heart, hosting everything from yoga classes to the occasional potluck where culinary skills vary wildly from gourmet to "What on earth is that?"

For those who fancy themselves as culture connoisseurs, there's the Indian Hills Historical Society. While it might not rival the Louvre, it's got a certain charm that's hard to resist. Here, you can peruse artifacts and photographs that document the town's quirky past. Imagine exploring a collection of items that includes everything from old mining equipment to a collection of vintage postcards featuring poorly drawn renditions of local wildlife. It's a time capsule of sorts, where you might even find the original blueprints for the world's least efficient treehouse.

Now, let's get to the good stuff: the best and worst things to see and do. If you're an outdoor enthusiast, you're in luck. Hiking trails snake through the hills, offering breathtaking views that can make you forget your worries—or at least distract you from your terrible life choices for a little while. Take a hike up to Mount Morrison, and you'll feel as if you're on top of the world—until you realize your legs are on fire and your water bottle is nearly empty. Pro tip: pack snacks, because "nature" won't feed you.

For those seeking a less strenuous activity, you might stumble upon the local farmers market, a gathering of proud vendors eager to showcase their kale and heirloom tomatoes. Here, you can taste organic honey, sample artisanal cheese, and listen to folks proudly proclaim that their produce is "100% organic" while simultaneously trying to figure out how to get their car to start without a jump. The farmers market is a place where small talk flourishes—everyone's discussing their favorite composting techniques as if they were discussing a hot new Netflix series.

But like any small town, Indian Hills has its quirks and pitfalls. If you're looking for nightlife, you might find yourself sorely disappointed. The locals have a reputation for being early risers, so don't expect much after the sun goes down unless you count the glow of the occasional porch light. The idea of "going out" generally means wandering over to a neighbor's house to watch a documentary about composting. Yes, composting, again.

Now, let's talk about the weather. It's a running joke that in Indian Hills, you can experience all four seasons in a single day. One minute, you're basking in glorious sunshine, and the next, you're dodging hailstones the size of golf balls. The locals have perfected the art of layering clothing as if they're preparing for an Antarctic expedition, all while pretending that they love the unpredictability of nature. "Ah, yes, nothing like a nice snowstorm in June," they'll say, wearing a sunhat and a parka at the same time.

In terms of culinary adventures, Indian Hills is home to a few quaint spots where you can grab a bite. The local café might not be Michelin-rated, but it serves up hearty meals that have the potential to warm your soul—or at least provide enough calories to power you through a day of hiking. But be warned: culinary experiments happen here. You might order a "house special" that turns out to be an unholy combination of quinoa, kale, and what you can only hope is a legitimate dressing. Remember, food is love, and love can sometimes be… surprising.

If you're lucky enough to visit during the town's annual events, you might just stumble upon the infamous Indian Hills Pancake Breakfast. This gathering is less about the pancakes and more about the gossip—people swap stories over fluffy stacks of pancakes, syrup, and the occasional whispered rumor about who has the best compost pile. Just try not to spill syrup on your neighbor's vintage quilt; trust me, it's a serious faux pas.

And as the day winds down, the true charm of Indian Hills comes alive. The golden hour casts a warm glow over the mountains, and the residents gather to share tales around fire pits, reminiscing about the day's adventures or the latest Netflix series. There's a sense of belonging that wraps around you like a warm blanket—a reminder that in this little slice of Colorado, life is less about grand escapades and more about enjoying the simple pleasures.

Jamestown

Ah, Jamestown, Colorado, a name that sounds like a quaint colonial town from a dusty history book, but instead, it's a tiny mountain gem nestled in the foothills of the Rockies. The name itself evokes images of 18th-century settlers wearing buckled shoes and frilly hats, which is amusing since the only frills you'll find in Jamestown today are the charming decorations in local cabins and the occasional resident's questionable fashion choices.

The town was founded in the 1860s during the gold rush, a time when folks with gold fever flocked to Colorado like moths to a flame. Jamestown was established by a bunch of miners who thought, "Hey, why not build a town here? We might just strike it rich!" Spoiler alert: they didn't strike it rich. Instead, they settled for a life of hard work, camaraderie, and maybe a few too many tall tales about the one that got away—or the gold nugget that was just a glinting rock.

The history of Jamestown is punctuated by its ups and downs, much like a roller coaster—if that roller coaster was built on a shaky mountain slope and only had a couple of enthusiastic riders. The town faced disasters, like the flood in 2013 that swept through, leaving many homes damaged. Residents rallied together, embodying the true spirit of small-town resilience, which can be defined as "let's all band together and complain about the weather while drinking some strong coffee."

In terms of museums, don't expect a sprawling metropolis of artifacts. Instead, you might come across the Jamestown Mercantile, which serves as both a store and a gathering place for locals. Here, you can find everything from groceries to quirky souvenirs. It's the kind of place where you might overhear a spirited debate about the best way to make homemade soap or whether a certain hiking trail is "totally doable" for someone with a questionable sense of direction. If you're lucky, there might even be a local historical display that includes faded photographs of residents dressed in their finest 1980s attire, a time capsule of sorts that serves as a reminder that every decade has its own peculiar fashion sense.

Now, let's dive into the best and worst things to see and do in Jamestown, which, by the way, could easily be categorized as the most charmingly chaotic list you'll ever encounter. For starters, the town is surrounded by stunning natural beauty, with hiking trails that could make even the laziest couch potato consider putting on some real shoes. Trails like the popular "Canyon Trail" will take you on a scenic journey where you might encounter deer, rabbits, and possibly a squirrel with dreams of stardom. Just be prepared for some uphill battles, both physically and mentally. After all, nothing says "I love nature" quite like panting at a scenic viewpoint and pretending that you weren't just regretting that second slice of pie from the local diner.

Speaking of food, the local dining scene is as eclectic as the town itself. The Jamestown Diner is a beloved establishment where the coffee is strong and the breakfast burritos are larger than your head. It's the kind of place where the decor seems like it hasn't been updated since the dawn of time, which is part of its charm. If you're not careful, you might find yourself engrossed in conversation with the locals, swapping stories and getting advice on which trails to avoid if you don't want to become bear bait. If you're feeling adventurous, order the "Jamestown Special," a mystery dish that may or may not contain something resembling edible food. They say you haven't truly lived until you've eaten something you couldn't quite identify.

On the flip side, if you're in the mood for an experience that might lead to mild existential dread, consider taking a trip to the nearby Barker Reservoir. The reservoir is beautiful, yes, but it also serves as a reminder of just how small you are in this big, chaotic world. Bring a picnic, but don't be surprised if you're joined by a flock of very assertive birds who have no qualms about trying to steal your sandwich. They seem to have an advanced understanding of negotiation tactics, which may include relentless staring and feigning innocence.

Jamestown is also known for its vibrant community events, such as the annual Jamestown Arts Festival. Picture local artists showcasing their crafts while a smattering of festival-goers attempt to decipher modern art that looks suspiciously like something you'd find in a toddler's art project. It's a perfect mix of culture and chaos, where you can sip lemonade, peruse questionable art, and engage in the time-honored tradition of discussing your plans to build a tiny house—because apparently, everyone in Jamestown is an aspiring tiny home builder.

For those looking for a touch of the paranormal, you might hear whispers of ghostly legends surrounding the town. Some locals claim that the spirits of miners past still roam the hills, presumably searching for their lost gold. Or maybe they're just trying to find the nearest Wi-Fi signal, which can be a challenge in these parts. If you're feeling particularly brave, consider taking a midnight stroll, where the shadows dance around you, and you might just convince yourself that you're being followed by a specter—or possibly just a raccoon with an unusual interest in your backpack.

And then there's the weather. Ah, the weather! If you're not prepared for rapid shifts between sunny skies and sudden thunderstorms, you might find yourself caught in an unexpected downpour while wearing sandals and a t-shirt. Jamestown's weather could be described as "enthusiastic" at best, and locals have mastered the art of discussing it with all the gravity of a science project. One moment, you'll be basking in the sun, and the next, you'll be seeking shelter under the eaves of the mercantile, shaking your head in disbelief at the sheer unpredictability of it all.

In the end, Jamestown, Colorado, is a little slice of paradise that feels like a secret known only to those who dare to explore its quirky depths. The combination of rich history, stunning scenery, and a community that truly embraces the peculiarities of life makes it a town worth experiencing. Whether you're scaling a hill, sipping coffee, or participating in a spirited debate over the best local hiking trails, you'll find yourself swept up in the charm that is uniquely Jamestown. Just remember to pack your sense of humor, because in a town where the only certainty is uncertainty, laughter is truly the best companion.

Come back soon, ya hear?

Thank you for joining me on this delightful exploration of every municipality in Colorado, from Akron to Jamestown. It's been a whirlwind journey filled with fascinating stories, quirky names, and a rich tapestry of history that each town has to offer. Together, we've uncovered how these places got their names, dived into their histories, discovered their museums, and noted their populations, all while enjoying the unique charm of Colorado's communities.

But this is just the beginning, because I couldn't fit them all into a single book! I invite you to join me for Volume 2, where we'll traverse from Johnstown to Yuma, uncovering even more hidden gems and local legends along the way. Your enthusiasm and support mean the world to me, and if you enjoyed this adventure, consider leaving a pleasant review at your favorite online book retailer. It's like sending a virtual cookie my way—sweet, simple, and completely free! Your kind words help fellow explorers discover these delightful municipalities, and I can't wait to continue this journey with you!